C0-ALL-192

# THE OTHER LIVINGSTONE

# The other Livingstone

**For the first time the story can be told of four men who played a crucial part in David Livingstone's discoveries - a part he attempted to suppress. This is a story of 19th century intrigue and rivalry which took place behind the scenes in Africa, away from the rapturous public gaze of the Victorians.**

## Judith Listowel

# CHARLES SCRIBNER'S SONS

### NEW YORK

HOUSTON PUBLIC LIBRARY

75-125536-5

R0l138 66415

Copyright © 1974 Judith Listowel

Copyright under the Berne Convention

All rights reserved. No part of this book
may be reproduced in any form without the
permission of Charles Scribner's Sons.

135791113151719 *I/C* 2018161412108642

Printed in Great Britain

Library of Congress Catalog Card Number 74-14007
ISBN 0-684-14130-2

To Richard who loves history.

# Author's note

In many cases there is more than one acceptable spelling of a 19th century African name. I have endeavoured to use the best known modern English spelling, except in direct contemporary quotations. Sometimes even this, no doubt, has not always been possible.

Judith Listowel

London
January 1974.

# Contents

# Preface

This book is not another Livingstone biography. There is no need for one, as an excellent critical assessment of the doctor was published in 1973 by Tim Jeal. His research has included all available sources in this country, as well as documents held in Salisbury and Lusaka. But Jeal has not lived in Africa; he does not seem to know of the existence of László Magyar, nor to be aware of the position and influence of Senhor Cardoso. A realistic appreciation of Livingstone's importance can only be made by giving due consideration to the men who helped him and were associated with him in Africa.

Today, Livingstone is no longer regarded as a saint-like figure; but he is still frequently acclaimed as the first European to have gone to the heart of Africa. His reports revealed to an astounded public that the centre of Africa was not a hot, barren desert, but lush, fertile land, crossed by mighty rivers. Livingstone appealed to the sentiments of evangelical piety in Victorian England and awakened the public conscience to the horrors of the slave trade. Slavery, and trade in slaves, had been banned long before he spoke up, but it was his indictment that touched the hearts of ordinary people, especially the young, and mobilized public indignation to demand the enforcement of the anti-slavery laws. Under this pressure, the government and the Royal Navy saw to it that they were enforced.

But there is another side to the Livingstone story. He left out of his reports facts which did not fit in with his purpose of attracting Christian traders to the African interior. More particularly, he never acknowledged that he had been helped in his explorations by others who had lived or travelled in Africa, and who knew certain parts of it very well – men like Cotton Oswell, László Magyar and Senhor Candido Cardoso. It is the purpose of this book to give long-overdue recognition to Livingstone's helpers. Without their knowledge, ideas and suggestions, Livingstone's own achievements would have been different, and the history of Africa in the 20th century could have taken a different course.

It does not detract from Livingstone's feats that he listened to the advice and benefited from the experience of a handful of outstanding men, but it is significant that he never admitted his debt to others. By recognising his defects as well as his admirable qualities, we can see David Livingstone as a more credible person than the sentimentally pious Victorian presented by his biographers until quite recently.

This book came to be written as a result of a footnote I saw by chance in a book in the library of Royal Commonwealth Society in London. The footnote referred to a Hungarian, László Magyar, who had been in Angola in the 1850s. I began making enquiries about Magyar and found that the Hungarian Professor Gusztáv Thirring had written a biography of him in 1936. I then decided to read Magyar's diaries and letters and, in the summer of 1972, went for this purpose to Budapest. But the Magyar papers in the Hungarian Academy of Sciences could not be found. A thorough search was made – they had vanished.

On the same day a member of the British Embassy in Budapest invited me to dinner to meet Professor László Krizsán, who is president of the Afro-Asian Institute in Budapest and lectures on African history at Moscow University. When he was told about the missing papers he was able to give me photostat copies of the diaries and letters (except for 30 vital pages) which he had made in 1970, when the originals were still in the vaults of the Hungarian Academy of Sciences.

Having established that Livingstone must have known of Magyar, although he denied even having heard of him, I decided to look into some of Livingstone's claims. Donald Simpson, the Librarian of the Royal Commonwealth Society, gave me the book in which Edward Oswell published the letters and diaries of his father, Cotton Oswell, who took Livingstone with him as interpreter on the expedition to Lake Ngami. On his return, Oswell dropped Livingstone at Kuruman, and went off big game hunting. In Livingstone's two letters about the discovery of Lake Ngami, read out at the Royal Geographical Society, Cotton Oswell was not mentioned.

In his *Missionary Travels in Southern Africa* Livingstone related that a Portuguese judge, Senhor Candido Cardoso, first told him of

lake Nyasa. Later, when Livingstone decided to set up missions and
settle Europeans in the Shire Highlands, he wanted to be known as
the first European to have seen the lake. He stated that Cardoso had
never been there, that the information Cardoso had given him was
erroneous; in other words, that Cardoso was either a liar or a fool.
In view of Livingstone's treatment of Cotton Oswell and László
Magyar, I decided to go to Tete in Moçambique, where Cardoso had
lived, to find out whether he had been in a position to go to Lake
Nyasa. I tracked down several of his descendants, and found that he
could easily have gone to the "big lake" in the north. Moreover, his
descendants are sure that he gave all the information he had about
the lake to Livingstone.

I particularly wish to thank Mr Donald Simpson and Professor
László Krizsán. In their different ways their help has made the writing of this book possible.

# Part One

## CHAPTER ONE

# David Livingstone
# -early days

David Livingstone[1] was born on March 19, 1813 in Scotland.

A Blantyre man later voiced the local view when he said: "Dr Livingstone was no thocht to be a by-ordinary [unusual] laddie; just a sulky, quiet, feckless sort o' boy."[2] By feckless he probably meant what a farmer, who employed young David to herd his cattle, had meant when he said: "I didn't think muckle of that David Livingstone when he worked wi' me. He was aye' lying' on his belly readin' a book."[2]

The greatest influence in David's childhood was his crofter-born grandfather, Neil Livingstone, a natural story-teller. From him David heard about his great-grandfather, who died at Culloden "for the old line of kings"; about his uncles who fought against Napoleon and two of whom fell at Waterloo. The little boy was excited by the romance of his Highland ancestors and he well remembered his grandfather's saying "There never was a dishonest one among us, nor was there a donkey."[3]

Neil Livingstone also spoke of the island of Ulva, near Oban (in Scotland), which he had to leave because crofters were being displaced by sheep and the more profitable production of wool. David could sense his grandfather's nostalgia for his youth, when the crofter families used to move with their flocks at the beginning of each summer to the upland pastures, where they would camp until August. It was a rugged but singularly happy existence. Occasionally Neil Livingstone would also refer to the harsh customs of the islanders; to the woman who had unintentionally killed a child, and was sentenced to be tied in a sack and placed on Kirty's Rock, where at high tide she would be drowned. Unfaithful wives and immodest maidens incurred similar punishment. In Africa David Livingstone used to say that the extreme savagery of the "Cape Caffres" was like that of the Highlanders.

Neil Livingstone went into the Blantyre cotton mill, whose owner, "douce David Dale", gave him a responsible position, and his four sons received some education at the school maintained by the mill. David's father, also called Neil, was apprenticed to a tailor. He did not like the work, but he married his master's daughter, Mary Hunter, and eventually became a small tea-merchant who took his wares from farm to farm. He made few sales, and spent his evenings reading theological books and missionary reports, which left little time for his five children.[4] David's mother was a sweet-natured woman, who brought warmth and love into their poor home – like other workers, they lived in a "single kitchen apartment house", which meant one room with two sleeping recesses, into which seven of them had to squeeze at night. The family cupboard was usually bare, yet Mrs Livingstone kept the family wardrobe in remarkably good order. David inherited his mother's luminous eyes, but not her devotion to the family.

In the decades after the Industrial Revolution, and especially in the slump after the Napoleonic wars, the working classes led unimaginably harsh lives. To help the family, ten-year-old David had to go into the local cotton mill, where he was employed as a piecer. This meant walking back and forth between the reels of the whirring spinning-jenny anything up to twenty miles a day – much of it crawling and stooping. It also meant tying together the threads on the spinning frames if they looked like breaking, which needed good eyes and constant concentration. As the spinners were paid in accordance not only with the quantity but with the quality of their output, the children who did not piece satisfactorily were often beaten. And if at the end of a ten-and-a-half-hour day a little boy dropped asleep on his feet, he was either hit, or doused with a bucket of cold water. The mill-owners believed that heat helped in making fine yarn; the temperature in the factory was kept at 80° to 90° Fahrenheit, and most employees, women as well as men, worked half naked. There was a high incidence of bronchial illness and pneumonia. It is an indication of David's strong physique that he grew up without a single serious illness.

David gave his first week's earnings, two shillings and sixpence, to his mother. For this he had toiled six days from six in the morning until six at night, with an hour off for his mid-day dinner. Even then he did not fall into bed, but went for two hours to night school; and then did homework, until his mother forced him to get some sleep. In the state of fatigue in which these children attended night school it is not surprising that less than 10% achieved literacy. David was an exception as his father had already taught him to read and write and he even started Latin in his first year of schooling. When all the others had given up, he was the only one to stay on until the teacher, Mr McSkinning, stopped the class. So David decided to learn Latin and Greek on his own, and did it by propping up his grammar on the spinning machine. At the age of fifteen he had been promoted to spinner and the mill-girls had great fun pitching bobbins at the book, trying to knock it off the frame. But David was not to be easily diverted from his obsessive learning. From the library which Mr Dale maintained for his mill-hands, he borrowed the books he devoured – books on travel, geography,botany,chemistry. His father, who banned any form of light literature under the collective noun of "trashy novels" insisted that he read theological works. When David refused to read Wilberforce's *Practical Christianity*, he was given a sound thrashing.

There was strife between father and son. David was determined somehow to get out of his terrible life in the mill, and seemed to believe, instinctively, that education was the only way. According to his father, science – meaning botany, chemistry, and so on – was directly opposed to Godliness. Moreover, he frightened his son by constantly repeating to him the doctrine of predestination, that damnation would be his lot regardless of action or effort, unless he became an "Elect of the Lord". Terror of damnation never left David Livingstone until, at the age of nineteen, he by chance read Dr Thomas Dick's *The Philosophy of a Future State*, in which Dr Dick categorically stated that science was not opposed to Christian beliefs; on the contrary, they could go hand-in-hand. This made David's conscience considerably easier; however, complete relief came – unexpectedly – through his father. In 1832, soon after David had read Dr Dick, friends persuaded Neil Livingstone to listen to Henry Wilkes, a young Canadian preacher of liberal theological views. Wilkes made such a profound impression on David's father that he applied for membership of the church in Hamilton (two miles from Blantyre) where he had heard him preach. He became a friend of the Rev John Moir, the minister of this church, who held similar reformist views, and who took an interest in young David. When David also joined, Moir put him into the charge of a veteran congregationalist, Arthur Anderson. Week after week, for five months,

David tramped from Blantyre to Hamilton for instruction "in the doctrines" and prayer.

During this time he met a number of people from higher social strata than himself, who were corresponding with friends in America, and had heard of the new, even more liberal, theology which was becoming fashionable there. One of the most distinguished proponents of this school was Charles Finney, who greatly influenced Livingstone and further strengthened his assurance that "the Holy Spirit is promised to all who ask it."[5]

When Anderson recommended David for solemn public reception as a communicant, the Rev Moir spoke words to him he was never to forget: "It is the conscience of the Lord's people and not the power of man that drives us to seek the Lord's Kingdom." Christians must hold themselves apart not only from the world but also from the church, if the church becomes too worldly. The Congregational Church rejected all outer control, both ecclesiastical and secular, in order to become more dependent on the Lord's will. All members of the Congregation had the right to share in the direction of the church's affairs.

This creed suited David's wilful and individualistic character. With the passing of the years he had less and less use for profession and formal creed, and cherished more and more the one great test of the Saviour: "By their fruits ye shall know them". For David Livingstone this was the supreme test of worthiness in the eyes of God. Moreover, by then he firmly believed that he himself was one of the Elect chosen by the Lord to judge his fellows. It was for this reason that, when he got to Africa, he felt entitled to criticise his fellow missionaries and eventually parted company with the London Missionary Society.

In his letter of application to the LMS he gave a moving description of the distressing religious experiences he underwent until the age of nineteen. The letter is long and verbose, but it is so revealing of David Livingstone that it is worth quoting in full[6]: "Through merciful providence of a gracious God, it was my privilege to enjoy the Instruction, example and prayers, of pious parents, who still walk before god in the land of the living. These, however, had no effect on my desperately wicked heart, only serving to restrain me, in some measure, from outward immorality; when about my twelfth year, I was visited with great distress of mind on account of my sinfulness, and anxious desire to possess the peace of mind and happiness, which

I felt convinced, the true Christian alone enjoyed. This I could not attain, because of my looking continually within for an effect, which I thought must be produced there, by the spirit of God, ere I could be entitled to take the benefit of the gospel and the delusion being strengthened by some preaching which I then heard, my only course appeared to be, just to wait the good pleasure of God. Thus, continuing to look for another ground of hope, than the finished work of Christ, *I found neither peace nor happiness, which caused me (never having revealed the state of my mind to anyone) often to bewail my sad state with tears in secret.*[7] The anxiety of my mind after some time abated but a perpetual uneasiness, a soareness of heart still remained, which no amusement, nor pursuit could assuage."

Every adolescent has problems with himself, his family, his community, his world. In Victorian days, as before and since, the torments of youth led the young to try out their claws on their nearest and dearest. It is revealing that David Livingstone's troubles centred entirely around his faith, his relations with his Maker. He appeared respectful to but also remote from his parents; in fact he was thoroughly self-centred and self-absorbed. Yet he seems to have disguised his "soareness of heart" quite successfully, for he played wild games with his contemporaries, went rambling and searching for rare flowers and geological specimens, and whatever his spiritual torments, they did not preclude poaching – just as his God-fearing ancestors had found nothing wrong with cattle reiving. One afternoon, when he caught a salmon, he pushed it down the leg of his brother Charles's trousers. As they passed through the village, David joined in the sympathy the neighbours showed for the poor lad's swollen leg.

About this time David read in one of his father's missionary tracts the appeal of Karl F. A. Gützlaff, the famous German missionary in China, who had translated the Bible into Chinese, and whose medical skill had helped him over apparently unsurmountable obstacles. Gützlaff was asking churches of Britain and America for missionaries to be sent to China. David was deeply shocked when he realised that the English Congregational Church had to rely on German volunteers as there were not sufficient Englishmen willing to do the Lord's work in China. He could not get this out of his mind; eventually he decided to become a missionary, and to acquire, like Karl Gützlaff, in addition to theological qualifications, those of a medical practitioner. In the 1830s, medical missions were a comparatively

new idea; yet his father, who had hitherto opposed any medical training unless he put it to a specifically religious end, now conceded that
David had found a way of combining religion and science. When
David had saved enough money for the expenses of one term, Neil
Livingstone went with him to Glasgow to find accommodation.
David's room in a good quarter of the town cost 2/6 a week,[8] which
included some food, but his fee at Anderson College for his medical
studies alone was £12; Greek and theology he studied at the Congregational College and paid for it separately.

It was wholly in character that David Livingstone should have
made little progress in "scientific theology" – although his teacher
was the Principal of the College, the Rev Ralph Wardlaw, whose
belief was that atonement was available to all – if they were able to
receive the Holy Spirit, and who dissolved the last shreds of fear in
David's mind. But David was outstanding at his medical studies, so
much so that he became assistant to Professor Thomas Graham. One
of his fellow students had a bench and a turning lathe in his room; on
these David increased his knowledge of rudimentary engineering,
which he put to good use later in Africa.

But the money he had saved over several years was soon spent, and
in April, 1837, he was back in Blantyre, working hard at the mill, and
studying in his spare time. He had to borrow from his elder brother
to be able to return to Glasgow in the autumn, and it was then, on the
suggestion of Arthur Anderson, that he offered his services to the
London Missionary Society,[9] which provided training for its future
missionaries. In his letter of application to the LMS David Livingstone told not only of his early religious experience but spelt out his
creed, from which he never wavered to the end of his life.

"In my 19th year," he wrote, "it pleased god in merciful kindness and compassion to shew me my folly and error, by means of a
work, entitled 'The Philosophy of a future State'.[10] . . . If I bes-
towed on them a thought, Heaven had no attractions for me, and
Hell was never an object of alarm. But now full conviction of their
relation to me filled my mind, and I likewise felt that the atoning
work of Christ was the only ground on which I could hope to find
peace to my soul here, and enjoy the prospect of bliss hereafter,
and enabled by divine grace to cast myself on the mercy of God
through Christ, as peace and joy entered my heart, to which till
then I had been an entire stranger. This has been occasionally
interrupted by unbelieving doubts and fears, but with the help of a

gracious God, I have been enabled to dismiss these, by repairing to the only hope of the sinner, the lamb that was slain, and now, trusting that he will keep me from falling, through life, and believing he will save me at last, not for anything I am or can do, for I see nothing in me, nor about me, to merit such great mercy, but on the contrary everything deserving the wrath and curse of God through eternity, but solely, through his own sovereign grace and love, flowing through the propitiatory blood of Jesus Christ his son.

The scriptures of the old and new testaments are a revelation of the will of god to fallen man. . . . From these we learn that there is one god in three persons, Father, son and holy spirit, that he is the creator, preserver and moral governor of the universe – that man was created by him holy and happy, but broke his law and introduced rebellion into the world, thereby losing the favour and image of god, and entailing sin and misery on himself and all his posterity. . . . God's righteous law being violated, man might have been justly condemned to eternal punishment, the deserts of his sin. But god, in infinite mercy and love, devised a way, whereby the claims of his justice are satisfied and the sinner saved. . . . Those who choose to reject his salvation must perish. . . . Experiencing in some degree that happiness which the gospel imparts and feeling in some measure my obligation to redeeming love, it is my earnest desire to consecrate my whole life to the advancement of the cause of our blessed redeemer in the world thereby endeavouring to evince my love and gratitude to him 'who though rich, yet for our sakes became poor.'

David Livingston"

This application, dated September 5, 1837, was favourably received by the LMS; it was also backed by a letter from the Rev John Moir, still pastor of the Independent Church of Hamilton. Friends helped with the fare to London. Livingstone passed the LMS examination and was sent for three months' provisional training to Chipping Ongar in Essex. Here he made a poor impression on the Rev Richard Cecil, who was in charge of studies. Cecil was not at all sure that with his hesitant manner in conducting family worship, his ungainly ways at weekday prayers in chapel, and worst of all, his panicky flight from the pulpit the first time he was sent out to preach a sermon, Livingstone would make an adequate missionary. It is worth bearing in mind that from first to last, Livingstone was no preacher, and that his impact on the British public after his crossing of Africa from the Atlantic to the Indian Ocean, was due to what would now be called lecturing. He affected the young in particular by the simple, factual description of his experiences; by his methods of letting his audience draw its own conclusions – except on the burning need to abolish slavery. Even in describing the horrors of slavery, he was accurate to the minutest detail. This novel technique moved his Victorian listeners more than a direct emotional appeal would have done.[11]

Fortunately for Livingstone, in 1838 the Rev Dr Cecil's adverse report was not acted upon. An elderly member of the Board of Directors, who had had some words with the Scottish lad "ungainly in movement, slow and indistinct in speech", persuaded his colleagues to give him another chance. Livingstone was brought to London, where he concentrated on his medical studies. He came to know the son of the Rev Dr Bennett, Congregational Minister of the Silver Street chapel in Falcon Square, near Aldersgate, who was then a medical student, but who years later, as Sir J. Risdon Bennett, MD, LLD, FRS, became the President of the Royal College of Physicians. Of how he remembered Livingstone, Risdon Bennett came to say: "I was struck with the amount of knowledge that he had already acquired of those subjects which constitute the foundation of medical science. He had, however, little or no acquaintance with the practical departments of medicine, and had had no opportunities to study the nature and aspects of disease. Of these deficiencies he was quite aware, and felt the importance of acquiring as much practical knowledge as possible during his stay in London. I was at that time Physician to the Aldersgate street Dispensary, and was lecturing at the Charing Cross Hospital on the practice of medicine, and thus was able to obtain for him free admission to hospital practice as well as attendance on my lectures and my practice at the dispensary."[12]

At this time David Livingstone's dream was still to become a medical missionary in China, but the outbreak of the Opium War frustrated his hopes. Aware that he must redirect his plans he went one evening to a protest meeting against the slave trade. There he was introduced to Dr Robert Moffat, who had been a missionary in South Africa since 1816. Subsequently Moffat called at the boarding-house for young missionaries in Aldersgate where Livingstone was staying. This is how he recalled what ensued: "By and by he asked me whether I thought he would do for Africa. I said I believed he would if he would not go to an old station, but would advance to unoccupied ground, specifying the vast plain to the north, where I had sometimes seen in the morning sun the smoke of a thousand villages where no missionary had ever been. At last Livingstone said: 'What is the use of my waiting for the end of this abominable opium war? I will go at once to Africa.' The Directors concurred and Africa became his sphere."[13]

Livingstone hurried back to Glasgow, to sit, on November 15, for the examination to become a Licentiate of the Faculty of Physicians and Surgeons. It was a near thing, for his wilfulness got the better of his judgement, and he argued with his examiners about the use of the stethoscope. However, they passed him, and after a moving farewell to his family, he left for London to be ordained a missionary on November 20, and then go to South Africa.

From the Minutes of the LMS Committee of Examination it is known that on Monday, January 28, 1839, the members resolved that three candidates (Moore, Livingstone and Parker) having completed their probationary term, be fully admitted under the patronage of the Society. On July 8, 1839, the Rev Richard Cecil required information as to the intentions of the Board regarding Messrs Fairbrother, Moore and Livingstone; on July 22 the Board resolved that they should stay with Cecil until Christmas and then attend the British and Foreign School of Medicine, to fit themselves for some station in South Africa or in the South Seas. The next entry regarding Livingstone is dated September 14, 1840: "Resolved also that the ordination of Messrs Ross and Livingstone take place at Albion Chapel early in October, and the Rev Richard Cecil of Ongar, the Rev John Young, and the Rev J. J. Freeman engage in the principal part of the service." In January, 1841, the Missionary Magazine reported that on Friday evening, November 20, "Mr David Livingstone and Mr William Ross, missionaries, appointed to South Africa, were ordained at Albion Chapel, Finsbury. The Rev J. C. Potter, Rev J. J. Freeman, Rev John Arundel, Rev John Young, and Rev R. Cecil engaged in the service."

Albion Chapel, situated in London Wall, was pulled down in the 1930s. It was a small Presbyterian place of worship, which did not please Livingstone, who regarded "the Presbyterian Churches too lax in their communion and particularly the established Church." He also frowned on William Ross, formerly a school-master, eleven years his senior, and recently married. But his main resentment was that Ross was a member of the United Secession Church of Scotland

– in other words, a brand of Presbyterianism. To George Drummond, he wrote, "My colleague is a Secession man and has a good deal of the Act of Testimony in his composition, but I am determined to live in peace and goodwill. I will not quarrel on any account and may God give me wisdom to conduct myself aright. I see it is of great importance that missionaries should be united." But because of his stubborn selfrighteousness, he never lived up to his resolution.

The service consisted of solemn prayer and the imposition of hands. The candidates were then asked questions about their beliefs and asked to provide proof of their Christian faith. The questions addressed to David Livingstone were not revealed, but we can get an idea of what they must have been from the seventeen questions he had to answer before he was made a member of the Society. They were sent to him in writing, and together with his answers are preserved in the archives of the Congregational Conference of World Mission in London.

The first question read: "On what grounds have you concluded that you are a real Christian?" The answer was almost identical with the explanation of his creed given in his original letter to the LMS. Questions on the doctrines of the Gospel, Christian Baptism, the Church to which he belonged, and so on, were answered with elaborations of material from the same letter. A number of questions referred to his practical experience, such as engagement in prayer meetings; others referred to his birth, family, occupation, financial status, education, health; how long he had desired to become a missionary and what his geographical preferences were; the 12th question must have been most relevant to the service in the Albion Chapel: "What are the motives that actuate you to offer yourself to become a Minister?" Livingstone's written answer ran: "My desire is to see the Kingdom of the Saviour in the heart of all who are now in that state in which I once was; from compassion for their souls; from a desire to dedicate all my powers to the service of him – and if my sinful motives are mixed with this, to be purified of them."

Before his admission to the Society, Livingstone was also asked questions about the qualifications and duties of missionaries; about the temptations he might have to face; about the attitude of his parents; his status: married, engaged or single. To the questions about his financial position his answer was brief: "By working in the summer, I can maintain myself, but not pay college fees and books; I have no friend in circumstances to help me; my brother cannot help as he has a family to maintain."

Though the prayers doubtless struck a chord in David Livingstone's inner being, the ceremony in Albion Chapel could not have meant much to him. Two years later, from Africa, he wrote to a friend, Manning Prentice, with revealing frankness, "I do not attach any importance to ordination. I only wish all had been ordained; it would have prevented some from despising others who remain here without that ceremony having been performed on them." (April 14, 1842.)[14]

On December 8, 1840, David Livingstone embarked with the Rev William Ross and his wife on the *George*, a steamer bound for the Cape and Port Elizabeth. Recently an anonymous donor sent a packet of faded letters to the Blantyre Museum – they were David Livingstone's letters to a girl called Catherine Ridley, with whom he was very much in love and to whom he had proposed marriage. But she turned him down, and soon after his departure married one of his close friends, T. Lomas Prentice.

Throughout his life, David Livingstone maintained the legend that as a young man he had been so dedicated to his missionary career that he had never even been interested in a woman. When he did marry, he soon had to choose between his family and his missionary and exploratory work – and he chose the latter.

## CHAPTER TWO

# Livingstone's years as missionary

On March 15, 1841, Dr David Livingstone – medical missionary – stepped on African soil at Simon's Bay. For four weeks he stayed in Cape Town with Dr John Philip, an ardent Congregationalist, who had become a controversial figure because of his strong championing of the indigenous people. Not only the Boers but also his fellow missionaries were critical of his passionate stand; not so Livingstone, who was much impressed by Dr Philip's reasoning. He said as much, and with great vehemence, from the pulpit. This somewhat tactless outburst was especially resented in a novice, and naturally the Boer community reacted indignantly. Remnants of these feelings survive to this day, although Field-Marshal Jan Smuts, after the first world war, went out of his way to pay tribute to Livingstone. It was significant that Livingstone took up the cause of the African almost before he had set eyes on him, and remained his friend to the end of his life. He got on appreciably better with Africans than with white men, who never took to his leadership.

Six weeks later, Livingstone arrived by ox-cart in Kuruman, the mission station which Dr Moffat, who had started life as a gardener, had beautified with flowers and fruit trees. On the way Livingstone had learnt to shoot, and had started to describe in his diary everything he set eyes on. Nothing escaped his attention; he had not only the gift of precise observation, but of relating the smallest detail so as to make the reader see it. Of the organisation of the Kuruman mission he was decidedly critical. Barely three months in Africa, he declared that it was wrong that so many missionaries should live in safe and comfortable localities in the south, while innumerable villages to the north remained unvisited. And why was not more use made of African workers? This reprimand from the newcomer annoyed some of his colleagues, and their relations became strained.

As the Moffats were delayed in Cape Town, Livingstone went with a senior missionary, Roger Edwards, on an expedition to find a suitable place for a new settlement. In the first year they covered 700 miles. The Bechuana tribes, terrified of Mzilikazi, who was thought of by many as the dreaded Matabele marauder, were glad to have a white man live amidst them, hoping he would give them security. Livingstone showed his talent for languages by learning Sechuana in three months; he gave proof of his courage by preaching his first

The Moffat's mission house

sermon to the Bakaa, a tribe that had recently murdered four white men. They gave Livingstone no trouble. This further strengthened Livingstone's conviction that it was his duty to spread the Word of the Lord among the African heathen – he could do it where others would fail.

Travelling through the fringe of the Kalahari desert, he and Edwards had a friendly reception from Sekomi, the Chief of the Bamangwato, the great-great-grandfather of Sir Seretse Khama, President of the present-day state of Botswana. From the time he first arrived in Africa Livingstone studied tribal customs, and treated Africans with patience and tact; though tactless, even overbearing with Europeans, he seemed to have an instinctive understanding for the Africans. To this approach, coupled as it was with his calm courage, practically all Africans responded.

Eventually Livingstone decided, without paying much attention to Edwards's views, that the new mission station was to be set up at Mabotsa,[1] in the land of the Bakgatla tribe, 220 miles north-east of Kuruman, roughly where Mafeking now stands. It was well situated and had plenty of water. The district was thickly populated, and the people excelled at iron work. But they showed no interest in the message of the Gospel, except for their Chief, Sechele, who became Livingstone's first convert.

At this time Livingstone had an adventure that nearly cost him his life. He had shown a somewhat cavalier attitude towards lions: "Nothing I have ever heard of the lion would lead me to attribute it either the noble or the ferocious character ascribed to it", he had written to a friend. But he was confronted by a fully-grown lion, which was crouching on a knoll above the road along which Livingstone and an African teacher, Mebalwe, were walking. Livingstone gave the lion both barrels. While he was reloading, the wounded animal sprang and knocked him to the ground. Later he wrote: "Growling horribly, close to my ear he shook me as a terrier dog does a rat. It caused a sort of dreaminess in which there was no sense of pain or feeling of terror, though I was conscious of all that happened. As he had one paw on the back of my head I turned to release myself and saw his eyes directed to Mebalwe."[2]

The teacher fired twice. He missed, but the noise distracted the lion who sprang at the African and bit him in the thigh. A second African who tried to help was also wounded. At last the bullets took effect and the spear of a third African finished the work. For three months Livingstone suffered excruciating pain and never regained full use of his left arm. The poorly-set humerus could at times be seen sticking up under his coat. In later years Sir J. Risdon Bennett, the famous surgeon, was to comment upon this incident in the following terms: "The account he gave me of his perilous encounter with the lion, and the means he adopted for the repair of the serious injuries he received, excited the astonishment and admiration of all the medical friends to whom I related it, as evincing an account of courage, sagacity, skill and endurance that have scarcely been surpassed in the annals of heroism." Sir Risdon also said: "His letters to me, and indeed all the records of his eventful life demonstate how great to him was the value of medical knowledge with which he entered on missionary life. There is abundant evidence that on various occasions his own life was preserved through his courageous and sagacious application of his scientific knowledge to his own needs, and the benefits which he conferred on the natives to whose welfare he devoted himself, and the wonderful influence he exercised over them, were in no small degree due to the humane and skilled assistance which he was able to render as healer of bodily disease."[3] This is perhaps one of the more succinct analyses of Livingstone's success with the Africans, and why his memory among them is still alive. Like Pierre Savorgnan de Brazza in West Africa, in Central and East Africa Livingstone was one of the few explorers[4] – for explorer was the role he really sought for himself – who achieved his results without bullying Africans.

His probing mind was interested in many things. At one time he even studied astrology, but as he wrote to a friend, it was perilous ground "for the dark seemed to my youthful mind to loom towards 'selling my soul and body to the devil' at the price of an unfathomable knowledge of the stars." Had he read his own horoscope, he might have discovered that a great change in his life was imminent. At last the Moffats arrived and with them their eldest daughter Mary, about whom he had heard a lot as she had been born and brought up in Kuruman. David Livingstone and Mary Moffat fell in love,[5] and on January 2, 1845, Dr Moffat married them in the old church which is still standing. Her husband described Mary as "a little thick, black haired girl, sturdy, and all I want." Her charming features deserved more praise. She was scrupulously tidy in appearance, and in the trying conditions of African travel she always managed to create some semblance of comfort in her wagon.

In their first home at Mabotsa the Livingstones had to contend with all the hardships besetting settlers in those days. Mrs Livingstone struggled on with her infant school, while Dr Livingstone preached earnestly and never ceased from his labours of saving Africans for God. He was keener than ever to use trained African evangelists, and submitted to his colleagues a scheme for a seminary. They would not hear of it; some of them accused him of wanting to curry favour with the Directors of the Mission for his own advancement. Much later Livingstone's plan was carried out by others; it would have improved relations with the Africans had it been done in the 1840s.

Then there was trouble with Roger Edwards, who had had his fill of Livingstone's wilfulness. He drafted an indignant letter to the home Directors stating that he was not prepared to play second fiddle to a junior. In the end he did not send the letter, but he certainly had a case. Livingstone tended to dominate in whatever company he found himself: with his Highland pride he was apt to appear domineering and seldom seemed to feel the need to explain: his conviction that he was right was unshakable.

At this stage the Directors of the LMS thought him unbalanced and impulsive, and were not inclined to support his plans. Yet neither criticism nor reprimand had much effect upon him. He solved his problem with Edwards by surrendering to him the station he had laboured so hard to build. As his next mission centre he chose Chonuane, a village in the Bakwain country, forty miles further north, and once more had to build a house, a school and a church. He also had to provide for Mary and their first child. Then water was found to be scarce and Boer encroachments came nearer and nearer. In August, 1847, the Livingstones moved again, this time to the eastern edge of the Kalahari, where he built a house on a rocky eminence over the Colobeng river. At night the cold was intense, and by day flies tormented his children, of whom there were now two; the flies "settled on the eyes of the poor little brats". Yet the Livingstones spent the happiest five years of their family life in Colobeng.

A difficult side of Livingstone's character was that he could not forget and forgive. Having had to give up Mabotsa rankled, and he took refuge in dreams about the unknown north. If only healthy sites could be found there, he would establish a home for his family more beautiful than Mabotsa had ever been, and mission stations that the Boers could not spoil since, with their cattle, they could not risk facing the waterless Kalahari desert. So his ambition grew to become a missionary pioneer and explorer. But how was he to start on this great venture on an annual salary of £100?[6] And what was he to do with his family, especially with his children when they reached school age? There seemed no answer to these insuperable difficulties. And then, completely unexpectedly, the hunters came, and through them new, almost miraculous, possibilities opened up. Livingstone regarded them as answers to his prayers.

Several of them passed Chonuane and Colobeng, enjoyed Mary Livingstone's hospitality and sought the doctor's advice about the country and its people. Livingstone made friends with Captain Thomas Steele, Mungo Murray, W. F. Webb, and perhaps the most charming of them all, William Cotton Oswell. In view of the far-reaching effect Oswell was to have on David Livingstone's life and of the part he was to play in the affairs of the Livingstone family until his death in 1893, Cotton Oswell's life story must be told – at least in broad outline.

## CHAPTER THREE

# The story of the hunter

No greater contrast could be imagined than that between the respective backgrounds of David Livingstone and William Cotton Oswell. Oswell's parents, on both sides, came from wealthy, well-established families. His father, William Oswell of Shrewsbury, traced his descent directly from St Oswel (Oswal or Oswald) of Northumbria; one of his ancestors had fought with Harold against William at the Battle of Hastings in 1066. William Oswell went into business in London, and became a successful trader with Russia. As he had to be daily at his office, in 1806 he bought a house in Leytonstone, Essex, which was suitably near London. One of his neighbours was Joseph Cotton, a country squire, whose family had close connections with the East India Company, the Indian Army and the Bank of England. His son, William Cotton, was elected a Director of the Bank in 1822.

The Cottons were a tightly knit, devoted family, in constant touch with each other. Judging by their journals and letters – which they had time to write and space to store – they cared deeply for each other, and discussed their smallest problems together.

William Oswell met Emily Cotton at her first dance, when she was 18 years old, and fell in love with her at first sight. Next morning, he wrote her a long, romantic letter, which began: "It is with an anxious, trembling eagerness that I take up my pen, but oh! with what language shall I address my dear Miss Cotton to acquaint her with the sentiments of a heart which is entirely at her disposal . . ." According to the custom of the day, he added a page for her father's benefit outlining his financial position. He had an income of £1,400 a year[1] and no income tax to pay. Three weeks later he asked John Cotton for his daughter's hand in marriage, and their wedding took place on August 20, 1807. The young couple settled in a spacious house in Leytonstone. It was disappointing that Emily bore four daughters in succession when they longed for a son, but at her age this was no tragedy. A more serious problem arose when friends, to whom William Oswell had loaned large sums of money, could not repay him, and in 1816 he lost half his fortune. The Oswells had to move to a smaller house and retrench their way of life. They were compensated for this misfortune by the birth of one son on April 22, 1818, baptized William Cotton, and the birth of a second, Edward Waring, two years later. William Oswell worked hard in the city, steadily retrieving his losses, so that in 1821 the family were able to buy back the house they loved.

At the beginning of 1822, William Oswell had a severe illness, from which he appeared to recover completely. But he had two relapses, and on October 22, 1822, he died, leaving Emily Oswell a widow at the age of 33. This was only the beginning of her tribulations: one after the other her four daughters also died, and the death of the third, her favourite Emily, left her disconsolate. Her family rallied around her; her father offered to put her up with her two sons, saying there was plenty of room for all of them in his home; eventually her brother Benjamin bought a large house he knew Emily liked, and asked her to run it for him. "For the next fifteen years Benjamin Cotton devoted himself body and soul to the service of his sister, and became a father in the best and truest sense to his young nephews."[2]

Both the Oswell boys were apparently charming, but William – ever since his school days known as Cotton – was the image of Victorian manhood – tall, handsome, athletic, highly intelligent, with excellent manners. At the age when David Livingstone had to work ten-and-a-half-hours a day under harsh conditions, Cotton Oswell lived comfortably at home with a private tutor; then he went to Dr Oke's school in Walthamstow for two years, from there to Mr Delafosse's at Hackney for three. At both he was very popular, and was outstanding as a cricketer. At home he had his own pony and groom, and bred retrievers. When he was nearly fifteen years old, his uncle Benjamin took him for an interview with Dr Thomas Arnold, the great reforming headmaster of Rugby, where mathematics were taught in addition to Latin and Greek, and, as compared with other "Establishments", corporal punishment and bullying were kept under control. In February 1833, Cotton Oswell passed the entrance examination, and was admitted to the House of Mr Grenfell, regarded as one of the best masters.

From the first, Cotton enjoyed Rugby. In his first letter to his mother he wrote, "I am much obliged to you for your offer of milk for my dogs, but do not let them have it without barley meal or some other substance as it makes them thin. . . . I hope you will have got me another horse by Midsummer. Do not get one too small. I should like one about fifteen hands high." And to his brother Edward he wrote a fortnight later, "I am particularly comfortable here at Rugby sitting in a little study of my own with a capital good fire. In this study I have breakfast and tea. . . . There is not half so much fagging as I thought there would be. I believe I can lick all the house I am at. . . . Our regular number of half holidays are three in a week. We usually have four, often five. We have 330 boys here – a pretty tolerable number I consider. We ought to have a good XI at cricket and we have got a very good one indeed by all accounts. There are about thirty fellows with thick whiskers, obliged to shave every morning, which according to my calculation must be a great bore; they are much older than I have been accustomed to. . . ."[3]

What Cotton did not mention was the impression he made on the boys at Rugby. Many years later, Judge Hughes gave this description of him:

"To my boyish imagination the one who stood out from the rest as Hector from the rest of the Trojan Princes: and this hero was William Oswell. It was not from any personal knowledge of, or contact with him, for we were at different boarding-houses, and at opposite ends of the school; and I doubt whether he ever spoke to me in his life, though I often shared his kindly nod and smile when we met in the close or quadrangle. It was the rare mixture of kindliness and gentleness with marvellous strength, activity and fearlessness which made him *facile princeps* among his contemporaries. I don't believe he ever struck a small boy or even spoke to one in anger. And so there was no drawback to the enthusiasm with which one watched him leading a charge at football, or bowling in a big side match, or jumping two or three pegs higher on the gallows than any other boy. He *cleared* eighteen feet nine inches in Clifton Brook, which means, as you know, twenty feet from take-off to landing. No doubt his good looks added to the fascination; he stood six feet high in his stockings when he left school, at eighteen, but did not look his height from the perfection of his figure – broad in shoulders, thin in flank, and so well developed that he was called 'The Muscleman'."[4]

Oswell left Rugby at the end of the Summer Term of 1835, and after a few days at home, joined his uncle Joseph Cotton at Tunbridge Wells, who, travelling in his own carriage, took his nephew to all the principal ports and manufacturing centres of England. They remained at each town until Cotton had "seen and digested everything it had to show". But Cotton was not inclined to take to business, he longed for a military career, and would have liked a commission in the Indian Army. Then another uncle, William Cotton, a director of the Bank of England,[5] secured him a job with the East India Company – to the sorrow of his mother who would have liked him to stay at least in England, if not in Essex.

Cotton went to Haileybury, then the Training College for the Company's service, in January 1836, with the highest recommendation of Dr Arnold, and his house-master, Mr Grenfell. Today Dr Arnold's views read somewhat amusingly: "It is very true that by our distinctness we have gained very much – more than foreigners can understand. A thorough English gentlemen – Christian, manly, enlightened – is a finer sentiment of human nature than any other country, I believe, could furnish." William Cotton Oswell lived up to all Dr Arnold's expectations.[6]

Oswell spent eleven months at Haileybury, and left with a prize in Classics, and high distinctions in other subjects. "The College Council, in consideration of his Industry, Proficiency and Conduct, place him in the First Class of Merit, and assign him the rank of Second on the List of Students now leaving College for the Presidency of Fort St George." Thus stated the concluding paragraph of the diploma he received, signed by the Principal, J. H. Batten, on December 6, 1836.

He spent the next five months enjoyably visiting friends and relatives, until on September 14, 1837, he sailed for India, where he was to spend the next seven years of his life in the Indian Civil Service, then the civil section of the East India Company. He shared the pleasant life of the well-to-do young gentlemen of the India of pre-Mutiny days. He worked hard, and soon learnt Tamil so well that he could discharge his public business without an interpreter – a rare accomplishment at that time. It also made him very popular with the Indians, who talked to him freely of their manners, customs, history and religions. During his up-country tours he was forcibly struck by the high mortality rate among the peasants from trivial diseases, and the amount of unnecessary suffering they endured. As there were no doctors outside the towns, he began to study medicine, which became a source of profound interest to him, and its application stood him in good stead during his travels later on in Africa, South America and even in Europe.

But Cotton Oswell was also capable of enjoying himself. He hunted, played cricket and racquets, went in for boxing, pig-sticking and shooting. In India, as at Rugby and Haileybury, he was much admired by his friends and colleagues.

Towards the end of 1843, while out on a shooting excursion on the banks of the Bhavany river, he was struck down by a virulent fever and for two months his life was in danger. His constitution saved him, and he regained his strength rapidly, soon riding daily, but his mind remained confused. When he tried to catch up with his accumulated arrears of work, the fever returned. He rallied again, but had constant relapses. At last he gave in, and accepted the advice proffered on all sides that he should take two years' leave and go to South Africa. He sailed on September 2, 1844. By then he had lost so much weight that he had gone down from twelve stone to seven. He was so weak that he had to be carried on board; he could not even raise his head, and was frequently comatose. But during the seven weeks' journey he improved so much that he arrived in Cape Town on October 26, 1844, in good spirits.

## CHAPTER FOUR

# Cotton Oswell's explorations

"I have met and been introduced to more friends and strangers since my arrival than for the last seven years of my life," Cotton Oswell wrote to his mother from Cape Town on October 26, 1844. "I shall I fancy gain much from a little rubbing together with my kind for I was I am afraid getting very rough and junglefied in India. The mere having to wear a coat seems to civilise one to a certain extent."[1]

Again it was from others that Emily Oswell heard how popular her son had become in a short time. His skill as a shot and as a horseman were the talk of Cape Town society; invitations poured in, especially from mothers with marriageable daughters. However, social life had never attracted Cotton Oswell. "After having lived a stirring life for seven or eight years, without some strong excitement, of which the Cape is destitute, I find it tedious in the extreme to remain in one place, and have already made two or three short trips into the country," he wrote to his mother four months later. "I am now on the eve of sailing . . . in the direction of Graham's Town in company with a Mr Murray,[2] and purpose wandering about in search of amusement and sport for some four or five months. For that period our wagons . . . will be our only home, and I look forward to the trip with the most sanguine hopes."[3]

A war, which had broken out between the Griquas and the trekking Boers forced Oswell and Murray to cross the Orange River much further south than they had intended. They found the countryside barren, "as if lately upheaved from the burning bowels of the earth, bearing in nearly every part strong marks of volcanic action," he wrote to his mother and brother in June 1845. "The only thing that puts me out at all is the privations our oxes, horses, and I may add we ourselves have to put up with for want of water." About 300 miles north of Colesberg, Oswell and his companion paid a visit to Kuruman: "We stayed a short time at the station of that grand old patriarch of missionaries, Mr Moffat, where we received all the kindly hospitality, attention and advice possible from him and Mrs Moffat – verily the two best friends travellers ever came across. I shall never forget their affectionate courtesy, their beautifully ordered household, and their earnest desire to help us in every way. He advised us to go to Dr Livingstone who was then stationed at Mabotsé – 220 miles or so to the Northward, and obtain from him guides and counsel for our further wanderings."

In this way the friendship with Livingstone began. Cotton Oswell, with his friendly and generous disposition, was enthusiastic about his new acquaintance: "After staying two days with the Rev Mr Livingstone, the best, most intelligent and most modest (a rarer virtue is modesty than you suppose) of the missionaries, and having by his advice taken a direction which led us at first rather to the westward, and eventually to the north east, for three months we revelled in the finest climate, the finest shooting, and anything but tame scenery. . . . We were fully repaid for our long journey, for we penetrated further than anyone had done before us, saw as much as we could with one pair of eyes a-piece, and last, not least, slew game in abundance – elephants, rhinoceroses, hippopotami, giraffes, *et hoc genus omne*."

It was typical of the carefree, gentlemanly and leisured attitude of Cotton Oswell that he did not trouble to record in detail his first African exploration, although the map he attached to the letter sent to his mother showed that he and Murray had penetrated some 400 miles northwards into the interior, where no European had been before them. For many weeks Oswell hunted with a group of Bushmen, and from them learnt much about the local wild life. He described them as "upright, tall,[4] sinewy fellows", and thanks to the Bushmen's skill and the abundance of game the party never suffered hunger. "I was very fond of them; they tell the truth, and instead of being mere pot-hunters, are enthusiastic sportsmen, enjoying the work as much as yourself," Oswell wrote to his brother on November 29, 1845.[5]

His own alertness and powers of observation greatly impressed the Bushmen, who recognised him as their equal in the skills of the chase, and gave him the name of *Tlaga*, meaning "on the lookout, wary, as of game", which clung to him throughout his travels in Africa.

Oswell and Murray had three months' magnificent sport among the Bakgatla, whose country Oswell mapped; then they moved on with their wagons to the Bawangketsi. Here Oswell had one of his

William Cotton Oswell

Cape Town

less pleasant experiences: out to shoot some game as food for the fourteen dogs they had with them, he got lost in the bush, and narrowly escaped attack by a lion in the dark. Half frozen in the cold night, he eventually found his way back to the camp guided by the sound of shots fired by the anxious Mungo Murray.

Oswell and Murray then made their way to Bamangwato territory, where they had a poor reception; thanks to Oswell's cool handling of the arrogant chief they extricated themselves from a fight with the tribe. In spite of the Bamangwato, they reached the Bakaa hills, about which they had heard, and which were the ultimate objective of this first expedition. But the Bakaa people were in a pitiable condition: the crops had failed and many were starving. At their chief's request, Oswell accepted 600 men, women and children, all in a terrible state of emaciation and sickness, and started for the hunting grounds. Seven weeks later he was able to send them back to their kraals well fed and relatively healthy. They had to requisition porters to help them carry large faggots of sun-dried strips of meat. On the return journey Oswell and Murray shot their way down the Limpopo; calling at Mabotsa "to shake the dear old Doctor and Mrs Livingstone by the hand," they reached Cape Town in December 1845. Had Oswell been in the least ambitious, he could have sent an important and arresting report to the Royal Geographical Society, for he had covered and mapped a considerable area which was then still blank on the official maps of Africa. If the Portuguese had reached it from their settlements along the east coast, they had not recorded it.

In March 1846, Cotton Oswell went on his second African expedition, with the aim of exploring the Mariqué river, a small tributary of the Limpopo. It was an added attraction that the area was rich in game, and Oswell was out shooting almost every day, sometimes for 36 hours at a stretch.

One early morning in May, an African brought him a letter fastened in a cleft stick from a Captain Frank Vardon, of the 25th Madras Native Infantry, suggesting that they join up and shoot together. Oswell's first reaction was that this unknown newcomer might not be a desirable companion, and he sent a cool answer. But an hour later he regretted his churlishness, and sent another letter begging Captain Vardon to ignore the first, pardon his selfishness, and join him as soon as possible. "To the end of my life I shall rejoice that I did so, for in three days the finest fellow and best comrade a man ever had made his appearance," he wrote many years later. "I will not attempt to describe him. Let every man picture for himself the most perfect fellow-traveller he can imagine, and that is Frank; brightest, bravest-hearted of men, with the most unselfish of dispositions, totally ignorant of jealousy, the light of camp fires, the most trustworthy of mates; a better sportsman and a better shot than myself at all kinds of game save elephants."[6]

Oswell shot a prodigous number of elephants and had the ivory piled up under his wagons. When a party of Boers, who hunted on the other side of the Mariqué, came to visit them and noticed the ivory, they would not believe that it was all Oswell's booty. "A poor lean fellow like you could never have shot such a splendid lot of tusks," one of them said. When the drivers convinced the Boers that Oswell had indeed shot all those elephants, they proposed that he should join and shoot with them, and take half of the ivory killed by the whole party. With difficulty Oswell persuaded the Boers that he was not interested.

Together Oswell and Vardon were the first white men to record the

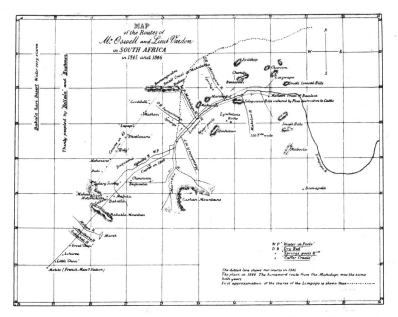

Map of the routes taken by Oswell and Vardon in 1845 and 1846

Mokolo, an important tributary of the Limpopo. There they first met the *quebaaba*, a rare type of rhinoceros, and the tsetse fly, which decimated their animals. Oswell also had a terrifying experience with a white rhinoceros. Riding his favourite horse, Stael, he fired both barrels at the beast, but instead of dropping or bolting, the rhino began to walk towards the smoke. Oswell tried to turn his mount but a thick bush was pressing against its chest. Before he could free it, the rhinoceros drove its horn in under the horse's flank, threw horse and rider into the air with terrific force and the point of its horn pierced the saddle. As they fell, the stirrup iron scalped Oswell's head with a gash four inches in length and breadth. He scrambled to his knees, and saw the horn within the bend of his leg. With the energy of self-preservation he sprang to his feet, but he tripped and collapsed on the ground. The rhinoceros passed within a foot without hurting him. At that moment his after-rider rode up, Oswell somehow managed to mount his horse, and galloped after the rhinoceros. Wringing the blood from his eyes, and keeping back the piece of scalp with his left hand, he held his gun to his shoulder with his right hand, and killed the rhino. Then he returned to Stael – so badly mauled by the rhino that he had to put a bullet into its head immediately. He took the saddle from Stael's back, and walked for ten miles, making his after-rider do likewise. When they eventually reached the wagons and explained what had happened, the Africans apparently burst into tears.

By the autumn of 1846, Oswell and Vardon were back in Cape Town, and both promptly set sail for India. Oswell had received an official notification that unless he returned by a certain date, his appointment would be cancelled. By then he was two months overdue – and on arrival found that his job was lost. But he was offered two other good posts, which he refused as he planned to go back to England – and then to Africa.

Early in 1847, the *Madras Journal of Literature and Science* asked him to write a report on his wanderings. He agreed and sent his account with a sketch map of the areas he had traversed. The *Madras Journal* commented:

"On the first occasion, with Mr Murray, Mr Oswell reached the Ba-Kaa mountains, and returned by the valley of the Limpopo. This line nearly coincides with the track of Mr W. Hume in 1830. In his next journey he was joined by Captain Vardon and they together explored the course of the Limpopo to a greater extent than had been done by any previous travellers. Mr Oswell was at first led to suppose that the stream pursued a more northerly course (indicated by the red line on the map), and he had placed their turning point in the Lingwapa mountains somewhere between 20° and 21° S. Lat. But subsequent consideration, and the result of a communication from Mr Livingstone, the enterprising Scotch Missionary in the Bechuana country, induced him to exhibit the direction of the river as it now stands. 'This sketch,' observed Mr Oswell, 'is not supposed to be strictly accurate. We laid down the course of the river Limpopo as correctly as we could from the tops of the hills, etc. with a compass, but having no other instrument, we are aware that many errors may have crept in, and only hope that others, more carefully provided, may some day or other give the world a better [sic]. The present will serve to show the wanderer where water may be obtained at a distance from the river, and information such as this even, is not to be despised in Africa. The lines dotted and plain mark the track of the wagons, but the country was well quartered on horseback for forty or fifty miles on either side. The Limpopo is supposed to reach the sea at, or somewhere a little to the North of, Delagoa Bay.

The Bekoa and Bumungwato tribes whom Mr Oswell visited in his first excursion mentioned three other people as living to the north of them, viz. the Makalakka, Mancupani and Mashuna. They were also familiar with the existence of the great Lake,[7] and had frequently visited it. They described it as lying in a WNW direction from their location, at a distance of twelve or fourteen days' journey for a man on foot (which would be about three hundred miles) or a month with the wagon."[8]

This indicates that Cotton Oswell was fully informed about the existence of Lake Ngami, and that he toyed with the idea of going to it on his next expedition. But before he could make this further expedition, he had to return to England, because his mother – as his family had written to him – had, although only 58 years old, become a very old woman, worn out with grief and pain. He took her to Torquay, hoping that the warm air might revive her. With every day the gulf of their eleven years of separation narrowed. When she was too tired to talk, he read to her. On January 7, 1848, on her 59th birthday, Mrs Oswell seemed completely exhausted, and next morning she died in the arms of her "best-loved boy".

Eight months later, Cotton Oswell wrote to Dr Livingstone, "I received your long letter yesterday. Many thanks for it; it has cheered my heart wonderfully. D.V. I propose being at the Cape by the middle of December. . . . With God's blessing I will be with you towards the close of May 1849." By now, Cotton Oswell was firmly intent on the exploration of the large lake in the north.

## CHAPTER FIVE

# Lake Ngami discovered

Oswell reached the Cape at the end of 1848, and immediately began to prepare for the journey. He engaged ten servants, bought two wagons, twenty horses and eighty oxen; and on February 10, 1849, he embarked for Port Elizabeth. From there he went to Grahamstown, where he purchased supplies: 300 lbs. of coffee, 400 lbs. of tea, 100 lbs. of salt, 400 lbs. of sugar, two cases of brandy, three bottles of mustard, a box of soap, 10 lbs. of pepper, numerous pots, pans, kettles, dishes, cutlery and buckets, a thermometer, a telescope, a sextant, not to mention gunpowder and cartridges.[1] The preliminary expenditure amounted to £600.[2] One entry says: "For Mrs Moffat: cauliflower, peas, broccoli, cabbage, spinach, carrots, turnips, Jerusalem artichokes."

In March 1849, he and his safari reached Colesberg, where he had to wait nearly four weeks for his friend, Mungo Murray. He wrote to his family, and received letters from two friends, Captain Thomas Steele and Captain Frank Vardon. In his hurried note Vardon said, "what about the lake – to be or not to be?" and many good wishes that "it shall be". Then nothing was heard from Cotton Oswell for nearly a year. Meanwhile the world learnt from David Livingstone, who joined Cotton Oswell's safari north of Colobeng, that the expedition had been a success.

Clearly, Oswell had discussed with Livingstone his idea of finding "the big lake to the north", about which the doctor had also heard. But on his own, with his meagre salary of £100 a year, always in debt to the LMS, Livingstone could not seriously have considered going there. To pass through the Kalahari desert, even along its fringe, was only possible with a well equipped expedition. This was utterly beyond his capacity. So when Oswell invited Livingstone to come with him, it was again like an answer to a prayer. Yet at once Livingstone also began to worry that he would have to share credit for discovering the lake – or that Oswell might get more recognition than he. This emerges from his letter to his brother Charles, written on May 16, 1849, in which he complained about the drought and his own poverty. Then he said: "However, there are unknown regions beyond, and I set off in a week or two in order to penetrate to a large lake which lies beyond us. If it has no alligators, won't I roll in its water as we have done in Christie's Burn.³ There are canoes upon it, and seven men came to us about a fortnight ago inviting us to visit them. I would have been off there now, but an English gentleman, who presented us with a waggon worth £50 sent an express begging me to delay until he came to accompany me. As that is not the only instance of his liberality I felt under obligation to wait. *The honour of discovery will probably be given to him*." (Author's italics.) In a letter to his parents, referring to Oswell, Livingstone said: "Others less closely connected may be more highly favoured."

Back from Lake Ngami, Oswell dropped Livingstone at Colobeng. The doctor lost no time in writing up the successful expedition in three letters. He made spelling mistakes and the vivid style was reminiscent of his grandfather's story telling. The first letter, dated September 3, 1849, was to Arthur Tidman, the Foreign Secretary of the LMS:

"We left Kolobeng on the first of June last, in order to carry into effect the intention of which I had previously informed you, viz. to open a new field in the North by penetrating the great obstacle to progress called the Desert⁴ which, stretching away on our West, North-West and North, has hitherto presented an insurmountable barrier to Europeans. A large party of Griquas in about thirty waggons made many and persevering efforts at two different points last year, but though inured to the climate, and stimulated by the prospect of much gain from the ivory they expected to procure, want of water compelled them to retreat. Two gentlemen to whom I had communicated my intention of proceeding to the oft-reported lake beyond the Desert came from England for the express purpose of being present at the discovery, and to their liberal and zealous cooperation we are especially indebted for the success with which that and other objects have been accomplished. While waiting for their arrival, seven men came from the Bataoana⁵, a tribe living on the banks of the Lake, with an earnest request from their chief for a visit. But the path by which they had come to Kolobeng was impracticable for waggons, so declining

William Cotton Oswell

Lake Ngami

their guidance, I selected the more circuitous route by which the Bamangwato usually pass, and having Bakwains for guides[6] their self-interest in our success was secured by my promising to carry any ivory they might procure for their chief in my waggon. And right faithfully they performed their task. When Sekhomi, the Bamangwato chief, became aware of our intention to pass into the region beyond him, with true native humanity he sent men in front of us to drive away all the Bushmen and Bakalahari from our route, in order that, being deprived of their assistance in the search for water, we might, like the Griquas above mentioned, be compelled to retire. This measure deprived me of the opportunity of holding the intercourse with these poor outcasts I might otherwise have enjoyed. But through the good Providence of God, after travelling about 300 miles from Kolobeng we struck this magnificent river on the fourth of July, and, without further difficulty in so far as water was concerned, by winding along its banks nearly 300 more, we reached the Bataoana on the Lake Ngami by the beginning of August."

Livingstone sent a similar letter to his parents, and a more detailed one to Captain Thomas Steele. The Tidman and the Steele letters, read out at the Royal Geographical Society, caused a sensation, and overnight Livingstone became famous. Of Cotton Oswell, the true organiser of the expedition, virtually nothing was heard.

In response to letters from relations and friends, upset because Livingstone described the discovery as though it had been exclusively his own effort, Cotton Oswell at last wrote to his uncle, Benjamin Cotton, on January 16, 1850:

"When I started I had a definite object, but did not mention it, as it would not have enlightened or interested you much in England, and my failure would have gratified some of the good folks here. There have for many years been reports received through natives from time to time of the existence of a Lake in the interior of Southern Africa. In 1835, I think, an expedition was fitted out by the Government, and headed by a Dr Smith, purposely for its discovery. They grew discouraged and turned homewards. Many others have since *talked* of making the attempt, and the Griquas, a mixed race living to the North of the Orange River, have repeatedly tried it, but always failed for want of water. Two hundred miles beyond Dr Smith's farthest point I had pushed in my former wanderings, and heard of the existence of this Lake and its direction, from many of the natives; this time I determined to make for it, for I felt persuaded the difficulties were not insurmountable, and the more arduous the task, so long as we accomplished it, the better. With horses, oxen and wagons I waited at Colesberg, the last of the frontier towns, for Murray, and inspanning immediately on his arrival, passed onwards to Kolobeng, the most Northern Missionary Station, situated in 24°30′E. Long. Here our party was increased by Mr Livingstone, the Missionary, and a Mr Wilson.[7] A party of Baquaina, the tribe residing at Kolobeng, accompanied us, and one of them who had in former years been at the 'Great Water' was appointed guide through the pathless wilds. For the first hundred and twenty miles, to the hills of the Bamungwato, a people whom we all had previously visited, the course took a N.E. direction. From this point the road was unknown save by report. Two days' travelling through heavy sand covered with low bush and clumps of mimosa, in a N.N.E. line, brought us to a spot called by the natives Serotli.

It was here our first difficulties began. Serotli stands on the extreme verge of the Kalahari Desert. Our oxen had already been without water for two days on our arrival, and there was no apparent possibility of their obtaining that necessary. The place itself was a sand hollow with no signs of water save about a pint in one small hole. We had eighty oxen, twenty horses and thirty or forty men, all thirsty. Unpromising as was the appearance of the spot, the old guide assured us that if we dug we should obtain a supply. Spades and landturtle shells were accordingly set to work, and at the close of the day we had sufficient to give the horses a sip each. For two days longer the poor oxen had still to remain without, but four pits being at length opened to the depth of eight or nine feet, a sufficiency for all our beasts was obtained. Watering them, we once more moved on. The sand was distressingly heavy and the sun fiery hot. The oxen moved so slowly and with such difficulty that I was at times afraid we should fail even in the very outset, but fortunately, considerably before we expected it, on the third day we came by chance upon a small pool of rain-water. The poor beasts were nearly exhausted, but a day's rest and three or four good drinks recruited [sic] them. The most trying, because the heaviest, part of the Kalahari was behind, but a hundred miles was still between us and any certain supply of water. Another small rain-water pond and a little spring, however, furnished us with what we wanted, though not without our having to do twice, three days without. You will perhaps wonder at our being so long in covering so short a distance, but a wagon is not a steam-carriage. Water was excessively scarce, its whereabouts unknown, and the sand, occasionally for miles together, over the felloes of the wheels. I shall never forget the pleasure with which whilst riding out ahead of the wagons, on the 4th of July we came suddenly upon a considerable river (the Zouga), running, as we struck it, N.E. by E. The wagons reached it the same evening, and our troubles were looked upon as past, for we were informed by the natives, with whom we managed after much trouble to open a parley, that the water flowed from the Lake we were in search of. Their information was correct, and holding up the course of the stream for two hundred and eighty miles, and meeting with no difficulties to speak of, save from the denseness of the bush and trees in particular tracts, through which we had to cut our way, we at length reached the object of our expedition, and were fully repaid.

None save those who have suffered from the want, know the beauty of water. A magnificent sheet without bound that we could see, gladdened our eyes. Animal life, which had in the Desert been confined to one or two of the deer tribe which do not require water, and Bushmen, who inserting a reed three or four feet below the surface, suck it up, was here and there along the river, greatly increased. A new nation, speaking a language totally distinct from the Bechuana, inhabited the islands, moving across the water in their canoes and living principally on fish, and animals taken in the pitfalls which lined the banks of the stream. Among the *ferae* the elephant and buffalo were the most numerous, the latter roaming in immense herds, and every accessible drinking place in the river being trampled with the spoor of the former. I had not much spare time to shoot, but a few capital specimens fell to my gun."

After a description of the fauna around Lake Ngami, Oswell wrote: "From knowing where to dig for water, our route back was not so harassing as our inwards one, though want of water made us longer than we otherwise should have been. I could write at much greater length on this topic, but will spare you." What Oswell did not tell was that at one point they were as good as lost in the desert, and almost at the end of their strength for lack of water – when he spotted a Bushman woman and induced her to show him water. There was a large pool at eight miles' distance, and this saved the expedition.[8]

David Livingstone arrives at Lake Ngami (*Mansell Collection*)

As for the future, Oswell wrote, "You will think it about time that I should say how I intend disposing of myself for the current year, and will, I am afraid, be rather disappointed at my persisting in a life of vagrancy; but the accounts from home are so good, and my love of vagabond life so unsatiated, that I purpose again diving into the interior and trying to reach the Portuguese settlements on the Zambesi, by an overland route. Mr Livingstone, the missionary will again accompany me, Murray will not. Of our intended course I will give you some idea in a letter which D.V. I will send to my brother from Colesberg."

The Oswell family was thrilled by this letter, and his cousin, Louisa D. Cotton, was the first to write to him as much, adding: "Now that Frank Vardon has seen your letter, he intends to be at the next Geographical meeting and put in a few words for you, the prime mover in the great discovery, whereas through the London Missionary Society, Mr Livingstone seems to have more than his due."[9]

On Frank Vardon's insistence, Cotton Oswell's letter was read out at the Royal Geographical Society on April 8, 1850, but by then the news was cold. Everyone had heard that Dr Livingstone had discovered Lake Ngami; he had captured the limelight, and there was no interest for anyone else. And this suited the London Missionary Society, which hoped to obtain funds as a result of the Livingstone publicity – indeed it did raise a considerable amount of money at this time. Livingstone's letter to Arthur Tidman was published in the *Missionary Chronicle* of March 1850, having been read out at the Royal Geographical Society on February 11, 1850. Livingstone received an award from Queen Victoria, and a gift of 25 guineas from the Royal Geographical Society of which Arthur Tidman informed him in a letter dated August 5, 1850. No one bothered to ask how Livingstone could have financed his expedition.

Cotton Oswell gave a much better description of the fauna and flora of the lake, and of some of the tribes living on the islands in it, than did Livingstone. The doctor was taken up almost entirely with the implications that two rivers, the Tanumakle which flowed into the Zouga, and the Teoge which flowed into the north-western end of the lake, indicated a large river system in the north. This is how he put it in his letter to Arthur Tidman of September 3, 1849: "The fact that the Zouga is connected with large rivers coming from the north awakens emotions in my mind which make the discovery of the Lake dwindle out of sight. It opens out the prospect of a highway capable of being quickly traversed by boats to a large section of well peopled territory. The hopes which that prospect inspires for the benighted inhabitants might, if uttered, call forth the charge of enthusiasm – a charge, by the way, I wish I deserved, for nothing good or great, either in law, religion or physic, has ever been accomplished without it. However, I do not mean the romantic flight variety, but that which impels with untiring energy to the accomplishment of its object. I do not wish to convey hopes of speedily effecting any great work through my poor instrumentality. I hope to be permitted to work as long as I live beyond other men's line of things, and plant the seed of the Gospel where others have not planted."

Then he related how the Batawana chief prevented their crossing the river and going further north. He said that he could have swum across, but "landing stark naked and bullying the Bakoba for the loan of a boat would scarcely be the thing for a messenger of peace, even though no alligator met me in the passage. These and other thoughts were revolving in my mind as I stood in the water, for most sorely do I dislike to be beat, when my kind and generous friend W. Oswell, Esqre, with whom alone the visit to Sebituane was to be made, offered to bring up a boat at his own expence from the Cape, which after visiting that chief and coming round the north end of the Lake will become missionary property. To him and our other companion, W. Murray, Esqre, I feel greatly indebted, for the chief expense of the journey has been borne by them." This was something of an understatement, as Livingstone was not in a position to make any financial contribution. The purpose of this statement emerges in the next sentence: "They could never have reached this point without my assistance."[10] As will be seen, in the following year Cotton Oswell returned on his own to Lake Ngami without any difficulty.

In the next year, too, as soon as the rainy season was over, Livingstone set out with his family from Colobeng without waiting for Oswell's return. True to his promise, Oswell, for his part, purchased the boat, and at the agreed time left the Cape to join Livingstone and carry out with him the programme they had arranged five months previously. On reaching Colobeng he found that the heat and drought had warped and damaged the boat to such an extent that it was impossible to launch it in a serviceable condition, and that the doctor had left a month before with Mary and the children.

As Oswell concluded that he had no chance of overtaking the doctor, he took his safari to the Zouga, the river discovered the previous year, shooting at his leisure. He followed the south bank on his way to Lake Ngami, and then passing around the lake, returned by the north bank.

It was May 1850, when he heard that Livingstone and his party were within 50 or 60 miles of him. He hastened to them and escorted

Oswell map showing Lake Ngami

them to Colobeng, to the immense relief of Mary Livingstone who was in the ninth month of her pregnancy, and gave birth to a daughter, Elisabeth, practically on arrival. The accounts of Oswell and Livingstone about this rescue operation are remarkably different. In an undated letter to his cousin, Louisa Cotton, Oswell wrote:

"I rode to meet Livingstone, who was returning, having given up all hopes of proceeding further at that time. He had, perhaps rather unwisely, taken with him his wife and children, and the latter together with many of his camp-followers, had been attacked with fever. He told me he did not believe I should be able to obtain guides as the Ba-Towana, from whom I hoped to procure them, were afraid that Sebitoané might take offence at their showing the white man the way through his dominions, and as he is a chief of great power they were unwilling to anger him. This I found to be the case, for later, messengers came from them telling me that some of his people had arrived there with orders from their captain not to return without seeing a *makooa* or white man. I was not above a hundred miles from the Ba-Towana when the news reached me inspanning, therefore, at once, I rode thither in four or five days. I was at first in great hopes that these men would show me the way themselves, but they asserted, whether truly or only awed into saying so by the Ba-Towana, that their chief wished to hear their report of the white man before seeing him. I remained three or four days with them, but the same story was persevered throughout, and finding it useless to tarry longer, I through them, sent a present to Sebitoané, bidding them tell him that I should attempt to reach him after the lapse of six moons. Without guides the road would be impracticable for wagons and oxen, or even on horseback, as in particular spots, which unless you had someone to tell you, you would not find out until too late, the tsétsé (the fly destructive to horses and cattle) is abundant, and even if I were lucky enough to escape the tsétsé and find the *road*, without an interpreter – I had counted on Livingstone for this – I was hardly likely to be able to make Sebitoané understand, and should then in all probability have been looked upon as a spy. I was thus forced to turn hunter again."[11]

Livingstone told no one that the Moffats (Mary's parents), who knew enough about that part of Africa, had objected to their pregnant daughter and their small grandchildren being exposed to the rigors and discomforts of a trip into the unknown interior. Once Livingstone had made up his mind, nothing could shake it. "Providence seems to call me to regions beyond," he wrote on August 24, 1850, to the LMS Directors in London. The hardships of the journey were all the Moffats had predicted; moreover two of the children caught the fever (malaria) that raged among the porters. Livingstone had to remove his family as fast as he could from the unhealthy atmosphere of Lake Ngami; the dry air of the desert helped to restore them. But water once more became a desperate problem, and Oswell, with his well-equipped caravan, literally saved them. Yet all that

Livingstone thought to write to Arthur Tidman was, "In returning
we met our friend Oswell at the ford by which we recrossed the river.
We hastened back to Kolobeng, and in re-crossing the Desert suffered more from want of water than we did in going in. The rainwater
was all dried up. If Mr Oswell makes any discovery, I shall inform
you of it."

In a letter dated July 8, 1850, to his father-in-law, Dr Moffat,
Livingstone said, quite untruthfully, "Oswell was excessively anxious that I should promise to let him accompany me next year, but I
declined, yet I don't know how to get quit of him. He returned a bill
of £40 which I sent to purchase supplies saying he never intended to
use it. What can be done, I don't know. As regards my own feelings, I
am regardless of fame of discovery. Looked at the Lake last year with
no emotion, but felt enthusiastic when I saw the River Tanumakle
and now feel an unquenchable desire to introduce the gospel into the
immense and well peopled region beyond. I think Oswell will renew
his importunities when he comes out. He said he would hunt about
the place where we met him till he killed 25 elephants, then return. He
might ride out a day or two on horseback to the north, but no
further."

To J. J. Freeman, a LMS Director, Livingstone wrote at the same
time: "We met Oswell on our return. Brought supplies for us from
the Colony, and returned a bill of £40 which was to be spent on purchasing them. Seemed very anxious to get me to promise to allow him
to accompany me on the next trip. I do not well know how to get rid
of him, and he feels he cannot go any distance alone. I sometimes
think I might employ him to find a way down to the sea coast."[12]

From Livingstone's own letter to Arthur Tidman (September 3,
1849), in which he says that Oswell promised to bring the following
year a collapsible boat so that they could cross the Zouga, it is clear
that Oswell, not Livingstone, was closer to the truth. The conclusion
is inescapable that Livingstone went off without waiting for Oswell,
as he had no intention of sharing the glory, even if it meant risking
the health of his family. It is strange that he did not realise that if the
recalcitrant chief at Ngami did not change his mind about a crossing
of the Zouga, no further crossing would be possible without Oswell's
boat.

Tim Jeal, in his admirably documented biography of Livingstone,
interprets the relationship between Oswell and Livingstone as follows: "Oswell was no mindless young man with a private fortune and

little else. He was exceptionally generous, modest and completely lacking in personal ambition. The last two qualities provide the key to the success of his relationship with Livingstone, who had already proved himself incapable of suffering any European whose views conflicted with his own. Livingstone liked to get his full measure of praise for what he did, and Oswell conveniently never saw fit to press his own claims. Oswell's companion, Mungo Murray, who also came on the 1849 journey to Lake Ngami, was a man of similar character, who preferred doing things to talking about them afterwards."[13]

But let the last word on the Ngami expedition be that of Francis Galton, DCL, FRS, FRGS, an eminent geographer and explorer of the White Nile and other parts of Africa. From him a clear appreciation is possible of the leading role played by Oswell in an enterprise for which Livingstone had claimed credit:

"One of the most epoch-making of the numerous explorations was that which, by traversing wastes previously impassable to Europeans, succeeded in connecting the pastoral uplands in which great game had been hunted by many travellers, with the lakes and rivers of the equatorial part of the Continent.

This notable Expedition was made by a party of three – Oswell, Murray and Livingstone. Its furtherance required wagons, oxen, stores, and a capable leader, and these desiderata were mainly supplied by Oswell. Livingstone was at that time comparatively inexperienced, while Oswell had spent years in persistent travel, and had become the most dashing hunter and successful explorer of his time in South Africa. Murray was also a hunter, but by no means of equal experience. The idea of desirability of such an Expedition was not due to any one of the three alone: it was in the air, and shared by many others, but its achievement was due, first and foremost, to Oswell. Murray joined Oswell with his wagon. Livingstone accompanied them as a guest, most welcome on many accounts, and not least for his familiar knowledge of the language of the native races, and for the personal love and respect with which he was regarded by many of them. Still, the Expedition would have gone all the same without Livingstone, while Livingstone could not have moved without the assistance of Oswell and Murray, especially the former. Yet, notwithstanding Oswell's eminent services to geography, notwithstanding the loyal attitude of Livingstone towards him,[14] and, again, notwithstanding the attempts of many of his friends in England to induce the public to appreciate him as he deserved, his work soon began to pass into oblivion. The chief cause lay in his invincible laziness as a writer, which rendered him a deplorably bad correspondent, even to his nearest relations, who craved for tidings, and whom he dearly loved. His dilatoriness in these respects was enforced by a strange shrinking from publicity, and from even the most legitimate forms of self-assertion; and, again, he honestly took greater pleasure in ministering to the reputation of Livingstone than his own. It followed that the story of the Expedition was first learnt through the letters of Livingstone, which were published and widely discussed weeks before a scrap of information reached England from Oswell's own pen. . . . Murray, the third member of the travelling party, of whom little is known except his love of hunting, was also a man who never cared to write; he was hardly seen by geographers, and fell quite out of touch with them. I never to my knowledge had the pleasure of meeting him. . . . It was my good fortune to gain the friendship of Oswell after his final return from Africa, when I quickly appreciated the remarkable nobleness of his character. I was at that time closely and eagerly connected with the Geographical Society, so that I was brought into frequent contact with every contemporary traveller of note. Among these Oswell, with his clear-cut, aquiline features, keen glance, and lithe frame, suggested perhaps the most typical specimen of a man born to adventure. His striking physical gifts, combined with his aristocratic bearing and winning but modest address, seemed a living realization of the perfect and gentle knight of whom we read in old romances."[15]

## CHAPTER SIX

# They reached the Zambezi

In Colobeng, David Livingstone was faced with grave difficulties. Here, too, water had become scarce and the river had nearly dried out. His six-week-old daughter, Elisabeth, went down with what he called "inflammation of the lungs"; it was, in fact, a bronchial infection, which she had probably caught from the two elder children, Thomas and Agnes. They had been so weakened by it on the journey that they could not stand up unassisted. The new baby girl died screaming, and her final scream haunted Livingstone for a long time. In his Journal, he wrote: "It was the first death in our family but just as likely to have happened if we had remained at home and we now have one of our number in heaven."[1]

Mary became seriously ill with shivering, ear-ache and a temporary paralysis of the left side of her face. This was not surprising in view of what she had endured while pregnant on their last journey. Yet the doctor remained remarkably self-absorbed. In a letter of July 8, 1850, he described light-heartedly to his father-in-law that one day, when he and Mary were travelling in their wagon: "It turned clear over in a pitfall". The tribes round Lake Ngami snared game with deep pitfalls, and Mary, he went on, had often feared being crushed in this sort of accident, "but when it came she could not help saying to herself, 'Is this all?' "

On his mother-in-law's insistence, Livingstone took his family to Kuruman, where Mrs Moffat saw to all their needs. But she also spoke her mind about Livingstone's rashness in exposing his family to such appalling hardships.

The Moffats were outraged that Livingstone was discussing his plans for the next expedition north with Mary who, though no longer paralysed, was still a sick woman. Soon the strain between Livingstone and the Moffats was such that in February, 1851, he hastily moved his family back to Colobeng. There he received a letter from

Kuruman

Livingstone and family

Mrs Moffat. If anyone could tell the brutal truth about himself to David Livingstone it was his mother-in-law. She wrote:

"My dear Livingstone, Before you left Kuruman, I did all I dared to do to broach the subject of your intended journey, and thus bring on a candid discussion, more especially with regard to Mary's accompanying you with those dear children. But seeing how averse you and Father (R. Moffat) were to speak about it, and the hope that you would never be guilty of such temerity after the dangers you escaped last year, I too timidly shrunk from what I ought to have had the courage to do. Mary had told me all along that should she be pregnant you would not take her, but let her come out here after you were fairly off. Though I suspected at the end that she began to falter in this resolution, still I hoped it would never take place, i.e. *her going with you*, and looked and longed for things transpiring to prevent it. But to my dismay, I now get a letter, in which she writes, 'I must again wend my way to the far Interior, perhaps to be confined in the field.' O Livingstone, what do you mean? Was it not enough that you lost one lovely babe, and scarcely saved the other while the mother came home threatened with paralysis? And will you again expose her and them in those sickly regions, on an exploring expedition? All the world will condemn the cruelty of the thing, to say nothing of the indecorousness of it. A pregnant woman with three little children trailing about with a company of the other sex through the wilds of Africa, among savage men and beasts! *Had you found a place* to which you wished to go and commence missionary operations, the case would be altered. Not one word would I say, were it to the mountains of the moon. But to go with an exploring party, the thing is preposterous. I remain yours in great perturbation M. Moffat."[2]

It was characteristic that this letter increased rather than weakened Livingstone's determination to take Mary. He had tried to explain to the Moffats that this was no exploring expedition, but "one for opening the way to thousands of natives waiting to become Christians." He also maintained that finding a base from which to commence missionary operations had to take second place until he had discovered more about the network of the rivers to the north. The idea of missionaries punting their way up malarial rivers and bringing the gospel to a land lying on the wrong side of a sizeable desert seemed quite ludicrous to the Moffats. They knew well enough the struggle they had experienced to make their bare quota of thirty converts. This point in time marked the main breach between Livingstone and his in-laws.

And yet, although Livingstone pretended that no argument would have the slightest effect when it came to carrying out his work in the service of the Lord, the stern rebukes of Dr and Mrs Moffat had made an impression. When Cotton Oswell reached Colobeng in April, 1851, he wrote to his brother, "Livingstone was strongly in favour of accompanying me, but there were two obstacles to his doing so: the lack of a wagon, and his unwillingness to expose his children to the privations entailed by the scarcity of water for the first 300 miles of the journey."[3] Oswell dealt with the first objection by presenting the Livingstones with a new wagon, and the second by volunteering to precede them by several marches over the driest part of the route, in order to clear the old wells and to dig fresh ones. Livingstone was delighted to accept, and with his pregnant wife and his scarcely recovered children set out on his third – and as it turned out – his most important journey.

For Oswell too this turned out to be a momentous journey, and his last in Africa. In Colobeng he learnt that Livingstone had sent five men to Sechele, the chief of the Bakwain, and had gathered much information: he now knew that Sebituane, the Chief of the Makololo, lived on a river a little to the south of the Zambezi, having formerly lived on that river itself. On April 4, 1851, Oswell wrote to his cousin, Louisa Cotton:

"On this Zambesi, as perhaps you know, the Portuguese have considerable trading stations. Sebitoané has only seen one of them, who came seeking slaves, but with the under slave dealers he has had traffic for the last three or four years. Without wishing to appear philanthropic overmuch, if we can open the way, *via* the interior, to the slave country, will it not be easier to put an end to that trade at the fountain-head, than on the coast, whither the poor wretches have been brought many hundreds of miles? If we reach the Zambesi others may go further, and eventually, by persuading the great Chiefs of the interior not to dispose of their people or captives to the merchants from the coast, do something to end this sale of human beings. Don't misunderstand me, I would not have you think that such are the only motives that influence me in again making the attempt – nothing so praiseworthy – I have a love of wandering and have been once fooled. I have got, so far, about 300 miles from Colesberg and on my way again. Livingstone will, I believe accompany me, and, should it please God, we shall reach Sebitoané somehow or other. The people are now willing to show us the path, and we will not abandon our project without a struggle."[4]

Throughout May 1851, David Livingstone recorded in his journal how he and his family found water in every place they arrived at. For instance on May 15 and 16 he noted, "In the desert, and in the evening of 17th we reached Nkaoana. Mr Oswell's men opened another well which from long disuse had become filled up. . . . This well on being reopened afforded abundant supply for all our cattle."

On May 27, in a place called Maritsa, they met three Englishmen who had preceded them, and were anxious to get to Sebituane. J. H. Wilson, the trader who had accompanied Oswell and Livingstone on the original Ngami expedition; Sam Edwards, the son of the missionary with whom Livingstone had fallen out in Mabotsa; and a young naturalist called John Leyland.[5] But the Bakurutse chief refused to provide them with guides in spite of their offer to present him with three or four guns. Livingstone, determined that the three Englishmen should not beat him to Sebituane, pressed on to the Zouga, where at Nchokota a man called Kamati told him (in exchange for a musket provided by Oswell) that it was possible to reach the country of the Makololo – Sebituane's tribe – by striking north, instead of going west to Lake Ngami, and then north-east. There was, however, one difficulty: there would be very few wells on the direct route, and many of these might be dried up as it had been an unusually hot summer.

Livingstone, mindless of anything except to get to Sebituane first, was prepared to take the risk. It was his family who suffered. On May 29, they entered the saltpan of Ntwéwé, and had to go five days without water. With his peculiarly insensitive sense of humour, Livingstone wrote in *Missionary Travels*: "The less there was of water, the more thirsty the little rogues became." He did, however, concede that the possibility of the children "perishing before our eyes was terrible."[6] When they did find water, it was stagnant and full of rhinoceros dung. But people with swollen lips and blackened tongues are not fussy. They were then attacked by swarms of mosquitoes. "Their bite is more venomous than anywhere else," Livingstone wrote to his parents.[7] "They are really painful and pain continues for several days. Sleep is out of the question. . . . I could not touch a square half-inch on the bodies of the children unbitten after a night's exposure."

Early in June they had to axe their way through thick bush; to cap it all, their guide, a lighthearted Bushman, lost his way and vanished. "Not a bird or insect could be seen during these three dreary days," Livingstone wrote in his diary on June 10. But next day he began to observe birds, then footprints of animals, which meant water. From then on they found ponds, and on June 18 they struck the Chobe river, where an emissary of Sebituane, Tonuana, waited for them with the message that the king had come more than 400 miles to meet the white men, and was on an island thirty miles downstream. Livingstone and Oswell decided to leave Mrs Livingstone and the children with the wagons, and on June 21 paddled in the canoes Sebituane had sent for them downstream at the rate of eight miles an hour, arriving at three in the afternoon.

"Presently," Oswell wrote, "this really great Chief and man came to meet us, shy and ill at ease. We held out our hands in the accustomed way of true Britons, and I was surprised to see that his motherwit gave him immediate insight into what was expected of him, and the friendly meaning of our salutation. Though he could never have witnessed it before, he at once followed suit, and placed his hand in ours as if to the manner born. I felt troubled at the evident nervousness of the famous warrior (for he had been and still was a mighty fighter with very remarkable force of character). Surrounded by his tribesmen he stood irresolute and quite overcome in the presence of two ordinary-looking Englishmen.

Livingstone entered at once into conversation with him; but throughout that day and the next a sad, half-scared look never faded from his face. He had wished us to visit him, but the reality of our coming with all its possibilities and advantages, seemed to flit through the man's mind as a vision. He killed an ox for us and treated us right royally; he was far and away the finest Kafir I ever saw."

Livingstone wrote in his diary: "He told us that having been informed by the messengers he had sent to Mr Oswell and me of our vain attempts to penetrate into his country in the preceding year, he had in the present instance, in his eagerness to make our acquaintance, not only despatched parties to search for us along the Zouga, but also made considerable presents to different chiefs on the way, with the request that they should render the white men every assistance in their power, and furnish them with guides."[8]

Livingstone believed he knew why Sebituane was so anxious to have the white men visit him. His tribe, originally part of the Sotho, had been driven north by the Zulu during the three first decades of the 19th century. In 1824 they had been defeated by the Griquas near Kuruman. They had had to go yet further north, reaching the Chobe river, where they established themselves as overlords of the Barotse Valley and the Batoka Plateau. Here they were threatened by the Ndebele, another Zulu clan, who had been forced out of the Transvaal by the Boers.[9] Their chief, Mzilikazi, was a threat to all tribes within hundreds of miles, including the Makololo. Sebituane knew that Dr Moffat had twice visited Mzilikazi at his kraal, and established a remarkable influence over him. Livingstone was Dr Moffat's son-in-law, and Sebituane hoped to influence Mzilikazi, the only man who could endanger his position, through Livingstone.

During that first night, Sebituane came to visit Oswell and Livingstone alone.

"He sat down very quietly and mournfully at our fire," wrote Oswell. "Livingstone and I woke up and greeted him, and then he dreamily recounted the history of his life, his wars, escapes, successes and conquests, and the far-distant wandering in his raids. By the fire's glow and flicker among the reeds, with that tall, dark, earnest speaker and his keenly attentive listeners, it has always appeared to me one of the most weird scenes I ever saw. With subdued manner and voice Sebitoané went on through the live-long night till near the dawn, in low tones only occasionally interrupted by an inquiry from Livingstone. He described the way in which he had circumvented a strong *impi* of Matabili on the raid, and raised his voice for a minute or two as he recounted how, hearing of their approach, he had sent men to meet the dreaded warriors of Umsilegas, feigning themselves traitors in order to lure them to destruction by promising to guide them to the bulk of the cows and oxen, which, they said, in fear of their coming, had been placed in fancied security on one of the large islands of the Chobé; how the Zulu fell into the trap and allowed themselves to be ferried over in three or four canoes hidden there for the purpose; and how when the last trip had been made, the boatmen, pulling out into mid-stream, told them they could remain where they were till they were fetched, and in the meantime might search for the cattle; how after leaving them till they were worn and weak with hunger, for there was nothing to eat on the island, he passed over, killed the chiefs, and absorbed the soldiers into his own ranks, providing them with wives, a luxury they were not entitled to under Zulu military law until their spears had been well reddened in fight.

Then he waved his hand westward and opened out a story of men over whom he had gained an easy victory, 'away, away, very far from the bitter waters'; and to whom, when they asked for food, wishing to bind them with fetters of kindness, he sent a fat ox, and, 'would you believe it, they returned it, saying they didn't eat ox'. 'Then what do you eat?' I asked. 'We like beef better than anything.' 'We eat *men*,' said they. I had never heard of this before; but they were very pressing, so at last I sent them two slaves of the Macobes, the river people, who as you know, are very dark in colour, but they brought them back, saying they did not like *black* men, but preferred the redder variety, and as that meant sending my own fighting men, I told them they might go without altogether.' This was the only intimation we ever had that cannibalism existed in our part of Africa", Oswell concluded.

A few days later, Sebituane asked to be allowed to accompany Livingstone and Oswell to their wagons and to be introduced to Mrs Livingstone – "the Lady" – Dr Moffat's daughter. A warm friendship developed between Sebituane and the two Englishmen, and Livingstone wrote in his diary, "It is impossible to overstate the importance we attach to Sebituane." Then suddenly, on July 6, 1851, Sebituane fell ill of pneumonia. Livingstone visited him on July 7, but did not dare to treat him for fear of being subsequently accused of having killed him. When Livingstone took his leave, "Sebitoané lifted himself, saluted, and told one of the people to take Robert[10] to Maunko, his favourite wife, and get some milk for him. I saw him no more, for on the same evening his people removed him towards the Linyanti town, and when still on the way, just at the clump of date bushes at which we stood, he expired in his canoe. . . . I do not wonder at the Roman Catholics praying for the dead. If I could believe as they do, I would pray for them too . . . In the afternoon Mr O. and I went over to the village to condole with the people. They received our condolences very kindly and took our advice in good part. 'Do not leave us; though Sebitoané is gone, his children remain, and you must treat them as you would have treated him.' "

None the less, Sebituane's death made it necessary that they should obtain permission to proceed from his successor, his daughter Mamochisane. She, however, was living far to the north, and the

Makololo estimated that it would take about five weeks to get an answer from her. Livingstone decided to wait, but Oswell – who had promised his family to be with them in England in 1852 – felt that he should leave, as this long delay would prevent him from living up to his promise. The Livingstones – especially Mary – begged him to stay; the doctor stressed that having come so far, it would be a grievous pity to return without having reached their goal – the great river in the heart of Africa. Oswell allowed himself to be persuaded.

During the time they waited, Livingstone confided to Oswell his ambitions, his troubles and his anxieties.[11] The experiences of the journey on which they were now engaged, and of those of the two preceding years, forced him to the conclusion that he would not be justified in allowing his wife and young family again to accompany him in all the hazards of his wanderings to unknown countries. Oswell shared these views and approved of Livingstone's plan to send them to England. There was also the problem of educating the children. But here the question of money loomed large – Livingstone was badly overdrawn on his meagre salary of £100 a year, neither Mary nor the children had clothes fit to be seen in any European town. But how were they to borrow money for their fares and their outfits, not to mention their living expenses in England?

In the midst of this anxious discussion, on Thursday, July 31, 1851, a messenger arrived from Mamochisane saying that Livingstone and Oswell should be treated exactly as if Sebituane were alive, and that they should be taken wherever they wished to go. Their aim was the big river, but the area through which it flowed, so the Makololo told them, was cut by numerous small rivers, which made wagon-travelling impossible. Livingstone therefore decided to leave Mary and the children at the Chobe camp in charge of the headman, while he and Oswell pressed forward on horseback. On August 1 they left Linyanti; the country was generally flat, with evidence of extensive inundations. Nearing their destination they had to pass through fifteen miles of marsh, covered with tall grass reaching to their shoulders as they rode, and they swam their horses through the little rivers. On August 4 Livingstone's entry into his journal read: "In the afternoon we came to the beautiful Seshéké (which proved to be the Zambezi) and thanked God for permitting us first to see this glorious river.[12] All we could say to each other was . . . How glorious! How magnificent! How beautiful! And grand beyond description it really was – such a body of water – at least 400 yards broad, and deep; it may be stated from three to five hundred yards wide. . . . The town of Sesheké appeared very beautiful on the opposite bank. The waves were so high the people were afraid to venture across, but by-and-by a canoe made its way to where we stood . . . In crossing, the waves lifted up the canoe and made it roll beautifully."

Livingstone either did not know at this stage, or deliberately put it out of his mind, that the Portuguese had been on the Zambezi for four centuries. He was near to tears, but was afraid that the old man conducting them over the river might think that he cried because he was afraid of the crocodiles. He soon heard about a huge waterfall called Mosioatunya – often called "the smoke that thunders" – but did not go to see it.

Oswell and Livingstone both observed that in Linyanti and in Sesheké Sebituane's followers were dressed in green baize, red drugget, calico, and cheap gaudy cloth, some in garments of European manufacture. These they had obtained, it soon emerged, from the Mambari, African agents of the Portuguese traders who lived near the Portuguese coast in the west, and who excelled at the slave trade. Livingstone wrote in his diary: "Pity this market is not supplied with English manufactures in exchange for the legitimate products of the country" (meaning ivory, honey, beeswax, cotton, tobacco and sugar cane). He continued in his diary (on October 1, 1851): "If English merchants would come up the Zambesi during the months of June, July and August, the slave traders would very soon be driven out of the market." Livingstone deluded himself that during these months there was no fever – yet his son Thomas had had a bad attack of malaria the previous year during June and July. As for his "determination" that English merchants could come up the Zambezi, this was to cost him dearly in the future.

"If it is profitable for those who are engaged in the coast trade to pass along in their ships and pick up ivory, beeswax, etc. those who may have enterprise enough to push into the interior and receive the goods at first hand, would surely find it much more profitable. The returns for the first year might be small, but those who for the love of their species would run some risk, would assuredly be no losers in the end. The natives readily acquire the habit of saving for a market. . . . Give a people the opportunity they will civilise themselves, and that too more effectually than can be done by missionary societies. The slave dealer must have his due. All the Mambari come decently clothed; we never saw a party of Bechuanas or Griquas of whom so much could be said."

After discussing all this with Oswell, Livingstone wrote to the Royal Geographical Society, "Our plan was that I should remain in pursuit of my objects as a missionary, while Mr Oswell explored the Zambesi to the East. For such an undertaking I know none better suited than my friend Mr Oswell. He has courage and prudence equal to any emergency, and possesses moreover that qualification so essential in a traveller, of gaining the confidence of the natives while maintaining the dignity of a gentleman . . ."[13]

Both projects, however, proved unattainable. Livingstone could not speedily find a suitable spot for a mission among the Makololo, and as he knew that the date of Mary's confinement was approaching he had to hurry to rejoin her. Oswell found the immense marshes and the tsetse fly, which abounded in every direction, insuperable barriers to his speedy advance, especially as he was anxious to keep the promise given to his family that he would return during 1852. So they made their way back to Linyanti, where they heard that Mr Wilson and Mr Edwards had just arrived on horseback. On the same evening they went on to the camp on the Chobe, and on August 12 started on their homeward journey.

When they reached the Zouga, Livingstone wrote in his diary on September 15: "A son, William Oswell Livingstone, born at a place we always call Bellevue." Not a word about Mary, or her labour, or even her general state of health. It was Oswell, who some years later at the British Association paid this tribute to her, "After spending two years in the company of Mrs Livingstone I am qualified to speak of her courage, her devoted attention to her husband, and her unvarying kindness to myself. . . . In regions thousands of miles away from a white person she cared for her children, and encouraged the prosecution of the expeditions. To myself she ministered many acts of kindness with a delicacy and consideration which only a woman can exhibit." At any rate this little boy lived, and was known all his life as Zouga.

When Mary and the baby were strong enough to continue the journey, Cotton Oswell left them in Colobeng, and went on ahead, to Cape Town. Both Livingstones felt very bereft – with the difficulties they were facing, they badly needed Oswell's support and encouragement. Mary was full of nervous fears; she had little experience of the home country and was very dependent on her strong-willed husband. She wept at the thought of the dangers he would face, and of her own loneliness during the months of separation. But when they reached Cape Town, looking very ragged in their bush clothes, they discovered why Oswell had preceded them.

On March 16, Livingstone wrote in his journal, "Reach Cape Town. Find our friend Oswell here before us, the outfit ordered, and he presented £50, £20, then £80, £20 = £170,[14] with the remark that as the money had been drawn from the preserves on our estate (elephants) we had as good a right to it as he. God bless and preserve him! . . . the best friend we had in Africa." To the LMS he wrote, "But for the disinterested kindness of Mr Oswell we could not have come down to the Cape. He presented supplies for last year's journey worth £40, for that to Sebitoane upwards of £20, also a wagon worth £55. . . . Most of our oxen are dead, and but for Mr Oswell's presenting a number worth £60 we could not have come down to the Cape. . . . He clothed Mrs L. and family in a style we never anticipated. This I state in confidence to you; it would offend him to make it public, but it makes me comparatively easy in mind."

In his letters to Arthur Tidman, Livingstone explained why he had to send his family back to England, and as he was going to open up new fields for missionary work, he asked him to intercede with the LMS that the Directors should provide Mary and the children with money to maintain themselves. On October 17, 1851, Livingstone had written to the Directors stating flatly that if they would not support Mrs Livingstone and the children in England, he would still go north "no matter who opposes." Perhaps he was relying on the ever forgiving and generous Cotton Oswell.

When Livingstone put his wife and family on a ship bound for England – Oswell had paid for their tickets – in April, 1852, he had still no reply from the Directors and therefore could not know whether they would help Mary. (Eventually they did agree to give her £150 a year, and even contributed £50 towards Livingstone's overdraft to the Society.) Livingstone knew that he could not take them back to the Zambezi, but his failure to wait and hear what provision the Directors would make was typical of his attitude of putting his wife and children after the achievement of his own obsessive plans.

Mary and the four children sailed on April 23, 1852. This is probably the date on which David Livingstone's career as a missionary ended, and that as an explorer began. He never gave up his medical work, and of course always regarded himself as the Servant of God. But he revealed his steely determination in a letter to his brother-in-law, in which he wrote, "I shall open a path into the interior or perish."

Typically of Oswell was a little scene enacted when he left for England. John Thomas, born in the Cape probably of slave parents, was a tall, handsome lad, who had attached himself to Oswell during his first expedition, and of whom Oswell had become very fond. When the time to say goodbye came, both men were strongly affected. To quote Oswell's own words about what followed: "I told John in part how I valued his services, and asked him if I could in any way repay my debt of gratitude. I had taught him to read in the Bush, but that was the only good I had ever done him. His answer came after some hesitation. He had heard so much of England that he should like of all things to go with me there. Two days later we were on board ship together."

## CHAPTER SEVEN

# Noble and generous to the end

Cotton Oswell never went back to Africa. On his return to England he found that his brother, Edward, was seriously ill and decided to nurse him. He wrote a long letter to Livingstone, explaining the situation.

Oswell had one gratifying experience – *La Societé de Geographie de Paris* awarded him their major silver medal "for your discovery of Lake Ngami. A similar medal has been awarded to your learned fellow traveller, the Reverend David Livingstone. We hasten to forward you this medal; pray accept it as a token of our hearty interest in your useful labours, and as some small recompense of your enlightened zeal for the progress of Geographical Science." The London Missionary Society had at last also felt that it should make some acknowledgement. Informed by Livingstone, Dr Tidman could, however, only write: "In the successive journeys undertaken by the Rev Dr Livingstone in South Africa, with a view to the extension of Missionary Operations in a Northerly direction, beyond the limits hitherto reached by foreigners, you have rendered such generous and efficient aid to our excellent and devoted friend that the Directors of the London Missionary Society feel constrained to express to you their deep sense of obligation. . . . Did not feelings of delicacy both to yourself and Dr Livingstone restrain us from advertising more particularly the many acts of disinterestedness and generosity rendered by you to your fellow traveller, thereby relieving him from much anxiety, it would have been gratifying to have made them the subject of special reference and acknowledgement."

Some members of the Royal Geographical Society were not satisfied with this. "Tell him, when you see him," one Board member told a friend of Oswell's, "that we are keeping our gold medal for him, but we must have some memorandum from himself." The message was passed on, but Oswell's reply was, "No, I won't write a line; I know quite well that Livingstone is working hard at his book; he wants this medal, let him have it; it means more to him than it could ever mean to me."

Another friend pointed out to him that a mere paper from him could not seriously affect any book Livingstone was writing, or inter-fere with any favours the Society contemplated bestowing on Living-stone, but Oswell's resolution remained unshaken. "However wretched my attempt might be," he said, "as I am the only man in England who can speak with authority on the part of Africa we visited together, I should take the wind out of my good friend's sails, and I would not do that for the world."

Edward Oswell, in his biography of his father, wrote: "Shyness perhaps, modesty certainly, disposed him to keep in the background; but it was more than this – a noble chivalry, surely – that prompted him to hide his own light completely, that his friend's might in the darkness to shine a little brighter."[1]

In October 1853, Oswell's brother, Edward, died, and after his long spell of nursing Cotton sought distraction in Paris, where he stu-died French. He was beginning to wonder in what direction to turn his steps next, when on March 28, 1854, war was declared on Russia. A month later his friend, Major Thomas Steele, then Lord Raglan's military secretary, wrote urging him to join him at Constantinople. Oswell joyfully accepted the invitation and sailed for the Turkish capital. In June, when it was necessary to convey despatches and secret service money from Constantinople to Colonel Lintorn Sim-mons in Shumla, Oswell at once volunteered for this hazardous enterprise, and within two hours was on his way. As night drew near, he sent his escort party to look for lodgings. They soon returned to tell him that they had found a deserted cottage. But Oswell detected recent occupation; questioning them closely, he extorted the sulky admission that they had turned a family out in order to make accom-modation for themselves and him. Late as it was, hungry, thirsty and tired as they were after a seventy-mile ride, Oswell would not allow a morsel to be eaten or a drop to be drunk until the poor folk were found – hiding in a wood in abject terror. On making them under-stand that his intentions were friendly, he ordered the men to clear his and their belongings out of the family's bedroom, and asked per-mission to sleep on the verandah. Such consideration was so unex-pected that the wife burst into tears and the man prostrated himself on the ground. The Bulgarians eagerly placed their little store of food on the table before Oswell, and were with difficulty persuaded to accept payment for it. His own soldiers regarded Oswell's conduct so incomprehensible and out of order that next morning they deserted, taking with them all his baggage. Knowing only three words of Turkish, and utterly ignorant of the road to Shumla, Oswell none the less reached his destination in 72 hours, having traversed a distance of 230 miles.

His mission completed, he left for Constantinople carrying despatches for Lord Raglan, but this time he went via Varna. "On my way to the coast I fell in with a cavalry regiment and the Rifle Brigade encamped near Devna," he wrote later on. "A sergeant saluted, and asked for news from the front. I turned myself half round to the right in my saddle to talk with him, and presently felt a hand placed very *gently, lovingly* on my left foot. John stood by my stirrup, his face a picture of affectionate triumph at having caught me again. He had taken service under an officer. We threw ourselves down under a bush and renewed old memories. The Major, near whose tent we were, called John, and finding from him who I was, most courteously entreated me, telling me how beloved John was by the regiment, and how well, through him, they knew my name."

John, on hearing of the war with Russia, had volunteered to serve with the Rifle Brigade and attached to a major, had gained the good will of the entire regiment.

Oswell was present at the battle of Alma; during the terrible winter of mismanagement and misery he assisted the overworked surgeons night and day on the field and in the hospitals, and devoted much of his time to visiting and cheering the sick and wounded. When anaesthetics and medical appliances ran short, the surgeons had none the less to operate. Oswell often said that he had had no idea what pluck meant until he saw men undergo, in cold blood, with all their wits about them, unflinchingly and unmurmuringly, the most agonizing operations. They would hold a bullet, a piece of wood, a handkerchief or a quid of tobacco between their teeth, and it was a point of honour with them not to let it drop until the doctors had finished with them.

On September 8, 1855, Oswell witnessed the storming of Malakoff, and the following day the fall of Sebastopol. Six weeks later he took his passage back to England, and on November 17 set out on a trip to South America. On board ship he met an attractive young woman called Agnes Rivaz, with whom he struck up a deep friendship. But it was only three and a half years later that he proposed marriage to her – and then her father would not give his consent because Oswell had loaned £6,000[2] to a friend who subsequently could not repay it, and did not have the income considered necessary to keep Agnes in the state to which she was accustomed. When his Uncle Ben found out the reason why the engagement was not announced, he offered to lend Cotton £6,000 at 4%, on the understanding that on his death this money would be Cotton's outright. Then his Uncle William also took a hand: knowing that his cousin, Catherine Clark, intended to leave Cotton a legacy, he informed her of Cotton's ill-luck with the loan, and she promptly placed the legacy to the credit of his account. The wedding day fixed for April 12, 1860, and Francis Rivaz wrote to his daughter: "No one but myself can know the exquisite happiness I have experienced in seeing your destiny identified henceforth with that of the most singularly gifted man it has ever been my lot to meet."[3]

For the next thirty years, Cotton and Agnes Oswell lived a happy, contented life. They had four children – two sons and two daughters, whom he adored, and was particularly proud when Edward, his younger son, took up exploring in South America.

Oswell's friendship with Livingstone continued, and he congratulated him most warmly on the success of *Missionary Travels*. "Everyone is talking of it and you," he wrote, "I know you don't care much for what others think, but we are all just slightly human, and the good words and the good wishes of this world are not altogether to be despised."

Livingstone kept up their correspondence, and wrote Oswell a glowing letter on April 2, 1859, from the Shire river about the ideal conditions for founding a mission on a high mountain called Morambala: "It is 4,000 feet high, and a fine point for a health station. It is well cultivated on the top, having hills and dales and flowing fountains there. Lemon and orange trees grow wild, so do pineapples." When the two missions founded on Livingstone's advice ran into disaster, Oswell defended him against the strictures of the Anglican Church, and of the thousands of ordinary people who were outraged by the death of Bishop Mackenzie and his companions. When Livingstone returned to England in 1864, Oswell agreed to edit his new book, *A Narrative of The Zambesi and Its Tributaries*.

Livingstone's last letter to Oswell was pathetically full of fantasy. "I will feel obliged if you will allow me to use your name on a fountain from which the Kafué rose at one place, and separated. Kafué is called Lunga, Loenge (hard g), Kafuje and Kafué. It seems to be one of four fountains rising very near to each other, and I am presump-tuous enough to think that these are the ancient fountains of Hero-dotus, of which we all read in boyhood and rejected as we became wise in natural philosophy. Mokantju was right and I have heard of the earthen mound at which the four fountains rise so often, and know pretty fairly the four rivers they form, that I venture to say I wait another year to rediscover them. When we heard Mokantju's tale, we were about 350 miles from the mound, but Liambai, whose fountain I call Palmerston's, and Kafué, whose fountain I call Oswell's, do most certainly flow into Inner Ethiopia. The other two, Bartle Frere's flows as R. Lufira into Lake Kamolout, and Young's (I have been obliged to knight him, to distinguish him from the gunner, as Sir Paraffin Young) goes through Lake Lincoln into Lua-laba, and North to Egypt. They thus enter the central line of drain-age. Webb's Lualaba into Petherick's branch. . . . I say the structure of the watershed is exactly what you and I found at Ntlotlé in the Kalahari. That and the enormous Lacustrine rivers and lakes, are the means which kind Providence arranged to regulate the grand old Nile; *but this is for you and Mrs O.*"[4]

If Oswell commented on the letter, his views have not survived. Apart from his own geographical knowledge (he had been a friend of Colonel James Grant, and was in constant touch with Sir Samuel Baker) Oswell probably sensed that poor Livingstone's theories about the sources of the Nile were far-fetched.

When Dr Livingstone's body was brought back to England, he was one of the people asked to identify it. Profoundly grieved, he doubted whether he would recognise his old friend, but not only was the broken arm unmistakable, but, despite the long journey since Livingstone's death, the features were unchanged.[5] He cut off a lock of the doctor's hair, dark brown still, scarcely tinged with grey. "He had so nearly done his work, but not quite," he wrote in April 1874, to his second son. "But still I know it was all for the best." Cotton Oswell and General Sir Thomas Steele were at the head of the eight pall-bearers in Westminster Abbey.

And yet, when Agnes Livingstone, who was like a daughter to him, asked Oswell to edit her father's last journals and letters, he refused. Admittedly, the later notebooks were hard to decipher, but his excuse that he was not fit to do the work was not convincing; his health had never been better. It is possible that Cotton Oswell had come to see the ungenerous references to himself in Livingstone's letters to Dr Tidman and the Rev J. J. Freeman, and for once even his feelings had been hurt.

The years were passing, and gradually Cotton Oswell's friends were dying. One day, in 1863, he was in his garden, when a tall man walked up to him unannounced – it was John, his devoted African friend, then butler in the service of a Sussex squire. It was a happy, nostalgic meeting. A few months later Oswell heard that John was seriously ill. At once he made preparations to go to him – and did go, 150 miles, although before leaving he received a telegram saying that John had died. Oswell paid for the funeral, and for a stone grave in Buckhurst Hill Churchyard, which bears the inscription: "In Memory of William John Thomas, born about the year 1825, died March 24, 1864. In early life he was the right hand of him who on this stone would record the unwavering fidelity cheerfulness and truth of a most unselfish Companion, Servant and Friend, tried amidst many wanderings, much need and some danger. May God In His Mercy, for Christ's sake, pardon master and man, and grant that they may meet hereafter as brothers."

It had always been Cotton Oswell's fear to live so long as to be no longer in full control of his faculties. He died quietly in the grey dawn of May 1, 1893, as handsome as ever at the age of 75.

On the day of his funeral there was not even standing-room in the church, so many had come. Letters poured in to Agnes Oswell and her children. Some were written by very humble people, who had little grammar; others by men and women of great distinction and high position. Sir Samuel Baker, one of the last of the "Africa friends", said, "When death seized my dear old friend Oswell it robbed all those who knew him of their greatest friend. His name will be remembered with tears and sorrow and profound respect. . . . His only fault was the shadowing of his own light."

A number of his friends and the Royal Geographical Society raised funds for a memorial with the inscription: "To the Glory of God and in remembrance of William Cotton Oswell this tablet is erected by the few remaining friends of his early life in England, India and Africa, who loved him as a brother, by the Royal Geographical Society in recognition of his discovery in 1849 of Lake Ngami in Africa with his friend and companion Dr Livingstone, and by his many friends in later years who will never forget his strength and gentleness, his ever ready help in need, his cheerful unselfishness and his great humility."

Livingstone had died twenty years to the day before Cotton Oswell; neither in his diaries and letters, nor, to our knowledge, in conversation, had he given adequate recognition to Cotton Oswell as an explorer and as the man through whose help, and thanks to whose modesty, he himself had become famous.

# Part Two

## CHAPTER EIGHT

# The unexpected stranger

On May 23, 1853, Livingstone reached Linyanti, the capital of the Makololo on the Chobe river. He had started from Cape Town almost a year earlier, in June 1852.

Not, this time, having Cotton Oswell's generous assistance, his equipment was modest; his wagons were overloaded with other peoples' goods and drawn by poor beasts – strong, healthy draft animals were beyond his resources. His bearers were mostly Bushmen, and his companion a coloured trader called George Fleming, who hoped to start trading with the Africans. Their journey through Kuruman Colony along a well-trodden northward track was pleasant, but took all of eight months.

On arrival at Colobeng, Livingstone had a great shock: Sechele's town had been raided and burnt down by a Boer commando of 600, headed by Andries Pretorius.[1] Sechele, almost alone among the chiefs, had dared to resist the Boers. They naturally believed that Livingstone had inspired his opposition and, what is more, that he had sold Sechele 200 rifles and a cannon. Actually, Sechele had only five rifles and the "cannon" was a big black pot. Sechele's tribe, the Bakwain, defended themselves bravely, and inflicted considerable casualties on the Boers, but their own losses were terrible: 60 killed, cattle confiscated and many young people sold into slavery. Chief Sechele himself managed to escape.

The Boers had resented the missionaries ever since the end of the 18th century because of their attitude to slavery and the indigenous population. The majority of the missionaries were English – the LMS having been the first in the field – and the English had abolished slavery, persecuted the slave traders, and passed liberal laws, so the Afrikaners tended to obstruct the missionaries wherever they could. Livingstone was known as a determined friend of the Africans, and was suspected even of providing them with arms; it was inevitable, therefore, that there should be a clash – either an attack on him personally, or destruction of his property. Livingstone is today still unpopular in South Africa with Afrikaners, whose attitude to the Churches and the missionaries opposed to apartheid has in some cases not changed very much.

The Boers also destroyed the mission-station; Livingstone's house lay in ruins, his precious records scattered and torn to pieces, his furniture looted. The Boers had had their revenge on him. Yet Livingstone's comment was typical and prophetic: "The Boers are determined to shut up the interior. I am determined to open up the country. We shall see who have been the more successful in resolution, they or I."

Livingstone also convinced himself (so he told Fleming) that his losses were all for the best, as now he could roam freely, without worrying over material possessions. Since Mary had returned home with the children, he could dedicate himself entirely to promoting Christianity and "Christian trade" among the Africans. And it was at Colobeng that news reached him of the Missionary Society's approval that he should continue his work in the country of the Makololo. This seemed providential – now he had the LMS's blessing to carry out his plan of exploring "the North".

Livingstone was 40 years old, full of energy and capable of enduring extraordinary privations. As he had written in his Journal on June 12, 1851: "I have drunk water swarming with insects, thick with mud, putrid with rhinoceroses' urine and buffalo dung, and no stinted draughts either, and yet I felt no inconvenience from it."[2] His ambition was now clearly to become a great explorer in the service of God. Nothing would be allowed to stand in the way. Perhaps the creation of his own legend was a part of this ambition.

From Colobeng onwards the journey became difficult. By March, 1853, they reached the Mohono bush, where for two days they had to hack their way through tropical forest. To avoid tsetse fly, they had to make a diversion, and cut another but longer path. Eventually they came to the Sanshureh; from his previous visit Livingstone knew it to be a tributary of the Chobe, which in its turn flows into the Zambezi. But there seemed no fordable place along its shore. Fleming was taken ill, and had to stay in his wagon, while Livingstone waded in water breast high to find a point where they could cross the Sanshureh. The Bushmen grew tired of these exertions and slipped away one night. A single man remained, with whom Livingstone set out in a pontoon and eventually reached a large sheet of water. Climbing a high tree he realised that they were surrounded by an immense wall of reeds six to eight feet high, and without any opening. Obliged to force their way through a layer of small but very tough papyrus leaves, they found a passage through the reeds torn by a hippopotamus. Then they came to a stretch of country dotted with

Crossing a swamp

thirty-foot-high ant-hills. From the top of one of these Livingstone saw an inlet into the Chobe and they paddled the pontoon from midday until sunset. Straining their eyes, they saw only tall reeds on both banks of the river. As the short twilight was falling, and Livingstone thought that they would have to spend a supperless night on their float, his Bushman companion noticed some huts on their left. Excited villagers appeared rushing to the river edge, staring at Livingstone and his companion. In their figurative way they shouted: "He has dropped among us from the clouds, yet came riding upon a hippopotamus. We Makololo thought that no one could cross the Chobe without our knowledge, but here he drops among us like a bird."[3] They had recognised Livingstone, for the village belonged to Moremi, a Makololo whom he had visited on his previous trip.

Moremi showed him and his companion how to retrace their steps back to Fleming, who had somewhat recovered, and a few days later a large party of Makololo came down from Linyanti to ferry all three of them across the river. They took the wagons apart, loaded them on a number of canoes lashed together, swimming and diving in high spirits among the oxen. And on May 23 they reached Linyanti to find that great changes had occurred since Livingstone's last visit.

King Sebituane's eighteen-year-old son, Sekeletu, was now in power. He had the same milk-and-coffee coloured skin as his father, but he was smaller – only five feet seven inches tall and lacked Sebituane's fine features.

The whole population of Linyanti, some 7,000, turned out to watch the re-assembled wagons in motion. They had never seen such a spectacle. Sekeletu sent Livingstone pots of *boyalwa*, the Makololo beer, quantities of food and put a hut at his disposal with a bed made up of branches and furs. But before Livingstone could sleep in comfort for the first time in weeks, the Court Herald, an old man who had held the same position under King Sebituane, insisted on an official greeting.

In the packed centre of Linyanti, he stood up and roared, "Don't I see the white man? Don't I see the comrade of Sebituane? Don't I see the Father of Sekeletu? Give thy son sleep, my lord." This was a reference to Livingstone's firearms; if he gave them to his hosts, they could sleep in peace.

Next morning Livingstone began to learn of the problems which were exercising the Makololo, and which kept Linyanti in a state of nervous tension. They concerned the succession. He knew that King Sebituane had, in his lifetime, installed his daughter, Mamochisane as chieftain. To prevent her from having a superior in a husband, he told her that all the men were hers, that she might take any one of them but ought to keep none. However, Sebituane had reckoned without the women; a Makololo proverb had it: "Their tongues cannot be governed." Their outraged opposition to Mamochisane's irregular mode of life so distressed her that after her father's death she begged her brother to rule the Makololo. Sekeletu knew that another member of the family, Mpepe, was determined to seize the throne; therefore he wanted Mamochisane to retain her position. Three days were spent in public discussion on what was to be done. Finally Mamochisane stood up in tears: "I have been chief only because my father wished it. I have always wanted to be married and have a family like other women. You my brother must build your father's house." Sekeletu agreed to take over the chieftainship, but he knew that he would have to fight Mpepe and he told Livingstone of his concern.

Mpepe was on friendly terms with the slave traders, who provided him with arms. This bore out what Livingstone already suspected – that the Makololo had begun to trade in slaves. Sebituane had explained to him that Arab and half-caste Portuguese merchants came more and more frequently into the interior, and were offering guns in exchange for slaves. Mpepe and his men had turned to raiding weaker neighbours to take prisoners whom they then sold in exchange for muskets.

Livingstone at once realised the infinite possibilities of evil in this new problem. It was all the more urgent that they should ascend the Zambezi which he and Oswell had seen in 1851, and continue their search for healthy land on which to build mission stations. Sekeletu offered his support as he wanted Livingstone to stay with him. Like the Tswana, the Makololo also lived in constant dread of Mzilikazi, the Ndebele Paramount Chief. It was well known that Mrs Livingstone's father, Dr Moffat, had acquired a considerable influence over Mzilikazi. If Livingstone brought his own family, Dr Moffat's daughter and grandchildren, to settle among the Makololo, Sekeletu could see life becoming secure.

Some sixty miles further on, near a town called Sesheke,[4] Livingstone and his party encountered Mpepe. Mpepe had told his supporters that he would kill Sekeletu – either at the first opportunity, or, should they meet to confer, when that discussion broke up. When Mpepe saw Sekeletu riding towards him on an ox, he rushed in his direction brandishing an axe. But Sekeletu was on the look-out, and managed to escape to a nearby village.

His first plan having failed, Mpepe was all the more determined to put into effect the second. The young king knew nothing of the plot. Livingstone happened to sit down between the two in the hut where they met. Having ridden all day in the sun, he was tired and asked where he should sleep. Sekeletu replied with great courtesy, "Come, I will show you." They rose together, and unwittingly Livingstone's body prevented the assassin's blow.

Mpepe's attendants divulged the intention to kill the young king, and Sekeletu put Mpepe to death the same night. It was done so quietly that Livingstone, who slept only a few yards from the scene, heard nothing. Mpepe was sitting by the fire in the hut. Nokuane, one of Sekeletu's friends, approached him with a handful of snuff, and Mpepe held out his hand. Nokuane caught hold of it, while another man seized his other hand. They led him some distance away and speared him.

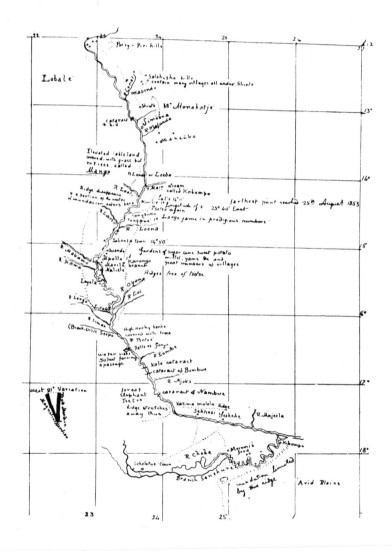

A map showing the Zambezi from Seketelu's town in the south to the Lobal country in the north

The excitement caused by Mpepe's death made it advisable for Sekeletu and Livingstone to return to Linyanti. A month later they set out again. This time Sekeletu was accompanied by many of the under-chiefs and also by his *mopato*, a regiment of young men of his age. They collected a fleet of 36 canoes, 30 feet long and 20 inches wide, and 216 men to handle them. Each canoe was manned by six paddlers, who stood upright and kept stroke with great precision. They proceeded upstream rapidly and soon were in Barotseland. In one village they met Mpepe's father and another man who had counselled Mamochisane to kill Sekeletu and marry Mpepe. The two were led before Sekeletu, who questioned Mpepe's father about his son's treachery. In the course of the inquiry Sekeletu suddenly sprang up, seized the old man, and handed him to his warriors, who also grabbed his companion. Livingstone had to watch while the two captives were hewn down with axes, and the pieces of their bodies flung into the river to the crocodiles. When Livingstone protested, Sekeletu's counsellors told him calmly, "You see, we are still Boers; we are not yet taught."[5]

It was also very disappointing for Livingstone that he saw extensive signs of inundation; the land was low-lying and marshy, and the villages were built on scattered mounds which seemed artificial. He continued his search to the farthest limits of the Barotse territory, but no healthy sites could be located.

Back in Linyanti, Sekeletu asked Livingstone what he hoped to get from him. Livingstone explained that his object was to elevate the Makololo and make them Christians. Sekeletu replied that he did not wish to read The Book, as it might change his heart and make him content with one wife; like Sechele – he wanted at least five.

When Livingstone asked for a canoe as a present, the young king gave him ten fine elephant tusks. Then they had to organise Fleming's return to Cape Town; he was not well physically and had had enough of rough travel. They also discussed whether Livingstone was to go first to the west coast, and from there traverse Africa, or whether he would be better advised to make his way to the east coast and go across from there. He was determined to cross Africa both ways, in order to establish from where supplies could most easily be sent to the mission station he was to open. This route was to be used by Christian traders, who were to ply their wares in understanding with the missionaries.

One day, when preparations had already made good progress,

Sekeletu told Livingstone, "There is a white man who wants to see you."

According to Sekeletu's subsequent account to the stranger, Livingstone seemed stunned, and did not want to believe that there could be another white man in this part of Africa.

"But there is," Sekeletu said he had insisted, adding, "He is a great admirer of yours; he has read of your travels, and he wants to greet you."

Livingstone was adamant, and suggested that the stranger was probably only a Portuguese trader, a half-caste, who had come to buy slaves.

Sekeletu replied that he did not think so. The man was known as *'Ngana Komo*, he had come from Bihé, and had waited a week in Linyanti to see Livingstone. He had had to go back to his camp, but now he wanted to return to pay tribute to him.

Livingstone, who spoke several African languages fluently, knew that *'Ngana* meant 'Why?', and *Komo* man or master. Why was the stranger called *'Ngana Komo*? Sekeletu explained that this white man had a habit of asking questions, always wanting to know why things had happened. Thus he had been nicknamed "Mr Why", *'Ngana Komo*. Sekeletu could have told Livingstone a great deal more about the stranger, but the only thing the doctor wanted to know was whether he was an Englishman. Sekeletu replied that he did not think so; he seemed to come from an even more distant country.

Although, according to Sekeletu, Livingstone would not meet *'Ngana Komo*, Livingstone wanted Sekeletu to find out the route by which the white man had come from Bihé to Linyanti, and how he had reached Bihé in the first place.[6]

During all his journeyings, Livingstone kept a detailed, lively diary. A brilliant observer, he described everything he saw, tribal customs, mysterious diseases, strange animals. His diaries contain detailed references to many hundred Africans he has talked to. As a writer Livingstone possessed all the skills of a gifted journalist. Yet there is not a single word in all his diaries about the white man who had been so anxious to meet him in Linyanti in the summer of 1853. Why did Livingstone refuse to see him?

## CHAPTER NINE

# The story of the white man

Sekeletu was right in thinking that the white man, who appeared so unexpectedly at Linyanti, came from a distant country. László Magyar came from Hungary. He was born on November 11, 1818, the illegitimate son of Imre Magyar and Anna Horváth. She was a peasant girl who worked as a domestic servant in Szombathely, where she met Imre Magyar. He was the son of a minor landowner, then acquiring farming experience on the nearby estate of Count George Festetics. Anna died three weeks after the birth of her son, and her grandmother, Appolonia Horváth, took the baby in her care. A shrewd, practical woman, Appolonia settled in a village between the rivers Danube and Tisza, near the 300 acre estate of László's paternal grandfather. She hoped that if Imre Magyar got to know and to love his son, he would eventually acknowledge him. At that time, Imre was working on another large estate some 600 miles away in the north of Hungary. Having built up a reputation as an excellent farmer, he soon obtained a job nearer home – as agent for the 40,000 acre domain of Baron George Orczy, uncle of Baroness Emma Orczy, of "Scarlet Pimpernel" fame. By the time Appolonia died, her calculation had proved right: Imre Magyar had grown so fond of little László that he adopted him, conferring on him the right to use his name – as an illegitimate child, he had been baptised László Horváth. Then he sent the boy to his own old school, that of the Piarist Fathers in Kalocsa, the largest town in the county.

The Piarists were the most progressive teachers of their day who, to prepare their pupils for a practical life, taught them not only doctrine, Latin, history and algebra, but also modern methods of agriculture, horticulture and viniculture, the rudiments of engineering, of road and of factory building, and of ship construction. Knowing that László Magyar, as an illegitimate child, would not inherit any of his father's money, they tried to direct him towards an industrial career, encouraging his interest in ships and shipbuilding. But Imre Magyar, although he must have been aware that his illegitimate son would never be accepted by the narrow-minded landed gentry whose company he himself greatly enjoyed, took the boy away from the Piarists, and sent him to a conventional school in Szabadka, the capital of the neighbouring county. Imre Magyar hoped that one day László would, like himself, become a first-class farmer, and establish himself as an expert on agricultural problems.

When years later László Magyar became known in Hungary as an Africa explorer, one of his former school mates, József Antunovics – by then a prominent journalist – collected the memories of his classmates about him. All of them agreed that in his early youth László was lively and naughty. Later – and on this too they were unanimous – he became reticent, never spoke about his feelings or reactions to anything, and did not even join in the frequent heated debates on whether or not the serfs should be liberated. Clearly László Magyar must have become aware that he was different from other children: although the eldest son, yet he was not Imre Magyar's heir. At that time in Hungary an illegitimate child could not become an officer, nor a government servant, nor hold office in the county administration. Under government law, formal adoption made it possible to overcome these taboos; but among the county gentry – patriotic, prejudiced, xenophobic – László Magyar would have found few openings. And he knew that it was all but impossible for him to marry a girl belonging to his father's world. All his former schoolmates related that László had three friends with whom he played a game in which he was invariably the captain of a ship and they the crew. In these games of make-believe, they sailed to far-away lands, overcame terrible storms and slew proverbial dragons. László harboured no illusions that these dreams would ever come true; he said so openly, but he could not refrain from talking about what he longed to do in order to get away from a society in which he was, and knew that he would always remain, an outsider.

At the age of sixteen, his father sent László to Pest University where, unlike his four step-brothers, he did not register. Until 1948 (over a century later) in Hungary anyone could attend lectures and obtain degrees without being formally a member of the university. Perhaps he deliberately avoided registration in order to keep secret from members of the faculty as well as from fellow students the embarrassing fact that he was illegitimate.

On his return home two years later, his father secured him a job in the Orczy Estate Office. Imre Magyar wanted to pass on to László his own considerable knowledge of farming – he had by then a national reputation for improving sandy soil by planting trees; for breeding prize sheep, and for producing wine appreciated in all parts of Hungary.

A reconstructed picture of László Magyar (from Prof. Thirring's book)

László made no secret of the boredom with which his desk-job filled him, and how tedious he found the endless talk about sheep – breeding sheep, fattening sheep, shearing sheep, selling sheep at the highest possible prices. He was no happier when his father got him an outdoor job as supervisor of labour in the fields. Judging by the recollections of his contemporaries, László took no interest in the serfs, whose hard life and brutal treatment had roused Hungarian liberals to fury, while the small landowners in particular were terrified of what would happen to them if they had to pay their labour. (As noblemen they were entitled to pay the serfs nothing.) These frightened Hungarians foreshadowed by thirty years the arguments of the planters in the American South; when the South feared that the

North were about to abolish slavery, they unleashed a civil war in an attempt to retain it. Imre Magyar was not encumbered by such prejudices; being a competent farmer, he knew that once he could pick and choose his labour – even if he had to pay his men – he would not only hold his own, but do better if some of his fellow landowners went to the wall. Having married a rich widow seven years after the death of his first wife, he now owned 3,000 acres of the most fertile land in Hungary, and was becoming one of the leaders of his county.

His son László had no appreciation even for the delightful side of the old régime – the constant entertaining, the gay parties, the shooting and riding, the long walks in the woods, and the temperamental arguments about any topic under the sun. He was a lonely, unhappy young man, who could see no way of escaping from an existence he thoroughly disliked. He confided in only two people – Karcsi (Charlie) Weber and Fani Gyurikovics. Karcsi's father was the assistant librarian in the Archbishop's library; the Chief Librarian, Cannon Nehiba, was passionately interested in biography and travel books, and saw to it that new works, both Hungarian and foreign, should be acquired. Mr Weber borrowed these, and Karcsi – mostly without his father's knowledge – lent them to his friend László. He read them so fast that they were returned without Mr Weber being the wiser. In this way László had access to many more books than the average boy of his age and background.

Fani Gyurikovics, who belonged to one of the most influential families of the county, had a very warm spot in her heart for László. She gave him the understanding he yearned for. Many years later, when already in Africa, he learnt of her death – she had never married – he wrote to his father, "I am mourning with all my heart the untimely death of Fani Gyurikovics, who was the sole comforting angel of my orphaned youth. Please tell me the exact date on which she died, for from now on I intend to spend that day every year in sad remembrance about her and about my own youth. May she rest in peace."

Imre Magyar was not only a go-ahead farmer, but also a fervent admirer of Louis Kossuth, who founded a paper, the *Pesti Hirlap (News-sheet of Pest)*. Kossuth, the editor, modelled his style on that of Victor Hugo. Like Hugo, he concentrated his attacks on the treatment of the *misérables*, in Hungary, the serfs. A born propagandist, Kossuth constantly exposed the fact that the stick was the only means of Hungarian education, whether in prisons or in schools.

A Royal establishment, southern Africa mid 19th century

Fiume about 1860

László was not interested in this controversial issue – he scanned the pages of the *Pesti Hirlap* for reports on engineering developments – the building of roads, railways and canals; on the growth of Hungarian industry, for the introduction of the industrial revolution was the aim of all enlightened Hungarians. Among many other schemes, Kossuth also wanted to create a Hungarian commercial navy, and it was largely at his instigation that the first Hungarian Naval Academy was set up in Hungary's main port, Fiume. On January 2, 1842, the *Pesti Hirlap* printed an appeal under the signature of Pál Kiss of Nemeskér, the Governor of Fiume, which said, "The Sea of the Hungarian Nation invites with patriotic love every young Hungarian, who has suitable physical strength and spiritual determination, to join the naval school of Fiume. It expects you to come in numbers, urgently."

When László read this news item, he knew that this was his chance, and he acted accordingly. The timid respectful son, who always consulted his father, resigned his position on the Orczy estate without a word to anyone. He packed his belongings and paid his railway ticket with money he had saved, and he was the first student to register at the Naval Academy of Fiume.

He loved every moment of his training. According to Pál Kiss, a friend of László's father, he was an outstanding student. But his real thrill came when the cadets were taken on their first cruise in the Adriatic. The sea lived up to all his expectations – only he longed to sail the high seas – the oceans of the world. With a certificate of graduation from the Naval Academy in his pocket, in 1843 he went to Trieste and enrolled himself on the postal steamer *Nautilus*, which carried 273 passengers – mostly emigrants from Croatia, Carinthia and Dalmatia – and was headed for Brazil.

His leave taking from his family was an unemotional affair. His father was certain that he would be back within a year, and even if he made the Austrian Merchant Navy his career, he would come home regularly on leave. Perhaps later, tired of travelling, he would settle down, marry a girl of good family, and take up farming. For his part, László was too excited at the prospect of his first real sea voyage to take the parting sadly. To his friends he confided his joy of having seen the last of sheep.

Of what followed he has written: "Having left Trieste on the mail steamer on which I had undertaken to serve as a cadet after a happy journey we dropped anchor in Brazil, in the bay of Bahia de Todos os

Santos. There having left the Austrian Naval Service, I set sail for the West Indies."[1]

At the age of 26, Magyar had broken out of his confined life in Hungary, crossed the Atlantic and shaken off the restraints of the navy.

## CHAPTER TEN

# Outward bound to follow Livingstone

For the next five years, László Magyar's family did not hear one word from him. From Brazil he went to the West Indies, and then to West Africa; back in the West Indies, he sailed to Java, from where

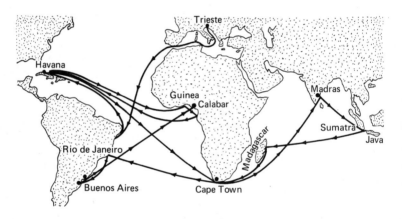

Magyar's travels from 1844, when he left Trieste, until 1849 when he went into the service of King Trudodat of Calabar

he made his way to South Africa; once more from the West Indies he journeyed back to West Africa, and eventually built a home in Angola, from where his first letter reached his father.

This is how he described his adventures:

"From Brazil I went by ship to Havana in the West Indies, and then sailed as ordinary seaman on a Spanish contre-bande[1] ship to the negro coasts of Guinea. I was incredibly lucky in this dangerous and damnable trade, for after a five months' journey though very ill, I returned to Cuba with a full purse. My 1,500 Spanish crowned thalers did not bewitch my soul that was yearning to learn. On the contrary, this money was my first implement for executing my plan to train myself for the work I intended to do. With this in view, I paid for lessons for six months with a distinguished professor of nautical sciences.[2] When I felt that I had acquired some mastery of these subjects, and I had purchased the necessary navigational instruments, I sailed on the *Albatros*, a Spanish ship, as second pilot to the East Indies. There the captain died[3], and I arrived through Sumatra and Java, in the Bay of Antongili, on the island of Madagascar.[4] There I fell so ill with yellow fever that I was at death's door when a French man-of-war took me on as passenger, and set me on shore at the Cape of Good Hope, where after a stay of some two months in the sailors' hospital, my health was restored. From the Cape I returned to Brazil, to Rio de Janeiro, on a Portuguese ship, already as a first pilot. Knowing that in this town was living a countryman of ours, a son of the town of Debreczen, József Vámosi, I thought it proper to call on him. This respected countryman received me with great kindness – as a result of several years of successful trading, he had amassed a considerable fortune. My friend Vámosi soon gave me to know that the Dictator of the La Plata Republic[5], Don Juan Manuel Ortez Rosas, had instructed one of his ministers, who was in Rio de Janeiro at this time, to engage on contract several suitable naval officers for the State Navy. This was good water for my mill; therefore armed with the necessary letters of introduction from my friend János Vámosi, I sailed to Buenos Aires, where as a result of my letters of introduction I obtained an audience of the Dictator who, informed of the object of my wish, set a date for my naval test. Having proved far more successful in it than I had dared to hope, I received a patent of lieutenant of the fleet as well as (La Plata) citizenship rights.

I never felt more joy than when I first saw glittering on my shoulders the decorative golden epaulettes, in which I saw the realisation of my childhood dreams. It is unnecessary to mention the conditions of the bloody war between the states of La Plata and Uruguay; the latter power, backed by the English and the French fleets, almost always came out victorious. On the river Plata, after a long bombardment, the above mentioned English and French fleets having destroyed the Buenos Aires flotilla, I fell into the hands of the Uruguayan enemy as a prisoner of war.[6] They put me before a military tribunal, which condemned me, and several of my fellow officers, to death. The main (but false) charge brought against me was that I too had participated in the massacre of Uruguayan prisoners of war; but thanks to the testimony of a noble-hearted commander of a French man-of-war, (whose name is de Lainé) I was saved. Having shared my fate, he demonstrated to the Military Tribunal my innocence, when being released and allowed to keep my rank as officer, I pledged my word: while the war was on, I would not again undertake service under the Buenos Aires flag against the Uruguayan state.[7] Thereupon I left Montevideo and went by ship to Rio de Janeiro. As I was used to a working life, a peaceful existence soon turned to boredom[8], and I set myself the task to travel in the interior of South America. Crossing the Cordilleras of the Andes, I wanted to explore *the country of the Incas*, or *Peru*, and to investigate the ancient treasures said to be lying all over the place. For the realisation of this plan I turned for help to a scientific society (which you mention in your letter) but I could not carry out this expensive trip unaided.''

On June 2, 1845, from Moldonado in Uruguay, László Magyar had applied to the Hungarian Scientific Society, soon to become the Hungarian Academy of Sciences, for funds for two expeditions. The first would have taken him from Uruguay across Paraguay to the Gran Chaco, Tucuman, Salta and Jujuz provinces, then crossing the Cordilleras, ending in Lima. The second would have started in Rio de Janeiro, from where he intended to explore the diamond and gold fields of Minas Geraes, then cross the Matto Grosso and the Andes, and through Lima make for the springs of the Orinoco, then the Chimborazo and the Kotopaxi regions. At the end of his journey, he wanted to sail down the Orinoco, and return to Hungary with the specimens he had collected.

Magyar asked for 12,000 pengö-forints[9] for his expenses, and 2,000 pengö-forints for purchasing the necessary equipment. On November 2, 1846, in Pest Count István Széchényi submitted to the Academy Magyar's request with his own backing, but owing to lack of funds, and because Magyar was completely unknown, the proposition was turned down. The Secretary of the meeting was, however, instructed to inform Magyar "of the Society's appreciation of his fervent efforts in the interests of science."

Exploring in Latin America, Magyar learnt several native languages; Spanish and Portuguese he already spoke fluently. But he felt that South America was not his chosen field. "Having only my Brazilian patent, I could not hope to be admitted for service in the English, the French or the North American war fleets without considerable loss in rank," he wrote in 1851, "and as I do not consider it right to exchange a horse for a donkey, I sailed to the West Coast of Africa, where I took service with the negro King of Kalabar, Dalaber Almanzor of Trudodat, as commander of his flotilla, and for two years earned the full satisfaction of His Black Majesty."[10]

Magyar described King Dalaber's fleet as consisting of 120 very long and narrow canoes, with up to 48 Africans rowing each one. He commanded this fleet from a schooner, and scored many victories against neighbouring African potentates. But his greatest victory was in a different field: from Calabar he made his first exploration in Africa.

László Magyar's account of his journey from Calabar up the Congo or Zaire river to the Faro-Szongo cataracts, was subsequently published by the Hungarian Academy of Sciences. In it he explained that *Congo* was pronounced by some locals Songo; *faro* – according to some tribes *nbvaro* or *bvaro* – meant boat; Faro-Szongo therefore meant "Navigable Congo". Magyar was told this by his Babuma servants, who also said that Europeans learnt from their guides that the cataracts were called Jellala, because they are near a village of the same name.

In his introductory paragraph Magyar stated: "In general, the great rivers of South Africa, which flow into the Atlantic Ocean, are of little use for sustained shipping. South of the Equator, the mountains running parallel with the coast cut across the riverbeds, which flow from east to west, invariably forming one or several cataracts in them. The smallest of these is sufficient to block shipping, especially here, where the charitable balm of civilisation has so far been ineffective in removing these obstacles. Therefore, contrary to general experience in other parts of the world, where great rivers are carriers of knowledge and civilisation, hitherto in Africa they have been of little use for spreading culture and increasing knowledge." Subsequently, Magyar noted accurately that owing to the many sandbanks,[11] seafaring ships could sail only ninety miles up the Zaire, not getting even near the cataracts. From Ponta da Lenha (of which we will hear more later on) goods had to be transported to Boma in barges.

Then he went on: "Having become fairly well acquainted with the language and the customs of the people of these domains, this pro-

African Naval Battle

Congo (Zaïre) rapids (*photo George Baker*)

mised good success for my aim to get to know the Kongo, one of South Africa's most powerful rivers, by sailing up its course. I knew that in the northern corner of the mighty delta lived the Kabenda, tribesmen famous for their sailing prowess and their remarkable ability and skill in building boats, with practically no tools. Many of the larger boats they built, have sailed to Brazil and the Antillas, burdened with 400 to 500 slaves. They are courageous people, who handle oars and sails equally well. Their many and independent chiefs have formed a defensive alliance, whose president is Mambuco Manitati, who lives in their capital, Malemba. The main god of their mythology is Many Panzve, the god of thunder, to whom they sacrifice animals, but no humans. They are polygamous and practice circumcision. They number some 30,000, and are on a higher cultural level than other Africans."

He engaged six brawny Kabenda oarsmen for his expedition. This cost little, and his salary was quite sufficient to provide for their food. His main problem was how to deal with the chiefs of the areas on the shores of the Zaire[12], who were on intimate terms with the slave traders. Magyar knew that he would have to buy their good-will with presents of cotton materials and barrels of brandy. To purchase these, he sailed from Calabar to Ambriz, situated on the waste, desert seashore south of the delta, consisting of some thirty bamboo houses of the slave traders who lived completely apart from the natives. "Foreign traders can only secure permission to settle at the price of very considerable gifts. But in spite of these, they are treated very badly by these arrogant, cunning and thieving people, who are in general subjects of the King of the Kongo. In the centre of this domain are to be found rich copper mines, which in future will provide lucrative commercial articles. Near the seashore the climate is extremely unhealthy because of the many swamps created by the flooding of the Ambriz river."

On May 9, 1848, Magyar set out from Ambriz,[13], sailing close to the coast. On May 10 he passed Muserra, a pyramid-shaped mountain about eight miles inland, reputedly containing rich copper mines. Next day he passed Mangue-grande and Mangue-pequena, where he saw a few European *factorias* – Portuguese commercial depots. On May 12 he rounded the Ponta de Padrao promontory, which forms the southern shore of the Zaire delta.

"Suddenly a magnificent panorama appeared before my eyes," he wrote. "The mighty river showed itself in all its beauty. At its six nautical miles wide estuary, the yellow water pours with immense speed into the sea, and for a distance of three nautical miles with horrendous power, it excellently retains its colour and sweet taste. Both its shores are covered by tall, thick woods; on the high north-west side are situated the negro villages of Kabenda and Manda-masia. The river's speed is seldom less than six or seven nautical miles an hour, therefore one can only sail upriver with a good wind and an incoming tide. Towards evening, but only with immense effort, I reached the English bay – Bahia dos Ingleses – so named after an English party which suffered shipwreck here."[14]

On May 13 Magyar noted, "With an incoming tide and a cool, good wind, I proceeded gaily between the two shores, covered in thick forest. In this wilderness, there was no sign of human beings. The deathly quiet was only disturbed by the screeches of birds and monkeys. This majestic wild scene caused feelings of sombre sadness in the soul of the traveller. On this occasion I remembered longingly the pleasant Hungarian countryside, with its well-cultivated fields, where even the smallest object talks to one."

On May 14, about ten in the morning, Magyar sailed past the Matampi river, one of the Zaire's large tributaries. The hitherto favourable wind dropped, and next day he made slow progress. Then he noticed inhabitants on the shores; promptly a fleet of boats, filled with smaller and bigger men, swarmed towards his barge. "In front sat women," Magyar recorded, "their heads shaved, and from their baskets offered manioc flour and bananas in exchange for cotton materials and beads. In the sterns sat men, clutching two or three long-barrelled rifles, and *zagayas* (assagaies), six inches long iron spears. They called themselves Mu-Sorongos, subjects of the King of the Kongo, but as I later discovered, only in appearance, as in fact they form an independent democracy, living under the leadership of smaller and bigger chiefs – *kukulu* – and around this river have the reputation of being fearsome pirates. Therefore I listened little to what they had to say. When some of them asked permission to board my boat, rifle in hand I flatly refused their request." Luckily at noon a favourable wind filled his sails, and his barge slipped away.

In the afternoon, Magyar passed the Island of Coconuts – Ilha dos Coqueiros – and next day he saw attractive bamboo houses, built on stilts, surrounded by well-cultivated maize, manioc, tobacco and *mandabi* (jinguba) fields:

"After six hours' of rowing, I reached the Ponta da Lenha – Point

Congo River village

View of Congo (Zaïre) from Isangila

of the Woods – *factorias*, where as a result of my letters of introduction to the factors who live there, they received me quite hospi-
tably, although I was utterly incapable of clearing away their
suspicions of my person, especially about the purpose of my
journey. My readers can imagine my position: I was alone, a Hungarian by nationality, who appeared unexpectedly through unknown routes among these piratical slave traders of some thirty
nationalities, whose language, mostly Spanish and Portuguese, I
could speak. But as I am a former naval officer, they regarded me
as their sworn enemy. What does this Austro-Hungarian dog seek
here, the ruder ones among them asked each other; others asserted
that I must be the spy of some English cruiser, and that I wanted to
ascertain the topography of their hideout, the number of slaves
they have bought, the time and place of their embarcation, as a
result of which it would be easy for the English not only to catch
them on the high seas, but knowing the route up-river and the location of their depots, raid them there.

I had almost lost hope that I would be able to continue my
journey up-river, when luckily opinions about me began to differ,
and I had the chance of gaining certain sympathies thanks to the
presence of an old acquaintance[15] whom I had met in my La Plata
days, and who was now carrying on his commercial activities in
Ponta da Lenha. During my sixteen days' stay, as a result of my
acquaintance's influence, I succeeded in soothing the ruffled feelings of these suspicious people."[16]

On May 17 Magyar noted in his diary, "Ponta da Lenha is well
known as an emporium of the slave trade in South Africa. This notorious settlement lies at some 70 miles from the delta, consisting of
some forty bamboo houses on stilts, as frequent floods turn the low-
lying shores of the Zaire into veritable swamps. The climate is
deadly; the damp, muddy ground is covered with dense vegetation,
baked by the boiling-hot sun of the equator. The miazma, steaming –
as it does – incessantly, endangers all human life. No European,
however strong his constitution, can stand this for more than three
years. The white slave traders only stick it because of their greedy
determination to make gigantic profits. And their way of life, which
consists of eating, drinking heavily and committing sexual excesses,
is killing them off rapidly – ten percent of these demoralised humans
die every year."

László Magyar had a sharp eye and missed little. "It is almost unbelievable what valuable goods are stored here; brought over from Brazil and the Antillas, they are eventually conveyed by the Zaire and its tributaries to various slave markets. From my own observations, I estimate the goods in the depots here are worth some two million Spanish thalers[17]; and the number of slaves dispatched from here to diverse parts of the Americas at about 20,000 per annum. From this it clearly follows that the English cruisers (cruzeiro), which are supposed to put a stop to this ungodly trade in human beings, have in spite of all their endeavours so far had little success."

On June 2 Magyar, having acquired the services of a good river

A view on the Congo

pilot, attached himself to a group of ships taking goods up the Zaire. But by the next day he had to stop at one of the islands, the *Ilha dos Palmeiras* – the Island of the Palmtrees – because he was writhing with chattering teeth in the grip of yellow fever. He ate *china sufas* – the medicine used against the disease at the time – and gave lavish presents to the chief, *mufuque*, so that when two days later he recovered sufficiently to continue his journey, the chief seemed to regret his departure. "He worried not so much about losing me, but my brandy, which he often praised with a deep sigh."

Magyar described the topography of the area, its flora, fauna and its reptiles, such as the terrible *crotalus horridus*, the surucucu, the fararakka (*vepra atrox*) and also the gigantic "boa constrictor". About the inhabitants, the Kabenda, he said: "Ruled by bigger and smaller chiefs – *mani mufuque* – they form an aristocratic republic in which a white cap, woven in beautiful taste from the roots of a smilax type plant, serves as distinctive emblem of a privileged body. These people are determined enemies of the Mu-Sorongo, who live in the southern part of the river." They were not only good-looking, but well dressed in bright coloured cottons, which they bought from the slave traders. In addition the women adorned themselves with many-coloured glass beads and yellow-copper arm and leg bangles. Magyar also gave an account of their agriculture, domestic animals, and religion – "a stupid polytheism, they have no priests but they pay generously their soothsayers who interpret their innumerable superstitions." Their main trading articles were slaves and palm oil, which they bartered with the traders for the things they needed.

On the evening of June 6, Magyar at last reached Boma, "one of the largest slave towns in South Africa, lying on the north side of the Zaire, on a gently elevated plateau. It consists of some fifty houses belonging to the slave traders. With the houses of their free negro servants, it forms a considerable township. Here the houses are not built of bamboo, but of thick wooden poles deeply bedded into the soil, on the outside padded with mud, the roofs covered with straw. Yet because security is precarious, they keep their goods on floats anchored in the river, and on the shore they display only the goods needed for their daily purchases. Well recommended to the traders who live here, I was received by them without any suspicion, and as a result I could easily acquire some knowledge of prevailing conditions."

Magyar spent three weeks in Boma, where the climate was much healthier than at Ponta da Lenha, and he fully recovered. But he suffered all the more spiritually from the horrors of the slave trade which he now witnessed at close quarters. "Every day from varying parts of Africa, slaves of both sexes arrive intended for sale, dragged here partly from the north-east, from areas beyond the equator, but mostly in boats, accompanied by armed men, called *quibuca* – slave drivers. Fully grown and strong slaves form groups of ten to twelve, who bear round their necks heavy iron rings, which have two loops, through which an iron chain is drawn, and they are manacled in such a way as to leave the space of one long step between every two slaves. These unfortunates frequently have to walk 120 days, completely naked, tortured by hunger and thirst, until they reach a slave market. Innumerable slaves die during these terribly fatiguing journeys. . . . But the most heart-rending spectacle is when five to six year old children who followed their manacled parents on the long, pitiful journey, as it were sharing their miserable existence, are torn without pity from the arms of their screaming mothers by the inhuman *quibuca*. Because no one has bought them at the market, the children are then dragged back into the interior, along roads soaked with bitter tears and blood. Many more beastly cruelties are committed by the purveyors of this godless trade in human flesh."

Magyar went on bitterly: "Envy and sadistic pleasure at other peoples' troubles, appendages of immeasurable greed, characterise the slave traders; hence there is no understanding among them, as a result of which they can fix no proper price for the slaves, because whatever they may settle among themselves in the daytime . . . they secretly change it at night, either by raising, or by lowering the agreed price. The local chiefs insist that the slave traders keep a considerable number of useless servants; a large *factoria* is normally compelled to pay at least ten francs a month to each one of 120 loungers, two-thirds of which money goes to the chief of the domain. In addition to these free negro servants, every slave trader has to employ so-called *linguisters*, who are well versed in this trade. Every night the *factor* gives them instructions how to receive the *quibuca*, who arrive from different directions; how many pieces of cloth they can promise for each *paket*, the name for the price of a fully grown, well built slave."

Then Magyar explained the technique of "the damned trade." "The *quibuca* are black men, who represent the chiefs in the interior, who capture people of their own blood, in order to sell them for profit. According to custom, they stop outside Boma and wait for the

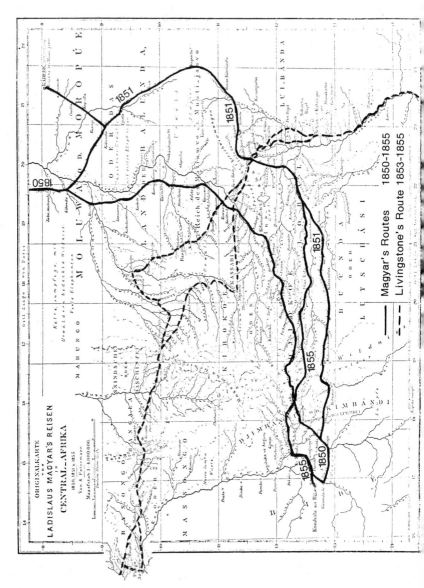

A map of Magyar's travels in central Africa between 1850 and 1855

*linguisters* who are instructed to bribe them with gifts and promises, and win them over for their masters often with as many as one hundred slaves, paying deposits of several lengths of materials and lots of brandy. Thus having settled the deal, at dawn the *linguisters* lead the slaves to their masters' yards, and no one else has now the right to buy these. . . . The traders treat the goods intended for the market with consideration; they clean them, they dress them in clothes made of two ells of cotton. But the slaves are guarded in strong yards surrounded by deeply embedded poles – *kubata* – by the so-called *mon-ngamba* (guards); at night the stronger men are forced to sleep in iron manacles in a fortified barn. The slaves are given plenty of good food; that they should not give way to despair, they are made to dance and sing to the accompaniment of their own music, until the ship arrives onto which they are packed by the hundred, thus being transported to America."

Magyar noted carefully the *paket* – price – paid for a well built, strong slave: it consisted of cotton, gunpowder, brandy, bone-handled knives, copper bangles, and so on. He calculated that in terms of money each slave was worth 80 Hungarian pengö-forints.[18]

This is what Magyar had to say about the locals: "The inhabitants belong to the Kongolese tribes, and speak their language; they are administered by a royal governor, called *Mani-Boma*, who pays an annual tax to the Kongolese king, but otherwise is completely independent. In general they are small, of attractive stature, they are clever, and used to the propinquity of white people with whom they are friendly. Their way of life and habits are common with those of the people I mentioned earlier, none the less I found that their marriage customs are different. As polygamy is customary, the girls who wish to marry are kept apart, in the company of several old women, in a place especially destined for this. There, as I was informed, in addition to some useful things such as agriculture and cooking, they are taught diverse sexually exciting motions. They go about completely naked, painting their bodies red with teak; for this the place where they are staying is called *kubata an kujuka* – the red house. The lad, who seeks a bride, chooses one of the girls through the intercession of the said old women – of course against a good fee. He takes his bride to his house but only with her agreement. Having lived together for seven days, if they like each other, he has to pay her relations a larger or smaller sum, according to her sweetness and looks. Then she becomes his property and at his home he presents her to his other wives and then makes her his own."

Magyar heard that further up-river the inhabitants were noto-riously dishonest and deceitful. Therefore, before resuming his explorations on June 27, he strongly armed himself and his crew. He had many adventures: one night his boat was nearly overturned by a hippopotamus; he had difficulties with the local chiefs about the toll he had to pay; and he met numerous boats loaded with slaves. But the inhabitants turned out to be friendly; in many places he heard shouts of: "*Evoe kindele!*"[19] (Look at the white man!) In one particularly attractive spot, which looked like a garden, he was taken to the chief, a fat, good-humoured man of 60 called Chiambassi, who asked Magyar questions about his name, his country of origin, the purpose of his journey; but he could give little information in return about areas further up the Zaire. All Magyar learnt was that his place was called Enganda, that the people were subjects of the *Mani-Songo*, to whom they paid an annual tax of resin and slaves, but who for his part had to pay tax to the *King of the Kongo*, who lived within a two-days journey, at Banza-Songo.

Chiambassi offered Magyar hospitality, giving him a dinner of goat meat and putting him up in a hut which had a comfortable bed made of plaited rushes. But Magyar could not sleep, because people danced around his hut all night, making a terrific noise, especially as there was plenty of *malufo* – palm wine.

On June 29, having given his host some presents, Magyar contin-ued his journey up-stream, and soon saw the Enganda mountains, whose Faro-Songo ridge causes the famous falls. He spent the night in a village called Zsimbi; next morning after tough rowing he reached a point where the river is squeezed between rocks and its cur-rent is so strong that the six hefty Kabenda could not move the boat any farther. They anchored by the shore, near a village named Kolo; early on July 1st he left four of his men in charge of the boat, and with two others, accompanied by several locals, set out on the rocky, pre-cipitous northern shore. They could already hear the roar of the waterfall. But it took them another four hours' climb to approach it. László Magyar crawled to the edge of the cliff overhanging the water. "Then a majestic scene of nature appeared before my eyes," he wrote in his diary. "The air was vibrating with the thundering weight of the water, which fell from a height of sixteen feet with the speed of light-ning. The greenish welter at the base of the fall dissolved into spray, which rose towards heaven, in which the sun transcribed rainbows.

An awe-inspiring spectacle, at which an ordinary mortal could only worship his Creator in amazement.[20] . . . I could not overcome the depth of impression this made on me; I watched for a long time in silence sunk into myself, the swollen waves rushing furiously, threatening to swallow everything. . . . Only after some two hours' contemplation did I notice that neither of my companions was with me. I even suspected them of having betrayed me. . . ."

A street in a Congo village

He found the two Kabenda at some distance, lying amid bushes. The men, normally brave, were at this moment trembling: "They explained to me nervously the cause of their fear," Magyar recorded. "They told me that the waterfall is the shelter of the souls of the dead, who inflict on every living person danger, curses and even death." Magyar's comment in his diary was, "Superstition fetters the souls of these unfortunate black people more tightly than the iron collars the *quibuca* put on the necks of the slaves they are driving."

When the Kabenda saw that their master had returned unharmed from the place they regarded as so dangerous, they shouted excitedly: "*Kindele! Kindele! Asai vakulus!*" (White man, white man, courageous, strong!)

The rest of László Magyar's diary regarding his Kongo expedition is missing, but in his Report he described the many areas he visited.

He wrote of the "Kongolese Kingdom", which had about one million inhabitants. Its main rivers were the Zaire, the Dande, the Ambriz, the Ambrizete and the Mutu-an-Kapuka, the river of the snakes. "The form of rule is a monarchy, restrained by an arrogant aristocracy," he recorded. "Succession goes through the daughters' children; the King of the Kongo, who has a great reputation as well as splendid titles, has no power to take decisions. These are in the hands of the stubborn nobility – *mani-mufuque*. The King is so poor that sometimes he does not know from one day to the next what is to be cooked in his house. These people have reached differing degrees of civilisation. The Muchi-Kongo, who live in the southern part of the country, and who have traded for a long time with the Portuguese, are decidedly the most cultivated. They barter their elephant tusks, yellow wax, malachite, palm oil and slaves for luxuries they want. They show exceptionally good taste in the production of certain materials."

Then he wrote of the "hordes of cannibalistic Fouti peoples in the Eastern parts, who live exclusively off robbery and hunting, selling their ivory to the *benguela*, the inland black traders." Further south, "no European, except for the Jesuits, has been able to cross the territory of the equally cannibalistic Mu-Sorongo; their chapel, called Santo Antonio de Mu-Sorongo, still stands and is greatly respected by these wild people. What is quite amazing, every year they repair it. Yet the Mu-Sorongo are polytheists. Muta Kalombo is their god of thunder; if in a rainy season the rain does not come, they sacrifice human beings to him; Lambalianquita is the god of the travellers and the hunters, to whom they sacrifice only game; their third deity is Hendée, the god of love, on the many festivities in his honour, which are regular Lupercalia, several selected virgins have to sacrifice their virginity to men chosen for them by the soothsayers, the *quimbanda*. Polygamy is general among them, although not circumcision."

Marriage required no ceremony, only agreement by the bride's relatives, who sold the girls to the highest bidder. Crimes were punished by fines; anyone who denied having committed the deed of which he was accused, was tried by the soothsayers with the so-called oath-drink – *bulongo* and *kablungo*. The soothsayers saved by an effective counter-poison those who paid the most in the form of slaves, while "the guilty" were sold into slavery with their entire families. The year was divided into only two periods, the first being the rainy season, called *Begi-Kamogi* (beginning September); the second the dry season, *Begi-Kambandi* (beginning in March). Magyar also portrayed their dances, musical instruments and curious funereal customs. He himself was nearly driven mad "by the hellish concert of the mourners", and took refuge in the woods until it was over. As, according to Congolese belief, there was no such thing as a natural death, the mourners then went to the soothsayer to find out who had killed the deceased. Of course for a consideration, he "found" the murderer, who was then tried by the oath drink.

The Congolese monarch's residence was in the capital, Banzaputu, (the San Salvador of the Portuguese) about 150 miles inland, on a high plateau, by the side of the Hokondo river. Its climate was very healthy, and it had some 5,000 inhabitants. It was made up of many small straw-covered houses, and had four large squares – *zsongo* – used for political meetings and for dances. They were surrounded by beautiful incendera trees, probably planted by the Jesuits, the remains of whose church could still be seen.

Magyar also explored "the domains of the Luba, Sinde, Jinga, Holo-Ho, Monzholo and the Jaga of Kasnadgyishi people, and the Inhanha swamps". On modern maps we can find few of these names: King Leopold of the Belgians merged them all into his Congo, now renamed Zaire.

Before returning to Calabar, Magyar had one more adventure which he related in his Report: "The Mu-Sorongo, of whom I have already written, are anxious to kidnap people. If their captives are not redeemed for a good ransom, they eat them. On my return from my expedition, I was chased for over an hour by some twenty of their canoes, and nearly fell into their hands. Only a sudden seaward wind, which swelled my sails, delivered me from this danger, as thanks to it I could leave with lightning speed."

Eventually Henry Morton Stanley completed the exploration of the Congo in 1877 and was met close to the delta by Alexander A. de Serpa Pinto, who steamed up on a gunboat with the backing of the Portuguese Governor. In their respective descriptions neither Stanley, nor Serpa Pinto, mentioned that László Magyar was the first white man to describe the Congo Delta in 1848, that is 29 years earlier.

Had László Magyar had the imagination to translate his diary (which at that time was still complete) about his Congo exploration into German, Italian, Portuguese, or Spanish, all of which he spoke and wrote easily, and sent it to the Royal Geographical Society in

London,[21] his fate – and that of Livingstone – would have been different. In 1848 no one had heard of Livingstone. Allowing time for
Magyar to translate his diary, the MS could have reached London by
the spring of 1849. At that time the Royal Geographical Society was
in financial difficulties and badly needed material to attract new
members. The new, able secretary, Dr Norton Shaw, would no doubt
have publicized Magyar's lively and accurate descriptions of the
Congo delta,[22] and, more important still, published the reports of the
slave trade he had seen in action at Ponta da Lenha and at Boma.
They would have caused a sensation, and Dr Livingstone's subsequent revelations would have been far less dramatic than they turned
out to be.

Unfortunately for Magyar, he sent his diary and many interesting
letters to Hungary, where owing to the glorious but unsuccessful
1848–9 War of Liberation, and the ensuing political oppression,
some were lost, while others began to see print only in 1850 – just
about the time Livingstone's first letters, read out at a meeting of the
Royal Geographical Society, caused a world sensation. Magyar also
heard about Dr Livingstone, and decided to meet him – even if it
meant travelling to southern Africa.

## CHAPTER ELEVEN

# Magyar, the explorer married to his job

László Magyar was probably unique among European explorers of Africa because he was able to move through different territories and communicate with their peoples almost as if he were one of them. His wife, Princess Ozoro, was the daughter of Kaiaia Kajangula, the Ruler of Bihé. Being, as it were, married to his job, Magyar the explorer thus obtained insights of Africa which were denied to other Europeans of his day. But before one examines the results of this marriage for the explorer's work, it is necessary to recount the events which led up to Magyar meeting his African bride.

"While in the service of the negro King of Kalabar," Magyar wrote in *A Short Resumé Of My Life*, "I was respected in my office, loved by my friends and provided with everything I needed, but eventually the deadly climate undermined my health to such an extent that I could not stay on without endangering my life. After a long pipe-smoking session with His Majesty, I asked and obtained indefinite leave, and having said my respectful goodbyes I travelled some fifteen degrees southwards, to the Portuguese colonies, in order to restore my health." Magyar arrived in Benguela on December 9, 1848.

At no time has he explained how he came to serve King Dalaber Almanzor of Trudodat. His friends in Benguela believed that he got to know him in 1844, when he first came to Africa on a Spanish slaver. There is some mystery about Dalaber Almanzor himself. The people of Calabar – and the author has consulted several old Chiefs who have extraordinary memories and are the repositories of their peoples' history – do not remember a ruler of that name, yet one of Magyar's correspondents said, apparently on Magyar's authority, that Dalaber Almanzor ruled not only over Calabar, but over the Gold Coast and Liberia in the north-west, and as far as the Congo (Zaire) in the south.[1]

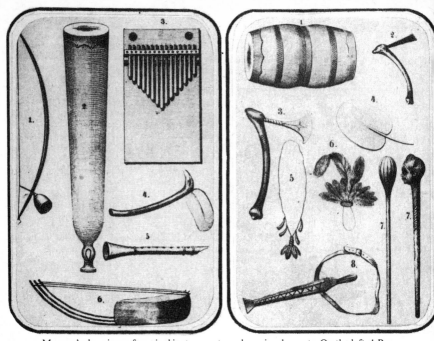

Magyar's drawings of musical instruments and war implements. On the left: 1 Burum-
bumba, musical instrument. 2 Ngoma, drum. 3 Viszángysi, musical instrument. 4 hoe.
5 Bendu, flute. 6 Kiszumbu, tambourine. On the right: 1 Kandinga, war drum. 2 Dia-
bite, pick. 3 Mutáka, war axe. 4 Temo, digging hoe. 5 Vihemba, gazelle's horns worn
around the neck. 6 Szala, war head ornament. 7 Hunya, club. 8 Mukuálo, short
throwing spear.

Canoes and paddles of Africa

In 1727 the *Boston News Letter* and the *Gentleman's Magazine* referred to Trudo Adato, King of Dahomey and Emperor of Popo. It seems that Dalaber Almanzor of Trudodat must have been descended from the African ruler about whom in the 18th century reports appeared in the New England press. It is difficult to dismiss the thought that this King of Dahomey and Emperor of Popo had provided slaves to the American colonists, which could explain the favourable references to him in the Boston newspapers. Dalaber Almanzor, whom László Magyar described as a highly intelligent and cultivated man, appreciated European merchandise; because of this he may have supplied "black gold" to the slaver on which Magyar served in 1844.

The parting between Magyar and Dalaber Almanzor was a sad occasion as they respected and liked each other. King Dalaber's farewell gift to his "Admiral" – as he called Magyar – was truly regal. In Benguela the Hungarian bartered the ivory, the lion and the leopard skins he had received from the King for goods worth 10,000 francs;[2] King Dalaber's gold he kept for an emergency. Magyar obtained from Portuguese traders 10,000 metres of cloth; one thousand litres of brandy; 20 forty-kilogram barrels of gun powder; one ton of bone-handled knives; three tons of salt; twenty rifles; several tons of glass and shell beads, mirrors and feminine trinkets. His acquisitions weighed 36 tons, which meant that he needed eighty porters, each man carrying a load of 45 kilograms.

Magyar had not gone to Benguela only for his health. To quote his own words: "During my stay here, I had occasion to confirm the enormous profits yielded by African inland trade (slaves, ivory, rubber, urzella, wax, etc.); equally I heard from reliable men that some 80 to 90 nautical miles inland, on a large, high plateau, lay beautiful territories, with the best and healthiest climate imaginable. Although the inhabitants are pagans, as a result of extensive trade in the centre of Africa, they are in contact with all countries; being cosmopolitans by nature, they accept newcomers; they are brave travellers and clever elephant hunters."[3]

Once or twice a year large caravans of African traders came to Benguela from the interior to exchange their wares for European merchandise. Magyar wanted to join one of these and make his way to Bihé, where the average temperature was 15° Reaumur (60° Fahrenheit), and the population numbered 50,000, ten per cent of whom were slaves. The Mbundu, the ruling tribe, were the only people between the Congo and the Kunene rivers who patronised European traders and travellers. Like other African traders, the Mbundu had "certain common interests" with the Portuguese colonists, of whom Magyar formed a poor opinion. The Governor, a pale, seedy-looking man, had a swollen stomach he attributed to bouts of fever which had damaged his liver and his kidneys. His staff looked equally puny. Magyar noticed that they all drank immense quantities of brandy and wine, and concluded that their poor physique was due not only to the climate, but to their alcoholic and sexual excesses. None of the Portuguese brought white women with them; they all "married" several black women, and in their homes brought up their mulatto children. Practically all medium and low-grade positions were occupied by their offspring and that of the traders; responsible posts were reserved for whites, both in government service and in commerce.

The Governor's palace was well-built; the rooms were tall and the earth floors dirty. The Governor did not even have a map of the interior; he asked Magyar to pay special attention to the course of the rivers and to the possibilities of river transport. The Portuguese aim was to find a means of connecting their west African colonies with Moçambique, their colony on the east coast.

Magyar was lucky that the next Mbundu caravan was headed by a Bihé aristocrat called Mursa, a tall handsome man, with short white hair and a white beard. He was a trader of high repute, well disposed to Europeans. He and Magyar took to each other instantly; the African not only offered to lead him to Bihéland, but to find him a good *Kisongo* – a majordomo-secretary-factor – on whose honesty and judgement every trader's fate depended. Mursa also promised to secure the services of a quick *kalei* – interpreter. Later in the day, Mursa introduced to Magyar a thirty-year-old relative called Pakasero, which meant "Ox Killer". The name suited the man, who was squat, with strong rippling muscles, and a hard body. Without uttering a word, he looked Magyar straight into the eye, and waited for the white man – according to local custom – to ask him three times: "Do you want to become my *kisongo*, to serve me faithfully, and if need be, risk your life for me?" Three times Pakasero answered, "Yes, I will." Then Mursa and the other relatives took Pakasero by the hand, led him quite close to Magyar, and recited in unison, "This is our brother, our son. From now on he belongs to you, and you belong to him. If you shed your blood, he must do likewise; if you die, he must die with you. Should he desert you in cowardly fashion, we will wash away his guilt with this." Each relative pointed to a cartridge placed at his feet.

Pakasero took an oath that he would become László Magyar's faithful *kisongo*. Putting into Magyar's hand a dark-red cartridge, he said, "Should I ever desert you in danger, or refuse to share danger with you, you must shoot me through the breast with this cartridge painted red with my own blood." From then on for sixteen years, Pakasero remained Magyar's faithful and quick-witted companion.

Pakasero first showed his mettle by collecting the strongest and most reliable porters, who packed Magyar's goods with experienced care. Pakasero arranged with them that each one of the 80 men should receive 40 ells of cloth and two bottles of brandy for carrying Magyar's 36 tons of wares over rocky mountains and swampy ground during a 40 day journey.

The caravan, which left Benguela on January 15, 1849, was systematically organised. In front walked some 150 armed guards, recruited from Bihé's best hunters; then followed about a thousand porters with their loads, which the Mbundu inspected as they would not allow any man to be overloaded; behind them came some 1,500 small traders, carrying on their backs their valuables and weapons; the rear was brought up by the "rich men" whose sole load was a rifle and many cartridges, and whose duty it was to shoot game when the caravan ran low in food.

The first part of the journey led through dry and desolate country, with scarcely any vegetation except *casonera* (a kind of aloe). Mursa saw to it that the travellers marched during moonlit nights, being at least spared the intense heat. Magyar described his experiences very interestingly;[4] two main events stand out on this journey. On Mursa's suggestion, he was elected leader of the caravan at a meeting "conducted so earnestly and in such good order as no one could have expected from people regarded as wild and primitive."[5] From then on, every night his flag – the Hungarian flag – fluttered in the centre of the restcamp, called the *zsonga*. The flag was easily made up, for the Bihé colours were red and white, hence only one green strip had to be added to the white one. Magyar was very proud of this honour, and proved himself a shrewd negotiator with the chiefs, through whose territories they passed, about the amount of toll – *kibanda* – the caravan had to pay. The second event was an amusing one: he discovered that the Mbundu regarded him as a kind of mascot who had "strong magic powers" and that he had been nicknamed '*Ngana Komo*, "Mr Why", because he asked so many questions.

Later on in the journey to Bihé they nearly had to fight one tribe, whose chief declared war on them, but thanks to a ruse thought up by Mursa, the caravan got away without a shot being fired. They were not so lucky in their encounter with swarms of red ants. Even elephants fled from this scourge.

László Magyar sadly had to part company with Mursa, who lived in the west of Bihé, while he had to go on to the capital, Kombala an Bihé, to obtain permission from the king, Kaiaia Kajangula, to settle in his country. Magyar's account of the ceremonies preceding his audience of the king, the formal dialogue between himself and Kaiaia Kajangula (Pakasero acting as interpreter), the granting of permission to stay because the king regarded it as an honour that a white man should wish to live in his domain, makes fascinating reading. So does the manner in which Magyar's fortified house – *libata* – was erected near Masisi an Kuitu,[6] the village of Pakasero's family, where Magyar decided to settle.

Before work could begin, a witchdoctor (Magyar's word) had to be called in to drive out the bad spirits, of course for a handsome fee. The house was built in European style, consisting of five main rooms, a larder, kitchens and laundries, and so on. Magyar said nothing about furniture; only much later, when already an exile in Lucira Bay, did he refer to "the patriarchal comfort in which we lived" and to the house from which "I watched my herds of cattle, sheep and goats".

Magyar was enchanted by the lovely countryside, the fertility of the soil and the gentle nature of the Mbundu. But it surprised him that the nearer he got to the capital, Kombala an Bihé, the fewer people he saw. However, when he discovered how the ruler dealt with his subjects, and the number of innocent people he killed in order to decorate the wall surrounding his capital with their skulls, he understood why most Mbundu put as great a distance between themselves and Kaiaia Kajangula as possible.

Thanks to Pakasero and his family, Magyar was soon comfortably installed, with a staff of thirty. His domestics were of three types: free men, whom he had to feed but to whom he paid no wages and who did only certain kinds of work; ransomed people who, in order to pay off family debts, had been pawned by the head of the family. In some cases, the head of the family pawned himself as well as his entire family. "Pawns" could not be branded or beaten, but they had to repay double the sum they owed. Finally Magyar bought a number of slaves, "who are treated like animals, are at the mercy of their owners who can sell them or flog them. Only if they kill a slave must they pay some blood money, but not much. The slaves do not have to be fed; on the contrary, they must feed their master by the game they shoot. But they can have free wives." László Magyar encouraged his slaves to marry free women, as they provided good food for their husbands, and their children were also free people. He wrote in his diary, "They seem only too anxious to comply with all my wishes."

Settled and contented, he made an effort to tell his father and his Hungarian relatives how he was faring. "My dear honoured Father," he began, "About the middle of last year, I wrote to you in great detail of the conditions of my life here in South Africa, in the hope that through the route I indicated I would receive the sweetly longed for answer. But vainly; already a year had passed since then, and an answer to my letter has not arrived. What can be the reason of this long abeyance? Perhaps, I thought to myself, some unsurmountable fatherly anger and curse, which follows me over a distance of several thousand miles?" Badly upset by lack of mail from his father, László Magyar sought an explanation in such ideas. Then he went on:

"I had already given up the smallest hope of ever getting news of my sweet country and of our family when these days a French man-of-war anchored in Benguela, with whose captain I became acquainted. From a batch of European newspapers he loaned me, I got to know of the great political events that have taken place, as well as of the miseries that have befallen my country. [He was referring to the lost War of Independence fought against the Habsburgs in 1848–49.] As owing to the shortage of time I cannot write at length [he was writing the letter on board the ship before its departure], I beg of you especially, my dear Father, that the letter you will write shall be a very long one, and that among other things you will tell me what has become of my excerpt, which has as its subject my journey to the Kongo, otherwise the Zaire, river, to the centre of Africa, and which I intended – through the good offices of Baron Ferencz Orczy – for the editor of one of the Hungarian newspapers for publication. Did it arrive and could I receive what has been published in my country's language?

I thought that in more quiet times my compatriots would read with pleasure reports of these wild and distant parts, the more so as from a geographical point of view this excerpt is not without merit.

I am satisfied with my fate, as since the time I left my fatherland I have made more and more headway in my beloved career."

He signed himself: "Your devoted son, László Magyar, Lieutenant of the Navy, on April 15th 1849".

Back from Benguela, he had the honour of being visited by Kaiaia Kajangula. But there was a price attached. The Ruler of Bihé confided to Magyar that he intended to wage war against his neighbours, the Ganguella tribe, among whom he had been born, although he was a Mohumbe, descended from the ancient Humbe race. He needed the white man's advice. Magyar was determined not to get involved in a tribal war, and with Pakasero's aid, the local witch-doctor enabled him to refuse without offending the king. Then Kaiaia Kajangula sent word that he had another honour in store for him. Pakasero translated the king's message: "I, Kaiaia Kajangula, the Furious Lion, am truly your friend. As it came to my knowledge that you are not married, I have decided to give you my own daughter as a wife. Her mother was born among white people, who brought her up; she has passed on to her daughter their customs and their manners. She will make a good and obedient wife to you."

For fear of the King's vengeance, Magyar thought he ought not to refuse. "I decided, although I had never even heard about my would-be bride, to tell the king that I was honoured to accept his offer," he wrote in his diary. "I said that his daughter could come to my house at any time and take up her position as mistress of all I possessed." Then he described his wedding: "As a result of all this, on May 23rd, 1849, my bride arrived, accompanied by numerous male and female slaves. After the *Kimbanda* (witchdoctor) had enacted many ridiculous, not to say impertinent, rituals, two of her brothers handed her over to me, before I had had the chance to exchange one single word with her. I married her as an unknown quantity, and now I can only describe her appearance. Ina Kullu (Princess) Ozoro is tall, slim, with a beautifully proportioned figure. Aged 14, her large eyes sparkle with life; in her shiny round black face, between her thick pink lips her teeth are as white as pearls. Her clothes are made of fine, bright materials. A white belt tied her flowing, fringed dress to her thin waist; her hair seemed embroidered with a great many coloured beads. But around her neck I noticed a thin golden chain, on which hung a golden cross of our Saviour. This sight gave me confidence and hope that under the Christian emblem worn by my bride, our union would be a happy one."[7]

László Magyar's marriage to the wife Kaiaia Kajangula's whim had forced on him, turned out to be a happy one. With his usual reticence, he wrote his family little about his relations with her, although in one letter he did say that his fears that Ozoro might, like other African women with powerful relatives, forget her "submissive position and become a veritable Xantippe" had proved unfounded. "She does not distract or torture me by causing endless trouble and confusion in the house, showing off and ruling with unlimited power over my other wives and my slaves, as other highly born African wives have done."

Aprons worn by women

Years later, he confided to his brother Imre Jr. something of Ozoro's background.

"My wife's mother was called Maria Duarte Monteiro, who had been born the slave of a Brazilian settled in the Domain of Kakonde. When already a grown-up girl, she was captured by a horde of Gualange robbers, and as the price of their booty, they handed her over to the ruler of the country, whose concubine she became, and bore him one daughter. Later on, after the death of that ruler, she came into the possession of the present ruler of Bihé,

Kaiaia (who is of Gualange birth)[8] and the daughter she bore him is presently my wife. On July 30th, 1854, a festive delegation arrived in my country, the country of Bihé, sent by the rulers of Gualange and of Shambosh, to greet my son, Shak-Kilembe Gonga, born to my above mentioned wife in 1851 in the land of the Morupoa. The purpose of the mission was, to recognise my son in the name of their lords, as a close relative, grant him the title of 'erombe' and the position and the rights that go with it.

My father-in-law, Kaiaia Kajangula, has 17 sons and 44 daughters. Almost each one had a different mother. All of them are handsome, tall, healthy, and none has any physical or mental defect."

In yet another letter there is a revealing sentence: "We have lived in undisturbed family harmony. . . ." In answer to numerous questions asked by his father, on December 25, 1853, he wrote, "Of the five children I had, only two are alive; the older one is three and a half years old, he is in Yak Quilem and is called Gonga. I would like to give him a European education so that in due course, as the grandson of the Ruler of Bihé, he should be able to take up his position with due dignity. Although polygamy is customary here, for a man without a retinue of wives is neither respected, nor has he any influence in the affairs of the people, I honour one woman only as my wife, the gentle and kind daughter of the Ruler of Bihé: Ina Kullo Ozoro. To the slave women who have born me children, I give their freedom and let them go as soon as they have breastfed them long enough." He added, "It has pleased the Almighty to lead me here that I should plant Hungarian seeds, which will – I hope – flower even in the distant future in the many members of my family."[9]

In answer to one more question from his family, he wrote: "I have sent Ozoro and my women slaves back to Bihé, and can obtain little news of them. Therefore I am not in a position to teach either my wife or my children anything. The Bunda and the Kalobar languages are spoken in my house."

In a long letter to his father, dated August 20th, 1856, we get a glimpse of Ozoro's position:

"The news that I intend to travel to my fatherland has caused a great sensation to my poor wife, Ozoro. But as I promised her to return, and as she understands the need to educate my son so that he should become a cultivated man, the kindhearted Moorish[10] woman replied, tears streaming down her face, '*Aláripon outnányom sonange* – go in peace, may the Almighty protect you.' But I did not have such an easy time with more than 200 relatives called together in order to inform them of my plans. After a great silence – which among these people is a sign of disapproval – they got up and ran off without a word, leaving me alone. Only slowly, after quite some time, helped by Ozoro's influence, did these wild devils become convinced that I had no intention of cheating them, but on the contrary, having educated and brought up my son to be a great man, I intended to bring him back here. Also I am leaving behind as proof of my intention my two sons, the smaller of them being only nine months old.

My wife Ozoro, whom I respect with all my soul, asks for an everlasting memento of her relatives living in a far-away cold land. I believe nothing would be dearer to her than to receive a portrait of your person, of your dear wife, and in general of the whole family. The daguerrotype can easily reproduce their likenesses, although it would be highly pleasurable to my entire African family if they were to obtain at least your own personal portrait not in daguerrotype form, but painted in lively oil colours, you wearing your splendid Hungarian attire. My dear Father, the pure love and gratitude of a son is inspiring me in making this request. This is also the wish of my wife, and it would be purposeful to bestow on her such an interesting memento for the future."

Imre Magyar complied with his son's request, but the pictures arrived (if indeed they did arrive?) in Africa only when László Magyar was already living on the shores of the Bay of Lucira, from where he could not even keep in touch with the wife who had remained in Bihé to watch over the interests of their sons.

Most of Imre Magyar's letters to his son, as well as László's own papers, have been lost. But one letter, which throws a good deal of light on László's personality and on the conditions under which he was living, did arrive and was subsequently published by the Hungarian Academy of Sciences. On April 20th, 1851, László wrote on the shores of the Kasai river he was exploring:

"Honoured dear Father, I received with joy your esteemed letter of January 27th, 1851, which was delivered to my hands by the leader of a caravan that had come here through Benguela. The reason for the long delay is the great distance – this place is some 500 geographical miles from the sea – caravans usually take 120 days to reach it. But there is no real happiness in life! My joy (over the letter) was terribly upset by the mournful news of the death of my beloved younger brother and friend of my youth, Józsi.[11] His sweet memory will live for ever in our hearts – may the remains of the dear one rest gently.

I know for certain that of my several letters, you received only one, therefore I consider it right first to answer briefly your esteemed missive and then shortly describe the conditions of my life, as I know my dear Father that your heart will be pleased learning that your son, struggling with the storms of life, always proceeding along the path of honour, has reached the place I wanted to be in already as a child, but which I doubt whether many of my compatriots would have got to.

It was necessary at last to get acquainted with the vast wilderness and the inhabitants of South Africa. Therefore I set myself the task either to explore them by travelling through these little known countries, and to inform the scientific world of my experiences, or to perish in my glorious undertaking. God is great. After some fifteen months of travel, I am already writing these lines in a place where no other white man has ever been,[12] and the same caravan that delivered your letter to me, will carry mine through Pungo-Adongo, to the Kingdom of Loanda (on the seashore) from where I hope it will reach you."

It sounds astonishing that on the Kasai river, which at this time figured on no map, caravans were coming and going with mail. And this was not all, for Magyar went on to say, "The mournful conditions of my fatherland – oh pain! – I know fully and in detail from the French and Brazilian newspapers, which reach me fairly regularly. I have faith in God that within a short time, the fate of my country will change for the better. For the time being it is best if I keep my political views about these events to myself." The attitude of a man, who a few years earlier would hardly listen to political discussions and was, at least in appearance, indifferent to the fate of the serfs, had changed markedly.

"You write, my dear Father," the letter continued, "that you trust my cleverness to extricate myself in the none-too-distant future from these barbaric countries and to return to my Hungarian fatherland. Oh, I believe and I hope that crowned with the fruits of my efforts, and respected by those who like geographical descriptions, I will return home."

László promised fully to inform his father about the physical, political, historical and statistical conditions of the countries he was exploring, and in which Imre Magyar was interested. He could not send his father his description of the Congo journey, as he had left the original in Benguela, "and some stupid hand has embezzled the copy I had posted to you."

A walled city

Bridge over the Kubango River

## CHAPTER TWELVE

# "Dr. Livingstone does not want to see you…"

When László Magyar first wrote to his father about his marriage, he had said: "I received no gold with Ozoro, but many good elephant and lion hunters." Their actual number was 285, and they were to prove very useful in Magyar's explorations of the Morupo country (whose capital, Kabebe, was in the area today called Katanga). He raised the funds for this expedition by hunting with his wife's bodyguard; as they were her slaves, according to local custom all animals shot or killed by them belonged to their mistress, that is to their mistress's husband. Magyar sent large quantities of ivory and skins to Benguela, in exchange for which he obtained gunpowder and such supplies as he needed.

While the preparations for this trip were going ahead, Magyar received the news that Kaiaia Kajangula had ten more nobles executed; to his horror, one of them was his friend, Mursa, whose skull was added to the row decorating the wall encircling the capital.

Magyar's caravan set out on February 20, 1850. On the third day he crossed the Kokema river; on the tenth he reached the Kuanza, which formed the eastern border of Bihéland.[1] Magyar decided to find its source, as he had heard from Pakasero and other Africans that it was in "The Mother Of All The Waters". After a very difficult passage through tropical forest, dense scrub and thorn, he and his companions came upon a strange tribe, who had "sooty yellow looking skin." The men were no taller than ten-year-old children, and had spindly legs; they were slight of figure although they had strong muscles; one third of their bodies was made up of a large, protruding stomach; their thin necks were topped by enormous heads. Their faces were flat, their noses consisted of two holes; their mouths were like a large slash across the lower half of the face; their eyes were tiny, their ears enormous, their crinkly hair divided into sparse ringlets. Magyar said their name was "Kaszékel" (Hungarian spelling for *casecle*), although in the south they were called Mukankala. Large numbers of Mukankala lived south of the Kubango river; few north of it as the Masongo and the Kibokue hunted them like game, to sell them as slaves. "I bought from the Bunda one boy and two little girls of this race," Magyar has written, "they are now grown-up and devoted to me. Although during my travels I often came near their own people, they never tried to escape, but distinguished themselves by their obedience. However, their mental capacities have not yet developed." Pakasero assured Magyar that the Mukankala were "good people, who never steal and never kill anyone. We know them," he said.

The Portuguese explorer, Alexander de Serpa Pinto, claimed to have discovered this extraordinary tribe whom he called "Cassequer". Magyar had described them quite accurately 25 years earlier; Pinto knew of Magyar's existence, although in his book, *How I Crossed Africa*, he misspelt his name and did not give him credit for this.[2]

A few days later, Magyar and his party reached the Olivihenda Mountains, and beyond them a magnificent plateau, shaped like a gigantic amphitheatre, framed by more mountains. The plateau was carpeted with soft, bright green grass, and every hundred yards or so there was a thin trickle of crystal clear water. For four days, Magyar and Pakasero explored it, and with the aid of his instruments, he established its geographical location.

Magyar realised that he had come to an important watershed; but he did not know that it was the most important of south-west Africa. Indeed not only the Kuanza and the Kasai rivers had their origin there, but also the Lungue-Bungo and the Luena, flowing into the Lulua; the Lumegi (or Luambegi) which is the main branch of the Leeba, which in its turn is the chief tributary of the Zambezi, is here called Leeambyé, and four more rivers.[3] Now Magyar understood why the Africans called the plateau "The Mother Of All The Waters". Unfortunately, it did not occur to him to sit down and describe it, with an explanatory map, however rough, to send to Benguela, from where his report could have been forwarded to any western capital – preferably to London. The opportunity was within his reach: at this juncture the traders who had attached themselves to his caravan decided to return through Bihé to Benguela.

Instead of informing the world of his achievement, Magyar pushed further north, to explore the Kasai river. For this he had to obtain permission from "the terrible Morupoa ruler, Muata Jamwo." A giant of a man, he received Magyar in his capital, Kabebe, in company of his 300 wives, and welcomed him as the son-in-law of a fellow ruler. Magyar had to witness the execution of hundreds of Morupo, some of whom were skinned alive, and their skulls placed on the wall surrounding the capital – just as Kaiaia Kajangula did in Kombala. Having been granted permission to travel in Morupoland, Magyar left Kabebe as fast as he could – the horrible executions had made him physically sick.

He met his caravan near a place called Yak Quilem,[4] at a considerable distance from Kabebe, and decided to make it his headquarters on the shores of the Kasai river, the largest tributary of the Zaire. Under Pakasero's supervision, his *libata* soon went up and his eldest son, Gonga, was born here. Magyar spent eighteen months in Yak Quilem, and as he wrote in his diary, "My main endeavour was to extend and complete our knowledge of the geographical and physiological condition of this unknown part of Africa, and observe the statistical and political conditions of its people. Finally, I regarded it as my duty also to carry out meteorological observations." In addition to this, thanks to caravans which came up from Benguela via Bihé, he sent for tobacco and potato seeds, and taught the Morupo how to cultivate these plants. He personally hoed his potato fields, setting an example to African men, who regarded all agricultural work as beneath their dignity, and only fit for women.

In the course of his explorations, Magyar visited the malachite mines of which he had already heard a good deal. He knew that malachite was a mineral connected with copper, and that the copper rings and bracelets worn in noses, on wrists, necks and ankles, came from this area. But in 1851 he did not find any extensive copper-mining operations.

In French and Brazilian newspapers, which the caravans also brought him, Magyar read about the sensation caused by the Scottish explorer, Dr David Livingstone. Then he heard from the traders that the great doctor intended to go from Linyanti to Loanda – the bush telegraph was functioning over distances of hundreds of miles. This was another decisive moment in László Magyar's life. With the same determination with which he had left the Orczy estate in 1840 to join the Naval Academy in Fiume, he now decided to meet Dr Livingstone.

In order to do this Magyar dissolved his harem, took Ozoro and

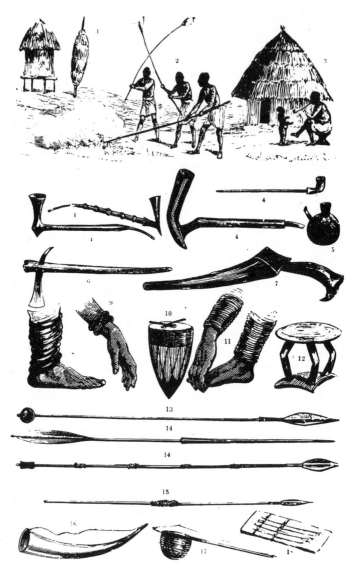

Styles: 1 storage of grain. 2 threshing. 3 small hut. 4 pipes. 5 "hubble-bubble". 6 war hatchet. 7 billhook. 8 leglets. 9 bracelets. 10 drum. 11 bracelets. 12 stool. 13 Manyuema spear. 14 Ujiji spears. 15 assegai. 16 signal horn. 17 guitar. 18 musical instrument.

his son Gonga to Bihé, and himself went to Benguela to dispose of his trophies, his gum-copal and moss dyes. But unlike in 1840, when his action led to complete success, this time luck was not on his side, and he was to pay dearly for his rashness. To start with, his barter deals did not yield as good a profit as he had hoped for. He therefore accepted a commission from the new Governor, Don José Caelho do Amaral, to map all the rivers he came across, and to clear up the origins of the Kunene[5] river, around which – according to African belief – "some oily fluid is in the earth".

Don José befriended Magyar, and confided to him that his real purpose was to find a river that could be used for inland transport and for effecting the *traversa* – the crossing of Africa from the Atlantic to the Indian Ocean. Don José, like his predecessor, was thinking of linking Angola with Moçambique.

Poor Magyar. It was his cherished dream to be the first to effect the *traversa*. On April 20, 1851, he had written to his father, "in the name of the Hungarian nation, write to me in detail if in my fatherland there are (as I do not doubt there must be) real lovers of our country's glory and its literature, who would provide some money for my bold and excellent plan to cross South Africa from the Atlantic Ocean eastwards until the Indian Ocean. Write to me the names of such patrons, and if possible, inform them of my personal aim as it is my duty as a patriot first of all to request help in my own country." He was certain that he could find Portuguese support, but then his achievement would no longer be a Hungarian feat. This to us almost incomprehensible attitude can only be understood if one bears in mind the brutal reaction going on in Hungary: Alexander Bach, in the name of the Emperor Francis Joseph, was trying to destroy everything Hungarian; as his father wrote to László Magyar, German had to be spoken everywhere, in all schools teaching had to be in German. (One can perhaps put oneself into Magyar's shoes by remembering what the Poles felt under Hitler's régime.) Saddest of all, although Imre Magyar did his best on behalf of his son, there was no response to his appeal: not one penny came in for László's plan to make the *traversa*; yet had he done it, the world would have had to take notice of him – for in the 1850s it meant the same kind of achievement as Lindberg's flying the Atlantic Ocean in 1927 in his small plane, with a schoolmap as his guide.

In May 1852, Magyar set out from Benguela with Pakasero and a handful of tested hunters, to meet the famous Scotsman. Pakasero

assured him that by following the Lumeri – by others called the
Leeba – river, they would get close to Linyanti, where Livingstone
was the guest of the Makololo. Pakasero was unaware that the Leeba
flowed into the Leeambiyé, as the Upper Zambezi was then called.
But because of his Portuguese commission, Magyar could not follow
this route; he had to bear south-east to the Kunene and the Kubango
rivers.

From the Kubango he turned east and set up a camp for his men
on the Kuitu[6] river, near a town the local tribe called Libébé, but
which others knew as Mukursu. Accompanied only by Pakasero,
Magyar then went on to Linyanti, the Makololo capital on the
Chobe river. Linyanti was also known as Sikeretu (which makes
reconstruction of events difficult), and could be approached from the
Kuando (not to be confused with the Kubango) as well. Both the
Chobe and the Kuando are tributaries of the Zambezi. Unfortunately, Magyar's diary from this point on – August 20, 1852 –
about this trip, has been lost, and the 30-page outline for the second
volume of his book, which in 1936 was still extant in the archives of
the Hungarian Academy of Sciences, has also disappeared. (Dr
Gusztáv Thirring, the author of the only well-documented book on
László Magyar, published in 1937, used all available material, except
some 70 letters in the possession of a relative of Magyar's living near
Dunaföldvár. Thirring's erudite study has only one drawback – he
had never been to Africa, and missed certain implications. In view of
the loss of the original material, any student of the Hungarian
explorer is greatly indebted to Dr Thirring.)

Reading Thirring's book, one can still sense the excitement felt by
László Magyar, when in October 1852, he approached the place
where he believed he would meet the famous Scotsman. He was
amazed to see the light-skinned Makololo; then he caught sight of
two men who had bright blue eyes, and seemed to be Europeans. He
rushed up to them, for he believed that one of them was Livingstone.
Magyar was disappointed when he realised his mistake, but pleased
by the warm reception given to him by Sekeletu, the young king,
whose guest he was for one week. To him he related how he had come
to the west coast of Africa; his journey to Bihé, his marriage to Princess Ozoro; his travels in Morupoland and up the Kasai river; and
the numerous countries he had visited: "the Hambo, Bunda, Kamba,
Oukanyama and Oukongari kingdoms; the lands of the Bailundo,
Andula, Kakingi, Zambuela, Kalunda, Lobar, Kibokue, Gambos

peoples", and those of many other tribes. He also explained to the Makololo chief the route he had taken from Bihéland to Linyanti, making it clear that there was a shorter, more direct route along the Leeambyé and Lumegi (Leeba) rivers. Sekeletu may have known about this route, for it was much used by slave traders. Africa at this time was criss-crossed by slave routes; the chiefs and their councillors in each area knew exactly how they were running, as they made a considerable income from the toll they charged. Sekeletu took Magyar to the great river Livingstone had seen the year before – the Zambezi; he invited him to stay until the doctor arrived, and offered to send him down to the Indian Ocean. Magyar said that he had to return to his camp near Libébé to look after his men, but his real reason for turning down with many thanks Sekeletu's offer was that he did not have the funds to pay the *hongo* – toll – that he would have been charged by the chiefs living between Linyanti and Tete in Moçambique. However, Magyar told Sekeletu that, having carried out his exploratory work on the Kunene and the Kubango, he would return in order to meet Dr Livingstone.

It was June 1853, when Magyar was back in Libébé, that he heard the news that Livingstone had arrived in Linyanti. Then came the shattering rider: "He does not wish to see you. . . ." This was the message sent by King Sekeletu. Magyar could not believe it, and dispatched Pakasero to find out what the situation was. Pakasero brought back the same message. Distressed and astounded at Livingstone's attitude, Magyar – still shy and reticent – would not risk a snub from the great man who, he was convinced, would have been glad to see him had he been an Englishman, and not a Hungarian.

But to come back to June 1853. While Magyar broke camp and went to Benguela to hand to the Governor his report on the Kunene and the Kubango rivers, three Portuguese settlers from the Bihé plateau were converging on Linyanti: Caetano José Ferreira, Norberto Pedro de Sena Machado, and Silva Porto.[7] Magyar knew all three – the handful of Europeans in Bihé were on friendly terms with each other. Two – Ferreira and Sena Machado – went south following the course of the Kubango and set up camp at Libébé, where Magyar's camp had been. The third, Silva Porto,[8] went north-east and then, hugging the shores of the Leeambyé (as the Zambezi was called) reached the Makololo capital.

On June 23, 1853, Livingstone noted in his diary, "A Portuguese

The Map of South Africa according to the latest discoveries. Pest 1857.

traveller arrived from Linyanti having come all the way from St Philip de Benguela. He wishes to pass across to Mosambique by way of Bashukulompo. He speaks no language but his own. His name Signor Caetano. Does not come to trade but only to see the country. He carries no instruments. He came by Libébé (Mucusso, on the lower Cubango) and was six months in coming, but the way is very crooked. . . . There was a contention between him and Port(o) about coming. If sent by Government he surely would possess instruments, but he has not even a common compass. Has my discovery of these parts awaked the suspicions of the slow Portuguese Government? . . . I have no doubt whatever but that they are both (Ferra & Porto) slave traders and both have their agents, in the Bashukulompo[9] country."

In his book *Missionary Travels In South Africa*, Livingstone wrote about Ferreira's visit: "When the *Mambari* [Africans from Bihé] in 1850 took home a favourable report of this new market to the west, a number of half-caste Portuguese slave-traders were induced to come in 1853; and one, who resembled closely a real Portuguese, came to Linyanti while I was there. . . . He seemed much disconcerted by my presence there. Sekeletu presented him with an elephant's tusk and an ox; and when he departed about fifty miles westward, he carried off an entire village of the Bakalahari belonging to the Makololo. He had a number of armed slaves with him; and as all the villagers – men, women and children – were removed . . . it is not certain whether his object was obtained by violence or by fair promises. In their case, slavery must have been the portion of these poor people."[10]

Silva Porto learnt of Livingstone's book only in 1867, when he read José de Lacerda's *Examination of Dr Livingstone's Journeys*, in which the author questioned some of Livingstone's claims. Silva Porto promptly published the following statement: "This man, Caetano José Ferreira, who has been so infamously abused, was my neighbour in Bihé, and is now living in the council of Dombe, in the district of the town of Benguela. Born in Barriero, a suburb of Lisbon, his name is Caetano José Ferreira, and he is as much a half-caste as Livingstone, the distinguished traveller. Ferreira left Bihé on November 20, 1852, with his companion Norberto Pedro de Sena Machado, who was born in Setubal. On January 16, 1853, their party went due south, to the Cuando river. . . . What consequences would not follow from an attempt to seize a whole Bakalahari village? I shall tell the reader: the leader of the party, his companion, and likewise all whites born in the country, and well over a thousand whites, would be massacred by the wrath of the multitudes in such regions, always avid for blood."[11]

As for the meeting between Livingstone and Silva Porto, this is what Senor Teixeira da Mota says:

"Silva Porto went to visit Livingstone at Linyanti, where they met on July 13 (1853).[12] The two met again the following month, when Livingstone went upstream to Katongo. . . . There are frequent references to Silva Porto in Livingstone's diary, . . . there is not the slightest indication that he considered the Oporto born Silva Porto a half-caste. On the contrary, in his first references to him, even before he saw him, he calls him a 'white man' on the information of the Africans. He also mentions that Porto was not engaged in slave trade. After meeting him, Livingstone wrote in his diary, on August 15, that 'Senor Porto is the first Portuguese who has seen the Liambae or Zambezi in the interior of the Continent.' We know, in fact, that since the end of the 18th century, several Portuguese travellers had seen it. In the last entries about Silva Porto in his diary, Livingstone already says that he purchased slaves, and declares that his desire not to travel with a slave dealer led him to decline Silva Porto's offer to accompany his caravan to Bihé;[13] none the less he did not refuse the liberal hospitality of the Portuguese settler's camp at Katongo. . . . "

Silva Porto did not set up his camp at Katongo by accident. On April 23, 1852, several "Moors" (as the Portuguese called the Arabs), who had set out from Zanzibar, arrived at Benguela. They had been found "almost lost" in the wilds of south-east Katanga by some of Major Coimbra's *pombeiros* – African serfs. The Moors asked to be allowed to accompany the *pombeiros* who were on their way back to the west coast, thus crossing the continent without having intended to do so. László Magyar, who was hunting in this area, took charge of the party, and led them to Major Coimbra, a friend of his, who was then shooting on the banks of the Lungue-Bungo.

Another Portuguese settler, Bernardino Abreu e Castro, realised the importance of the fact that the Zanzibaris had crossed the continent, and sent a report about it to the Governor, Caelho do Amaral (who commissioned László Magyar to write a report on the Kunene and the Kubango). Senhor Abreu e Castro's report was published in the Official Gazette, and with it the offer of a reward by the

Serpa Pinto

Silva Porto

Governor, Coelho do Amaral "to whoever proposes to accompany these fearless travellers (the Zanzibar Moors) when they return to the East Coast, so that there may be a circumstantial account, if not exact, at least as approximate as possible, of the different points through which they may travel, to enable the Government to make an attempt to establish communication by land between the west and the east coasts of Africa." The Governor then invited Silva Porto to perform the task of crossing the continent. Silva Porto immediately accepted, although he did not intend to do it personally: he meant to go as far as Barotseland, set up camp at Katongo, near Naliele, the Barotse capital, and send his *pombeiros* with letters to Moçambique so that they might return with answers from the authorities on the east coast. Porto told the Governor of his plan, and de Amaral accepted his conditions. Actually, the reward offered was so modest that Silva Porto had to organise a caravan on commercial lines.

But first he had to overcome the obstinacy of a chief directly to the west of Bihé, who wanted to impose himself as a middleman in the trade between the Portuguese and the Lui (Barotse) people. Having resolved this difficulty, Silva Porto set out on November 2, 1852, from Belmonte, his farm in Bihé, taking the Zanzibari "Moors" with him. He crossed the Kuanza near its source, and later the upper reaches of the Kuitu and the Kuando – all areas László Magyar had explored. In February, 1853, Silva Porto reached the Riambeje – another name for the Zambezi – and set up his camp at Katongo. From there he sent his *pombeiros* to trade in various directions, and on March 25 organized their trip and that of the Zanzibari, to Moçambique, from where they reached Zanzibar in November 1853. The *pombeiros* eventually returned to Benguela by sea; Silva Porto wrote up their experiences and his account was published in the Government Gazette of 1856.

Thus the Zanzibari "Moors" crossed the continent for a second time, now from west to east, together with Silva Porto's *pombeiros*. This was when Dr Livingstone started his journey from Loanda to Quelimane, where he arrived on May 20, 1856. But on this more in later chapters.

It was in Katongo that Silva Porto heard of Livingstone's arrival at Linyanti. As mentioned above, he went to see him on July 13, 1853, and this is how he described their first meeting in his diary: "After the necessary greetings, the distinguished traveller showed me his maps, some complete and others incomplete, and an early Portuguese map,[14] of small size, against whose author the distinguished traveller was vexed, as he had not marked precisely, as was his duty, the position and breadth of the Loanja river, showing it very far from its place. The distinguished traveller showed me a blank map, which he unrolled; he gave me a pencil to mark the position of Bihé and the main points where I had travelled. Another vexation for me, for I had to pass as ignorant in the eyes of the distinguished traveller, seeing that more than once I had to reply in the negative, saying that I did not have the necessary knowledge. He rolled up the map, which he kept, as well as the compass. Afterwards he showed me the letter from Chevalier Duprat, a kind of circular to the authorities and subjects of His Faithful Majesty, recommending the distinguished traveller. . . ."

Livingstone's account of his meeting with Silva Porto is very different. In his *Missionary Travels in South Africa*, he wrote:

"Mpepe [a chief living at Naliele, near Catongo, who was a rival of Sebituané's successor, Sekeletu] favoured these slave traders, and they, as is usual with them, founded all their hopes of influence on his successful rebellion. My arrival on the scene was felt to be so much weight in the scales against their interests. A large number of *Mambari* had come to Linyanti when I was floundering on the prairies south of the Chobe. As the news of my being in the neighbourhood reached them . . . the *Mambari* betook themselves to precipitate flight. . . . The Makololo enquired the cause of the hurry, and were told that, if I found them there, I should take all their slaves. . . . They went to the north, where, under the protection of Mpepe, they had erected a stockade of considerable size; there several half-caste slave traders, under the leadership of a native Portuguese, carried on their traffic, without reference to the chief into whose country they had unceremoniously introduced themselves; while Mpepe, feeding them with the cattle of Sekeletu, formed a plan of raising himself, by means of their fire-arms, to be the head of the Makololo. The usual course which the slave traders adopt is to take a part in the political affairs of each tribe, and, siding with the strongest, get well paid by captures made from the weaker party."[15]

This is the first passage involving Silva Porto, without mentioning his name. The second goes on to say, "Some of these *Mambari* visited us while at Naliele. They are quite as dark as the Barotse, but have among them a number of half-castes. . . . The half-caste, or native

Portuguese, could all read and the head of the party, if not a real Portuguese, had European hair, and, influenced probably by the letter of recommendation which I held from the Chevalier Duprat, His Faithful Majesty's Arbitrator in the British and Portuguese Mixed Commission at Cape Town, was evidently anxious to show me all the kindness in his power. These persons I feel assured were the first individuals of Portuguese blood who ever saw the Zambezi in the centre of the country, and they had reached it two years after our discovery in 1851."[16]

This was Dr Livingstone's description of Silva Porto's caravan organised at the request of the Governor of Benguela, to establish contact between the east and the west coasts of Africa – a gang of African slavers, led by half-castes, among them one who had European hair! It is in a footnote that Livingstone mentions the name of "the leader of the slave traders": "On asking the headman of the *Mambari* party, named Porto, whether he had ever heard of Naliele being visited previously, he replied in the negative, and stated that he had attempted to come from Bihé three times, but had always been prevented by the tribe called Ganguellas. He nearly succeeded in 1852, but was driven back. Now, in 1853, he attempted to go eastward from Naliele, but came back to Barotse on being unable to go beyond Kainko's village,[17] which is situated on the Bashukulompo river (the Kafue) eight days distant. The whole party was anxious to secure a reward believed to be promised by the Portuguese government. Their want of success confirmed my impression that I ought to go westwards. Porto kindly offered to aid me, if I would go with him to Bihé; but when I declined, he preceded me to Loanda, and was publishing his Journal when I arrived at that city. Ben Habib[18] told me that Porto had sent letters to Mosambique by the Arab, Ben Chombo, whom I knew; and he has since asserted, in Portugal, that he himself went to Mosambique as well as his letters!"[19]

There are three major errors in Livingstone's description of Silva Porto's party. The first is that far from wanting the reward offered by the Governor-General of Angola, Silva Porto, on September 16, 1853, while still in Barotseland donated to the Misericórdia of Oporto (where he was born) the money award and the patent promised by the Governor-General, to the person who should accomplish the communication with Moçambique, writing, "If the services that I rendered to conclude it are worthless, there is worth at least in the blessings of the hundreds of unfortunate people agglomerated in that pious establishment of my country."

Secondly, Silva Porto did not go to Portugal; he did not claim to have done so, nor to have reached Moçambique. The limits of his journey were Barotseland and Linyanti, which he described in his reports to the Governor, and which saw print in the Government Gazette of 1854.

Understandably, Silva Porto was indignant about Livingstone's statement that "some of these *Mambari* visited us while at Naliele." This is his comment, "I shall say that they cannot possibly be qualified, since the distinguished traveller was visited by me, and not by the Africans from Bihé. He thus falls short of what he owed himself as a gentleman, placing someone else on a level with savages."

Finally, this is Senor Teixeira's interpretation of why Dr Livingstone turned down Silva Porto's offer to go to Bihé with his caravan: "It was not because of the horror of accompanying 'slave traders', as he mendaciously says, but only because if he did so he could not appear before the world as the discoverer of the regions he would have to cross till they reached the territories under Portuguese sovereignty. He therefore ascended the Zambezi and traversed the Kasai and Kuango – but the Portuguese had long journeyed over all these areas, despite the fact that in his book Livingstone speaks only of '*Mambaris*' and 'half-caste slave traders', names whose dubious meaning we already know from the way in which he referred to Caetano Ferreira and Silva Porto."[20]

After all this, we have to return to László Magyar, and to the questions asked at the end of Chapter Eight: why did Livingstone refuse to see him and why did he pretend that he had never heard of him? Magyar's letters to Antunovics were published in 1852, 1853 and 1854 in the *Magyar Hirlap* (*Hungarian News Sheet*), later in the *Pesti Napló* (*Pest Diary*), the two best Hungarian newspapers of their day. These papers did reach the west; in Paris Bertalan Szemere, the last Hungarian Prime Minister of the 1848–9 War of Independence, was living in exile. He read Magyar's reports in copies of the *Magyar Hirlap* for the year 1852, translated them into English, and sent them to Father János Jácint Rónay,[21] who was living in exile in London.

Rónay was a Benedictine monk, who had served throughout the War of Independence as chaplain attached to the Freedom Fighters, but he was also a distinguished naturalist and a follower of Darwin. Szemere asked Rónay to draw the attention of the appropriate geographical authorities to Magyar's travels and reports. Father

Rónay took them to Sir Roderick Murchison, the President of the Royal Geographical Society, who on February 14, 1853, had them read at a meeting of the Society, and subsequently published in its Journal of 1854.[22] Through the British Legation in Lisbon, Murchison wrote Magyar congratulating him on his achievements, and enclosed an extensive programme for him, offering financial assistance from the Society if he were willing to carry it out. But it seems that Magyar never received Sir Roderick's letter, for he did not take up the offer, or even acknowledge the letter.

On December 12, 1856, Father Rónay met Livingstone in London at a reception in his honour, arranged by the Royal Geographical Society when he returned from Africa. On the following day Rónay had an interview with Livingstone, as he wanted to find out from him where Magyar was, for no news had been received from him for a considerable time. But Rónay reported: "Livingstone did not know anything about him; he said he had heard his name for the first time at the Geographical Society."[23]

A year later, on December 20, 1857, Rónay met Dr Livingstone again at the house of a Mrs Haldane. Livingstone promised the Hungarian priest "on his arrival in Africa not to forget about my countryman and to send word to me provided he would find him."[24] Rónay never received a word from Livingstone albeit he was normally ? voluminous correspondent.

Yet Livingstone must have heard about Magyar. In the first place, it is very unlikely that the Makololo should not have told him of Magyar, even if they referred to him as *'Ngana Komo*. They must have related to Livingstone that there was a white man who had come from Bihé, and who originated from a far-away, cold country.

Secondly, we know from Magyar's letters to his father that he was well informed about Livingstone's whereabouts, and of his nickname – *Munari* – among the Africans. Equally, Livingstone must have heard about *'Ngana Komo* and his exploits, and he could not have failed to realise that he was no mulatto slave-trader. Moreover, Sekeletu provided Livingstone with guides to Loanda, who acted on information received from Magyar. Again it is impossible that the doctor should not have heard of this. He spoke the Makololo's language, and was fully informed about their affairs. When Father Rónay asked him about Magyar, he must have realised that this Hungarian was the man he had heard described as *'Ngana Komo*.

As in the case of Lake Ngami, Livingstone was determined to

create the impression that he was the first European to travel from the Zambezi to the west coast of Africa, and that he did it without aid or advice from anyone. It is sad that to Magyar, as to Cotton Oswell, he would give no recognition. And yet, had Livingstone admitted that Magyar's prior experience had been of some use to him, this would in no way have diminished his achievement of travelling 1,800 miles through difficult terrain to Loanda, and from there returning with his Makololo to Linyanti, when he could have sailed to England, where an enthusiastic reception awaited him.

From Linyanti Livingstone effected the famous *traversa*. The whole world cheered, not least because he had the gift of communicating his discoveries to his readers. László Magyar was unable to continue his journey from Linyanti to the east coast, as he had not adequate funds; he also lacked Livingstone's gift of communication, and remained unknown while his fellow explorer became an international figure.

## CHAPTER THIRTEEN

# Magyar's achievements and tragic end

The rest of László Magyar's work and his tragic end must be recorded if we want to assess his importance as an explorer and his help to Dr Livingstone in Livingstone's trek from the Zambezi to the south-west coast of Africa.

In a letter to his father written on Christmas Day, 1853, Magyar summed up his life since his arrival in 1848: "During five years of travel, I explored South Africa from the Atlantic Ocean in the west to close on to the Indian Ocean in the east, from the southern Latitude of 4°–22°, to the eastern Longitude of 12°–34°. I will begin its systematic description, as well as rectifications of its map as soon as my health allows. I understand the long absence of any letter from you, also your surprise that not only have I settled among the wild people of Africa, but have also married here. Yet my dear Father, this should not surprise you, as otherwise I could not have achieved my set aim, and now when I have succeeded, I can say that there is no European power or treasure which by itself could enable the bravest of travellers to wander through this wild and deserted part of the world.

During these five years the armed slaves of my wife were my only companions."

He went on to describe how they had been brave and obedient, following him everywhere; but now most of them were dead, due to illness, wounds, and the hardships of the journey – hunger, thirst, wild animals. "I myself, beaten down by sickness due to the very hot African climate, have the appearance of an old man of sixty." He was 35 years old.

In mid-1854 Magyar was back in Bihé, from where he undertook his third journey, the exploration of the Lobal countries – situated to the south-west of what is today Katanga. He described their inhabitants as cannibals, who ate human flesh mixed with veal appetizingly prepared with herbs, and the way in which it took all his tact to avoid having to taste the delicacy of which the tribe was apparently very proud. On his way back to Bihé, loaded with ivory and other hunting trophies, he decided against Pakasero's advice to shorten his journey by crossing Ganguella territory. The Ganguella were the tribe that Kaiaia Kajangula had wanted to destroy in 1849; had Magyar been able to read the future, he would not have refused to help. The Ganguella attacked and robbed him of all his possessions, including the gold King Dalaber Almanzor had given him in 1847. His ivory had been of excellent quality and with the money he hoped to obtain for it in Benguela, Magyar had meant to finance his trip to Hungary with Gonga.

When Kaiaia Kajangula heard of what had happened, he swore vengeance and attacked the Ganguella. But his venture turned to disaster for himself and for his son-in-law. He was defeated, and Mu-Kinda, his ambitious and jealous nephew, (son of his elder brother Ochi, who never reigned) used the disgrace to depose and murder him.[1] Having mounted the throne himself, he banished Kaiaia's entire family, and made it known that if 'Ngana Komo dared to show his face again in Bihé, he would share his father-in-law's fate.

Against Pakasero's advice, Magyar none the less returned to say good-bye to his wife, and make plans for the future. He agreed that Princess Ozoro, who was living unmolested in a distant part of Bihé, should stay there to watch for any opportunity that would enable Gonga to regain his grandfather's throne.

Of course Magyar was seen, and his presence reported. King Mu-Kinda sent a party of soldiers to kill him. Thanks to Pakasero he got to neighbouring Hamboland, where his life was saved by Donna Isabel, whom he had first met two years previously when on a hunting expedition in Hamboland. One afternoon, while on an excursion, he had sat down among cedar trees, when unexpectedly someone spoke to him in Portuguese. He saw two African girls, dressed in semi-European fashion. They told him that their mistress, Donna Isabel, who lived near Kandala, a close-by town, had heard that a white man had joined the caravan that was going to Bihé. She considered it a great piece of luck and had sent him a present: sweet fruit on a tray, covered with a white, embroidered coverlet.

Magyar was pleasantly surprised, and asked the girls to tell him about their mistress. They replied that she would come to visit him and would tell him herself. They asked his permission on her behalf

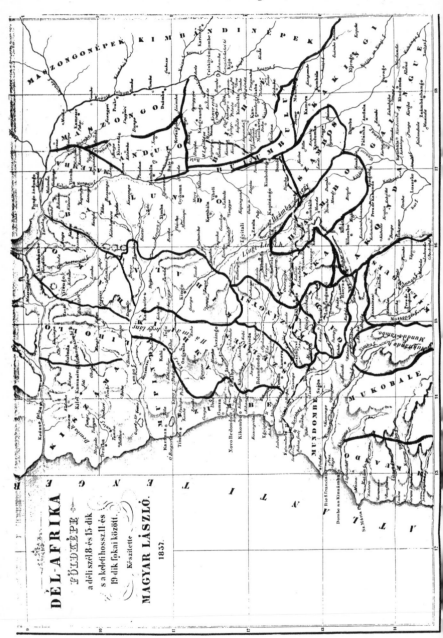

Landscape of southern Africa between 8° and 15° southern latitude and 11° and 19° eastern longitude. Drawn by László Magyar. 1857. Bold lines show some of Magyar's travels (on land).

that she should come to see him. He gladly granted it, then rushed to his quarters to put on his best clothes, and waited excitedly for his guest, who soon arrived.

From her litter, which was surrounded by several female slaves, a young woman of about 22 years descended. She had a yellow brown skin; and sat down on a rush-mat which her attendants spread outside his hut. Magyar greeted her in European fashion, placed his chair near her and sat down.

"It is so rare," she began in Portuguese, "to see a European in these parts, and when it happens, it is a real day of joy. Sir, I hope you will forgive me for disturbing you with my visit. I was born in Benguela, and grew up in the capital of Brazilia where I spent nine years of my life. Five years ago my husband, who traded with the interior, and I first settled in Benguela, and then we came here. But soon after that my husband died. I had grown used to this place, and to the healthy air and good water. I could not make up my mind to exchange all this for Benguela, so I stayed on and I am trading with the natives. I make my slaves do agricultural work, and with the fertile earth, I easily grow what I need for my household."

While Donna Isabel related her life history, Magyar had the opportunity to observe her. Her dark skin was not unattractive, but her thick, swollen lips and flat nose made a disagreeable impression. But these shortcomings were compensated for by her large, fiery brown eyes, and her small, even, pearl-white teeth. Her clothes, more African than European, were made of fine material in bright colours, floating robes held in over her waist by a white silken belt. She wore a pale blue shawl over her shoulders and a pretty, flowery material over her hair, tied like a turban. Round her neck and in her ears, she wore magnificent jewellery.

Then it was Magyar's turn to tell Donna Isabel of his journey, his family and the story of his life. In the evening he returned her visit. She lived in a simple house, well furnished. She loved visitors. After they had eaten a very good, typical European dinner, Magyar took his leave. Two years later she was to save his life, when her warriors chased the Mbundu thugs back to Bihé, and Magyar was eventually joined by Pakasero and some 60 of Ozoro's guards with whom he reached Benguela on Christmas Day, 1856, having lost his family, his home, and his possessions – everything he had built up during his nine years in West Africa.

Magyar hoped to receive funds from Hungary, and to go there

with Gonga, Pakasero and some of his slaves. He wanted Gonga educated either in his own country, or in England. None of these hopes was fulfilled.

Magyar first mentioned his wish to return home in a letter dated December 23, 1853. He was feeling far from well, having had eye trouble that blinded him for some weeks. A lion had mauled him; he bore the marks for the rest of his life. Imre Magyar's response was warm and sympathetic, although slightly worried as to how his son would maintain himself in Hungary. He informed him that in his will he had left him an annual allowance of 600 forints[3] and had sent him 150 gold pieces[4] through the Lisbon house of R. G. Batalha. He told László that he was greatly looking forward to his return, and advised him to plan his trip so as to arrive in the summer, when it was warm. According to Professor Hunfalvy, his book would be published by the Hungarian Academy of Sciences. "For the rest," his father added, "when you have with God's help got home, we will discuss what to do with your writings; if necessary I myself will have them published." A keen farmer, he asked László to bring him seeds of plants that might be introduced in Hungary, especially leguminous plants, millet, sorghum and raps.

On August 20, 1856, Magyar wrote at length about his planned return.

"I intend to bring with me, in addition to my older son, Shah Quilembe Gonga, a retainer and three slaves. Pakasero has been my friend and constant companion during the last six years of my adventurous travels. Not only was he my weapon bearer, but by his devotion and alertness, he saved my life more than once from certain death. Having heard of my inpending departure for my fatherland, he assured me with tears in his eyes that only death could part us. He had made up his mind to come with me to my distant, cold country. My two slaves are used to look after me personally; the third, Tsamunha, is a young lad whom the Ruler of Bihé had, according to local custom, given to my son, and who is Gonga's inseparable companion. According to the barbarous laws of this land, he is not allowed to outlive him. Were my son to die before him, he would be buried alive with him; but should I be absent when Gonga returns, it would be his duty to introduce him to his numerous relations here. All this will increase my travel expences; moreover, owing to my correspondence with the Portuguese Ministry [of Marine Affairs], once in Lisbon I will have to call on several important people, who will return my visits. For these reasons the 150 gold pieces that you have sent me may not be sufficient."

Magyar asked his father that the 600 forints annual allowance should be paid to him as of December 25, 1855 (that is from the previous year, when the will was signed); this would suffice for his travel and living expenses in Hungary. What worried Magyar was that the house of R. G. Batalha had gone bankrupt, and if his father had sent the money through them, what had become of it? He suggested that in future his father should send everything through Mr Norton Shaw, secretary of the Royal Geographical Society in London, who would forward it through the Portuguese Ministry of Marine Affairs. Then he explained the reasons why he could not leave Bihé at once – one of those quirks of fate that was to have unforeseen consequences: "I and my son must submit to several different barbarous ceremonies; we cannot avoid them, for he and I would lose all our rights as citizens among these wild cannibals, and what is more, they might easily suspect me, and murder me. But if we observe the local rules, my son will be recognised for the future, and when he has been trained as a naturalist, he will be able, thanks to the intercession of these numerous robbers and other relatives, feared by all other blacks, to travel easily all over Southern Africa. For these, and other reasons, with an aching heart, I have to remain here for at least a whole year."

Magyar's letter crossed his father's, dated April 12, 1857, which contained shattering news. Having heard from England that László had died, Imre Magyar had not sent the 150 gold pieces to Lisbon. When he later heard that he was still alive he wrote:

"Under the present dispensation, you cannot hope for any support for your own person, which would normally be due to you in view of the efforts you have made. Your book – published by the Hungarian Academy of Sciences over my protests[5] – caused a certain interest, but within a short time was forgotten. Do not imagine that a horn of plenty is in store for you here, and that any one will take care of you in a manner befitting your reputation. I cannot, to the detriment of your brothers and sisters, either give you a share of my estate, or assure you an allowance. Especially not when you intend to bring here, besides your son, a regal retinue of black servants. I can see that you did not take to heart my advice first to enrich yourself, although it is much easier to collect a fortune in Africa than it is here. And as you could not control your scientific ambitions, you should at least have put your talents to good use on behalf of Portuguese or English interests. I am afraid that as your reports have been published in Hungarian, you have closed the door to the possibilities offered you by the Portuguese and the English. . . ."

The last sentence was unnecessarily pessimistic, but it was followed by a shrewd passage:

"I confess that at first I was of a different opinion about your fate; thinking superficially, I considered it right that you should come home, that having built up a reputation and made a name, you should complete your career in peaceful comfort. But now I am of a different opinion. You must not only consider the years that lie before you, but the future of your sons and of your grandchildren. In other words, such influence as you wield in Africa must not be whittled away. It is your duty to maintain it and pass it on to your son, and use every means to achieve this. At present it is the determined aim of all European Powers to colonise; we see that the Russians and the English want to occupy and exploit Asia; the French North Africa; the Portuguese want to strengthen their colonisation of South Africa so that other Powers should not poach in their domains. For this the Portuguese need men – men like you, who know Africa, speak the languages and are in contact with their authorities. Accept the Portuguese offer of working for them however arduous the work may be; should your son be educated in Europe, he will never want to return to Africa, where if you play your cards well, he may even become a Deputy Governor."

Imre Magyar, the Hungarian country squire, who had never been further than Vienna – and that only in his student days – showed a surprisingly realistic grasp of nineteenth-century world politics. He added with equal realism: "Hungary has no trade, let alone any other connections, with Africa. Here men of your experience have no chance of any appointment. Should your work be published in Portuguese, you will still remain a Hungarian. Next April (April 1858) I will send you one thousand forints[6] through the Austrian Legation in Lisbon." Then he explained bitterly that while hitherto he had thought of himself as a well-to-do man, with a larger income than he needed for his way of life, now conditions had changed to such an extent that he was only just scraping along. He had to pay 3,000 forints in imperial taxes, which hitherto, as a nobleman, he had not had to do. Moreover, he was being incessantly harassed with new demands for payment: the wages of the agricultural workers and of the domestics had risen considerably; his estate yielded no more than 1.5% of its value. "With the best will in the world, I cannot spread myself any further."

László replied that he could not change his plans, as he had made all necessary preparations for sailing in November for Lisbon, which would take 70 days, and having no funds himself, if his father did not send him money to the Portuguese capital, this would greatly embarrass him. From this letter it emerged that he had managed to get his

A part of Magyar's handwritten manuscript: "A General Sketch of the Provinces of Munda-evambo, Lungo and Kapota of South Africa."

"A broadly spreading area, subject to different climatic influences; here it is terribly hot and the land is bare; on the western border, near the Atlantic Ocean, the air is moderate, the vegetation lush and very varied. I shall herewith provide a description of these provinces which, stretching eastwards, on the west are bordered by the Atlantic Ocean, and for this reason at first sight seem to have an easily accessible border. Therefore, although one is already in Africa, it seems that it will be easy to proceed across the area and provide a description of it. But whenever this sort of thing is assumed, the opposite usually happens. Different travellers of a scientific bent have attempted to penetrate these internal provinces, several hundred miles distant from the shore, so as to bring information to the scientific world."

son Gonga to join him in Benguela. Imre Magyar received this letter on December 23, 1857, and replied on January 15th, 1858. This letter reached Magyar with unexpected speed. In it he told his son that his situation was getting worse with every day: "soon our position may become worse than that of the Poles, and you know what that is like." He urged László to accept the Portuguese offer, and give up – for the time being – the idea of travelling to Hungary. It was all very well that in England Livingstone had received a gift of £50,000 from the Government (this was not true); Magyar hoped in vain for any kind of remuneration. When the Emperor Francis Joseph had visited Szeged, Imre Magyar had brought up László's explorations in Africa. The Emperor had been interested, but promised no grant.

So Magyar had to give up his cherished plan. He was desperately homesick – he longed to talk to his own people – no doubt he also wanted to bask in the kind of glory that surrounded Livingstone; his health was poor and he was convinced that in Hungary he would again get well, and that in the peace and quiet of his father's house, he could complete his book. Also, there he could obtain the books and maps he needed so badly to check his own findings. But his luck was out, and, as a final irony, Imre Magyar eventually did send his son 1,000 golden crowns[7] to pay for his own and his son's trip home, but Magyar never saw this money.

Surprisingly little is known about the last seven years – from 1858 to 1864 – of Magyar's life, although he made his headquarters in Loanda, Benguela and Moçamedes, from where mail went frequently to Europe. Between 1857 and 1861, he explored the Munda-Evambo, Lungo and Kapota countries; he hunted a good deal; then his health again troubled him and he devoted himself to farming – at last, seemingly, the training his father had forced on him began to pay off. But the weather ruined successive harvests, and rinderpest destroyed his cattle. So he eked out a living by collecting gum-copal and doing some trading.

In 1858 he wrote to the Hungarian Academy of Sciences, asking for financial support for another exploration, but again his proposal was turned down. However, sponsored by Professor János Hunfalvy, on December 15, 1858, he was elected a corresponding member of the Academy. Hunfalvy repeatedly wrote to Magyar, pressing him to describe his journeys in Hungarian, to give detailed accounts of tribal customs and geographical features, of the flora and fauna he observed.

At the end of 1858, the Hungarian Academy of Sciences received a large chest containing Magyar's diaries, maps, drawings and notes. The manuscript of the first volume of his planned three-volume *Travels In Southern Africa* had already been delivered to his father, and reached the Academy through László's half-brother, Imre Jr.[8]

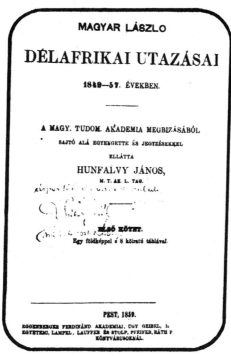

Frontispiece of Magyar's book: *László Magyar's Travels in South Africa in the years 1849–1857.* Commissioned by the Hung. Academy of Sciences. Prepared for printing and edited by János Hunfalvy, corresponding member of the Hungarian Academy of Sciences. Volume one. With one map and eight stone prints. Pest 1859. At Ferdinand Eggenberger, bookseller for the Academy as well as at Geibel, bookseller for the University, and Lampel, Lauffer and Stolp, Pfeiffer, Rath and Co. booksellers.

Edited by Professor Hunfalvy, this manuscript was published by the Academy in 1859, and he was granted an award of 140 golden crowns, which actually reached him. But the promised material for Volume II, which was to describe the territories between Latitude 3 and Longitude 19 and 27, and for Volume III which was to deal with the areas between the same longitudes but south of Latitude 20 (mostly desert areas) never arrived in Hungary. In a letter written from Lucira (on the coast of Angola) and dated November 16, 1858, Magyar related that after the murder of his father-in-law, he had moved to Benguela, and that he intended to send his son Gonga, baptized Arthur, to school in Moçamedes. Then he settled in a place called Gyiokolo Moino in Kurundtan, south of Lucira. On December 21, 1861, he wrote to Professor Hunfalvy: "The notification that I have been elected a corresponding member of the Hungarian Academy of Sciences, dated December 20, 1858, I had the pleasure of receiving only just now, that is with a delay of three years. My joy rose to the highest pitch over this undeserved honour. I confess, I lack the talent for this distinguished position, though not the good will nor the fortitude to make myself worthy of it. I always considered it my sacred duty to further the advantage and the glory of my dear Fatherland with every means of which I am capable." He thanked Professor Hunfalvy profusely for his help and support, and for editing his book. Then he went on: "I must admit I had thought that in my own country I had been forgotten. Moreover, I had also been hampered in any further work, and in sending you descriptions of my travels and results, by the information current about the conditions prevailing in my Fatherland – namely that everything had been placed on a German footing, and that even scientific literature could only be published and hope to arouse interest, if written in German. Because of lack of any correspondence for such a long time, I could not tell that this news was false, and with a distressed soul I put down my pen, and waited for happier times. But now, convinced of the opposite, I have decided to clean-copy the remaining parts of my work, which I will send you. . . ."

Six months later, on June 9, 1862, he wrote to the Academy's Secretary, Ferenc Toldy, for the first time revealing the immense difficulties under which he was labouring: "The terrible rinderpest is still taking its toll in South Africa. In the last five months, some two million head of cattle have perished in this area alone. I myself have lost several hundred animals. But this is not all. Emanating from the Mossamedes district, a frightful epidemic of a deadly disease called typhus is now raging; there are also several hundred white people among its victims. May God stop castigating this dessicated area with so many scourges, for believe me, dear Countryman, even without it, life here is a worse agony than Tantalus had to endure. . . ."

Then silence. Magyar did not even acknowledge the money Professor Hunfalvy had, at last, induced the Academy to vote for his return expenses, and which actually arrived in 1865 in Ponto de Cujo, the place he had moved to. But only in 1868 did the Academy begin to ask questions as to Magyar's fate; he was after all one of their corresponding members. Spurred on by Professor Hunfalvy, on April 23, 1868, the Academy requested the Ministry of Religious Cults and Education to make enquiries of the Portuguese Government through diplomatic channels, to establish where László Magyar was and how he was faring.

In October 1868, two answers from the Portuguese Government reached the Hungarian Academy in quick succession. The first, dated August 18, reported that in 1856–57, the Governor of Benguela had had many favourable reports about the said "Hungarian traveller". The second, dated August 20, stated curtly that László Magyar had died on November 9, 1864, at Ponto de Cujo, near Cape Santa Maria, leaving a minor son, whom his mother had taken into her care. "Probate has established that all László Magyar left were a few slaves, some clothes, and nineteen imperial gold crowns." This was insufficient – according to the Portuguese authorities – even to satisfy his creditors. What they did not state was that, aged 46, Magyar had starved to death. The faithful Pakasero had died a few weeks earlier.

There is no indication what Magyar felt or what he thought when, surrounded by the books the Hungarian Academy had sent him, his notes, his maps, and some hunting trophies, he must have known that the end was near. Did it fill him with bitterness that he would never see Hungary again, never tell his father and his friends of his adventures; never discuss with Professor Hunfalvy the two new volumes of his book; never breathe the rarified atmosphere of the Hungarian Academy of Sciences; never savour the triumph of having had a much more exciting life than the country gentlemen who had not accepted him? We are not likely ever to know, for even if his manuscripts were to turn up, he must have been too weak to have kept up his diary. Perhaps a farewell letter to his curiously loving, yet hard, father might have given us his last message.

Informed of László Magyar's death, at least the Academy did not let matters rest. It wrote again and again, through diplomatic channels, enquiring what had become of the money sent to Magyar, and demanding, indeed insisting, that at least his books, writings, maps and notes should be transmitted to it. It took the Portuguese

Government four years to answer. Its communication said nothing about the money, but it admitted that two large cases, containing Magyar's books and writings, had been found in his hut. These had been placed in the care of a Portuguese settler, Senor Joao Esteves de Aranjo. Unfortunately, it was stated, Senor de Aranjo's house had been burnt down, and with it Senor Magyar's two cases "with all their contents."

The members of the Hungarian Academy were sceptical of this statement. In his measured way, Professor Hunfalvy wrote, "Indubitably, the various communications of the Portuguese Government seem ambiguous, secretive and contradictory. But at this point of time, it would be useless to start an argument about all this. We must accept that László Magyar's writings and notes have been irreparably lost, and at this stage no one can lift the veil that covered so much of his life. In 1868 this might still have been possible, had a generous patron under-written the expenses of a reliable person to be sent to Benguela, to make energetic enquiries."

In Hungary the Portuguese Government's statement about the destruction of Magyar's two cases is doubted to this day. The Hungarian theory is that in the 1860s the Portuguese authorities, for some reason never fully comprehended, wished to prevent the English authorities from reading the information László Magyar had gathered.

On November 13, 1873, seven months after Dr Livingstone's death, at a formal meeting of the Hungarian Academy of Sciences in Budapest, Professor János Hunfalvy made a speech acclaiming László Magyar's efforts and achievements. The nine years' delay in the recognition of Magyar's explorations was partly due to the vague answers of the Portuguese authorities, especially concerning Magyar's papers which contained the material for Volumes II and III of his travel descriptions. The Hungarian public had no idea that the Academy had met; it had completely forgotten the man in whose honour the meeting was held – László Magyar.

As for Princess Ozoro and her five children, nothing further is known about them, except for one episode. In 1875, the *Deutsche Gesellschaft zur Erforschung Aequatorial Afrika's* (the German Society for the Exploration of Equatorial Africa) led by the Prussian Captain Hofmeyer, had as one of its members the Hungarian Lieutenant Antal Lux. Lux, professor of geography in the military lower-secondary school of Kismarton, landed in Loanda and there met one of László Magyar's sons. He did not mention it in his book, *Von Loanda nach Kimbundu*, published in Vienna in 1880, but in 1881 in a lecture to the staff at Kismarton about his African journey, he said: "After László Magyar had arrived on the West Coast of Africa, he entered into marriage with the daughter of the black ruler of Bihé. Magyar is already dead. But two of his sons – mulattoes – are still alive. I had the opportunity of talking to one of them in Loanda. Magyar was the second European who visited the capital, Kabébé."[9]

Lieutenant Lux's lecture was published in 1881 in the *Oedenburger Zeitung* (the *Newspaper of Odenburg*, the German name of the Hungarian town of Sopron), and the few words referring to László Magyar are in the 75th issue. Clearly, Lux had very little knowledge of Angola, and no appreciation of Magyar's achievements. Nor does he tell us which son he met – the older one, Gonga, later baptised Arthur, or the younger one called Julio? One does not know if he enquired about Princess Ozoro, and why she was then living in Kakonde; or how Magyar's sons earned their living, and what were the chances of their regaining the Bihé throne?

# Part Three

## CHAPTER FOURTEEN

# Livingstone crosses Africa

On September 20, 1854, Livingstone set out on his famous journey – the *traversa* – crossing the continent from west to east. Although several Portuguese halfcastes and Arabs had done it before him, no one at that time in the western world had heard of their achievement, and David Livingstone was the first European to accomplish it in the 19th century. László Magyar, who had come so near to it, could not complete his *traversa* for lack of funds to pay the *hongo* – the toll – charged by African chiefs for allowing travellers to pass through their territories.

Livingstone had turned down the offer of the Captain of the mail-packet, *Forerunner*, to take him to England on the grounds that he had promised his Makololo porters to lead them back to their homes. In fact it seems from his diaries that Livingstone had another reason for wanting to remain in Africa: he felt that his journey had been a failure. Instead of discovering a convenient way for supplying missions in central Africa, all he had established was that the 1,800 mile route was extremely difficult, and that because of rivers and marshes, wagons could not be used on it. He had no idea that in England his journey was regarded as a great achievement and that he would have been given a hero's reception.

In Loanda an Austrian botanist, Dr Friedrich Walweitsch, who was at that time working for the Angola Government, offered to accompany Livingstone. The doctor would not hear of it, and wrote ungraciously in his diary, "As it appeared evident to me this plan would afford Dr Walweitsch an opportunity of availing himself of all my previous labours – without acknowledging his obligations to me in Europe, I consider it would not be prudent to put such a strong temptation in his way."[1] This demonstrates Livingstone's suspicious nature – he had no evidence that the Austrian would not acknowledge his obligations to him – and his fear of having to share the limelight with another.

During his return journey Livingstone's health was better than on the way to Loanda, yet his progress was far slower. This was due to innumerable calls from Portuguese officers at militia posts for treatment against fever. In mid-December he was at Pungo Adongo, only 160 miles from the coast. Here he received a letter from Mr Gabriel, which enclosed one from Lord Clarendon, the Foreign Secretary, expressing pleasure over Livingstone's safe arrival, and a cutting from *The Times*, dated August 8, 1854, describing his journey as "one of the greatest geographical explorations of the age". Mr Gabriel also reported that the ship carrying his maps, letters and journal, written in Loanda, had been wrecked; had he been aboard, he would have shared the fate of his papers. For two weeks Livingstone stayed at Pungo Adongo to re-write from memory the letters and the journal that had gone to the bottom of the sea. Continuing his return journey, he once more passed by the Olivihenda Mountains without visiting the Mother of All the Waters, just as later on he was to miss the Cabora Bassa rocks, which made navigation up the Zambezi impossible. By mid-March, 1855, he was once more in the throes of a bout of fever. He was so weak that he could only proceed at the rate of seven miles a day. There was then another mutiny among his followers, which he put down by hitting the leading trouble-maker on the head with a revolver.

Livingstone reached Linyanti on September 13, 1855, and he received a warm reception from Sekeletu. This was a great relief as he had worried how the young king would accept the fact that he had had to give away his ivory in bribes in order to reach Loanda. Instead of money, he brought him a colonel's uniform with a gold braided cap. But Sekeletu was delighted with his outfit (and wore it until it fell to shreds). He demonstrated his anxiety to help Livingstone by promising him a hundred men to accompany him to the great water at the end of the river – to the Indian Ocean. Canoes with sixteen rowers were put at his disposal, and on November 3, 1855, he set out with 114 porters for Tete, at that time the furthest Portuguese stronghold inland.

And now, five years after he first heard about the great falls east of Seshéké, Livingstone reached Mosioatunya or "the smoke that thunders".[2] He was impressed, but far less than he had been by the Zambezi in 1851. The falls were fine to look at, but they fulfilled no useful function. His description in his diary was devoid of all adjectives –

Quelimane

Victoria Falls

later, in London, on his publisher's advice, he had to touch it up for *Missionary Travels*. In his diary at the time he wrote: "The falls are singularly formed. They are simply the whole mass of the Zambezi waters rushing into a fissure or rent made right across the bed of the river. In other falls we have usually a great change of level both in the bed of the river and adjacent country, and after the leap the river is not much different from what it was above the falls; but here the river, flowing rapidly among numerous islands and from 800 to 1,000 yards wide, meets a rent in its bed at least 100 feet deep and at right angles with its course, or nearly due east and west, leaps into it, and becomes a boiling white mass at the bottom ten or twelve yards broad."[3] Livingstone underestimated both the height and the width of the falls. Their width is 1,900 yards, and their height between 200 and 300 feet, both double his estimate.

Immediately after the falls, the Zambezi loops to the south before flowing east and then north-east. Livingstone decided to travel north, cutting out the loop altogether, mainly because he had heard that the area north of the Zambezi was high, fertile and healthy. This might be the place he had so long hoped to find for setting up missions and trading settlements.

As he travelled eastward across the Batoka Plateau, he became convinced that he had made a crucial discovery: the plateau was well watered but not swampy; it was high, therefore the temperature cooler than in the river valley, and it was dotted with trees and seemed suitable for cattle. Livingstone saw his dreams come true – provided he could persuade the LMS to hurry, and English traders to follow.

At the beginning of 1856, Livingstone entered what is today Moçambique. When he approached Zumbo, a deserted Portuguese settlement, native hostility suddenly increased. He had heard gossip about immensely wealthy and powerful traders in ivory and slaves, of Portuguese or Indian origin, of families or clans called da Cruz and Pereira. He did not know that at this time they were actually waging war on each other and the Portuguese authorities were unable to make them keep the law. In his diary, Livingstone commented on the activities of the da Cruz on the right side of the Zambezi; "Kisaka [Chisaka] continues the same system of plundering on the side of the Maganjas, preventing all trade, as he says he has conquered the country, all belongs to him."[4]

Further down the river he met Chisaka's men, who had crossed to

Sena to sell slaves, but sales were not going well, and the slaves had been there three days without food. None of the merchants considered the trade immoral, but Livingstone did discover that some of them had misgivings about the large quantities of arms and powder that were finding their way into Chisaka's hands.[5] Livingstone recorded that Chisaka could make his strength felt as far as Kariba and that he recruited some of his army retainers, the Batonga, from above Kariba and could close the roads from Tete to the Shire at will.[6]

In January 1856, Livingstone's main interest was to establish cordial relations with Chief Mburuma near Zumbo, so as to induce him to lend him canoes to cross the Loango at the point where it flows into the Zambezi. Livingstone spoke indifferent Portuguese, he had no knowledge of the peculiar relationship which existed between Portuguese, Africans and Indians, nor of the wars fought between powerful *sertanejos* – "backwoodsmen" in classical Portuguese, but in Africa meaning "settlers" – nor of the attitude of different tribes to the Portuguese or to other Europeans. But he noted in his diary that near Zumbo Africans were behaving very suspiciously "collecting from all sides, and keeping at a distance from us though professing friendship."[7]

It was on this occasion that he gave a notable illustration of his courage and determination. He knew that when his men forded the river, they would be split up and therefore at the mercy of the local natives. He was also alarmed when they refused to tell him why the Portuguese had left Zumbo. Had he understood the background, he would not have asked, as the Africans could not answer – lest they offended either of the powerful warring clans. After prolonged discussions with Chief Mburuma, he was offered two canoes, which would mean numerous crossings to ferry over goods, animals and 114 men. He took it for granted that an attack would be made when they began crossing and his followers were divided. It was now evening, and nothing further could be done until the morning. Livingstone wrote in his diary, untrammelled by modesty: "See O Lord how the heathen rise up against me as they did to Thy Son."[8] He toyed with the idea of crossing by night, but decided against it. That was not the way an Instrument of God's Providence should behave. "I will not cross furtively by night as intended. It would appear as flight, and should such a man as I flee? Nay, verily. I shall take observations for lat. and long. tonight, though they may be the last. I feel quite calm now, thank God."[9] Then he slept soundly.

This was the essential Livingstone – proud, brave, obstinate, fully confident in the Lord. "If I am cut off . . . my efforts are no longer needed by Him who knows what is best."[10] His belief that God controlled every event was so strong that it excluded physical fear. Yet there was the fear that God may not have intended him to take the course he was pursuing, and that he had rejected Livingstone.

The following morning Livingstone observed that the women had been sent away, and that a large number of armed men had appeared. Instead of two, only one canoe was provided, although he could see two tied up on the near-by shore. Getting all the goods, cattle and men across in a single canoe was a nerve-wracking experience. Surrounded though he was by natives with spears at the ready, Livingstone showed no fear and started to talk to them, showing his watch, lens and compass "to keep them amused, until there remained only those who were to enter the canoe with me." He was last to cross. He bore these Africans no malice, and in fact he said that they had probably been afraid that he might play some trick on them.

Beyond Zumbo lay Senga country, in which two chiefs, Mpende and Pangura, had their territories. Livingstone met Mpende, who explained to him that the Zambezi flowed due east for seventy miles and then turned sharply south-east; if Livingstone headed south-east at once, he could cut off fifty miles and reach Tete that much sooner. What is more, if he did not follow the Zambezi, he would avoid a hilly, rocky path, as well as "several Chiefs . . . who levy tribute on those who pass up or down."[11] It was in this way that he came to miss the Cabora Bassa rapids, and retain the illusion that the Zambezi was navigable as far as the Batoka Plateau.

The reason why Livingstone took this decision was his health: he was again plagued by fever, and he wanted to reach Tete as quickly as possible. In fact, eight miles from the town, he was so weak that he sent word to the Military Commander of Tete, Major Tito Augusto Araujo Sicard, to help him. Major Sicard, a local settler and a charming person, immediately sent a portable hammock and Livingstone was carried to his house. Here he spent two months, Sicard providing him with every possible comfort. What he did not appear to do was enlighten Livingstone about the dangerous Cabora Bassa rocks; for Livingstone wrote in his diary, "I was informed of the existence of a small rapid in the river near Chicova; had I known of this previously, I certainly would not have left the river without examining it. It is called Kebrabasa and is described as a number of rocks which jut out across the stream."[12] As it was, in a letter to the Directors he said, "The only impediment to navigation of the Zambezi is one or two rapids, not cataracts."[13]

Zambezi rapids

Livingstone's misunderstanding of the significance of the Cabora Bassa rapids is all the more strange since at Major Sicard's house he met all the Portuguese of any importance in the town, and several of them had seen the terrific rocks, extending over the river for thirty miles. It seems incredible that Cardoso, who knew the entire Rivers area well, should not have told him about it. He and Livingstone had many long conversations on a variety of subjects.

Livingstone recorded in his diary on March 22, 1856: "Senor Candido has sent off negroes to produce different medicinal roots which enter into the composition of a remedy for the wound of a poisoned arrow. It was made by a Jesuit and is said to be very efficacious." A week later he wrote, "Oil of Brother Pedro.[14] Received the following recipe for curing poisoned wounds from Mr Candido. It was invented by a padre, and he calls it Oleo of Frei Pedros. Oil of Ricinus communis, and the following roots: Calumba root, Musheteco Do., Abutua Do., Balatinva Do., Peregecamto Do., and root of

Itaca or Capende; equal parts to be put into a bottle and kept to be applied to wound as occasion requires. The really effective ingredient may be the castor oil, for the Bushmen make use of fat only for the cure of these poisoned wounds, administering it internally at the same time."

Although Cardoso's considerable medical knowledge gave him much in common with Livingstone, and though Livingstone noted in his diary everything he heard, he gives no indication of being aware of Cardoso's powerful connections. Cardoso was in fact married to Francisca Pereira, daughter of Dombo Dombo – Gonçalo Caetano Pereira – who was waging war against the da Cruz's. When informed of Livingstone's plans, Cardoso also told him of the big lake to the north, which he had visited. They parted the best of friends, and on April 13, 1856, Livingstone noted in his diary: "Mr Candido sends his broken watch spring to England that I may purchase another for him. This I have much pleasure in doing, for he has been very kind and obliging to me all along." Livingstone never saw Cardoso again, but later had many unpleasant things to say about him. What happened to the broken watch spring is not recorded.

By this time Livingstone was critical of the Portuguese. The Portuguese needed settlers with European wives, and enterprising people to exploit the iron, coal and gold deposits, not to mention the agricultural possibilities of this rich country. But Livingstone had far too little knowledge of the *prazo* system[15] and efforts made by men like Pereira and da Cruz, to realise that climate, malaria and the nature of the terrain had something to do with the lack of development.

For his part, Livingstone was determined that English missionaries and traders were to open up the country and drive out the slave trade, which the Portuguese authorities not only tolerated, but through which many of them waxed rich.[16] It was therefore an instinctive reaction to their shortcomings to call the Portuguese lazy, degenerate and corrupt, living exclusively on the proceeds of the slave trade.

Although Livingstone castigated the Portuguese with the harshest words he could think of, he accepted the generous hospitality of Major Sicard for two months. When he left in May 1856, he had to make arrangements for his Makololo porters. Again Sicard came to his rescue, providing them with land near Tete so that they could grow their own food; he also promised Livingstone that he would see to it that they did not starve. Livingstone set off downstream by canoe with only eight porters, and found the journey much easier than he had expected – although he had another very bad attack of fever. But at Quelimane he gathered strength remarkably quickly when he heard that English warships had called every few months to enquire about him.

These calls by the British Navy were the result of Mr Gabriel's letter to the Foreign Secretary, indicating about when Livingstone would arrive in the Zambezi delta. Also in Quelimane Livingstone heard that HMS *Frolic* had sent a brig to the mouth of the river to get news of him – it capsized in the surf that always pounded the bar and all eight members of the crew were drowned. Livingstone chose to regard this as an accident, not as evidence that the mouth of the Zambezi might not be suitable for shipping.

Another upsetting event was the suicide of Sebweku, his trusted Makololo interpreter, whom alone he wanted to take to England with him. But worse was to come. He received a letter from the LMS Directors, written on August 24, 1855, in which they said, "The Directors while yielding to none in their appreciation of the objects upon which, for some years past, your energies have been concentrated . . . are nevertheless restricted in their power of aiding plans connected only remotely with the spread of the Gospel. . . . Your reports make it sufficiently obvious that the nature of the country, the insalubrity of the climate, the prevalence of poisonous insects, and other adverse influences, constitute a very serious array of obstacles to missionary effort; and even were there a reasonable prospect of these being surmounted – and we by no means assume they are insurmountable – yet, in that event, the financial circumstances of the Society are not such as to afford any ground of hope that it would be in a position, within any definite period, to venture upon untried, remote, and difficult fields of labour."

Livingstone was heartsick and disgusted by the Directors, who made it clear that his explorations would not be followed up. His critics among the missionaries had long been saying that he was simply an explorer out for fame; now the Directors, by their new attitude, seemed to bear this out. Yet originally they had authorised his journey – which could only mean that they had intended to use it as a fundraising stunt. It needed all the acclaim he was to get after his arrival in England on December 9, 1856, to wipe the bitterness from his heart, especially since he learnt in Cairo, where he went from Alexandria to sightsee and pick up his mail, that his father had died. HMS

*Frolic* called at Alexandria for coal and water.

Fortunately Livingstone had no idea of the disappointments yet to come. He did not foresee the results of his obstinate determination to set up missions in Central Africa, and of his over-optimistic, seriously misleading statements in *Missionary Travels*, aimed at influencing young men to volunteer for this work. Moreover his violent criticisms of the Portuguese were to lose him the support of people who could have helped him; his disgraceful treatment of Cardoso was not only to hurt a friend, but one who was in a position to advise and to explain the difficulties against which the missionaries would have to battle.

CHAPTER FIFTEEN

# Help from the blue Cardoso eyes

Reference has already been made to the somewhat arrogant disdain with which, unhappily, Livingstone tended to regard most of the Portuguese; he behaved very badly to one in particular – Senhor Candido José da Costa Cardoso. As Senhor Cardoso kept no diary, and so far none of his personal letters have been found, his story has had to be pieced together from official documents; impressions of him from Livingstone and his party; the memories of Cardoso's descendants and of the Tete elders. All Portuguese sources bear out that he was a man of consequence, popular and admired in his day in Zambezia.

Cardoso was one of the Portuguese who welcomed Livingstone on his arrival in Tete on March 2, 1856, when the doctor stayed at the house of the Military Commandant, Major Sicard. Livingstone was only too glad to listen to Cardoso, who ten years earlier visited the great lake, about which the doctor had already heard from an Arab trader. Cardoso said that it was 300 miles from Tete; and was the source of the Shire. Livingstone opened his diary at a blank page and persuaded his new friend to sketch a rough map there and then to show the approach route. From the handwriting it is clear that the doctor annotated the map himself. On April 3, 1856, Livingstone wrote in his diary: "Mr Candido says that earthquakes have happened several times in the country of the Marawi at no great distance from Tete, or in the region of coal and hot springs. They are named 'Shiwo' in the Marawi tongue, and in that of this side of the river 'Shiteco-teco' or shivering. They have never been of more than a minute's duration, and never did any damage. Indeed, with huts made with poles stuck in the ground it is difficult to conceive what damage could be done unless rocks were rent and waters gushed forth. They have never happened on this side of the river. There are many great caves on the other side of the river, and chiefly in the

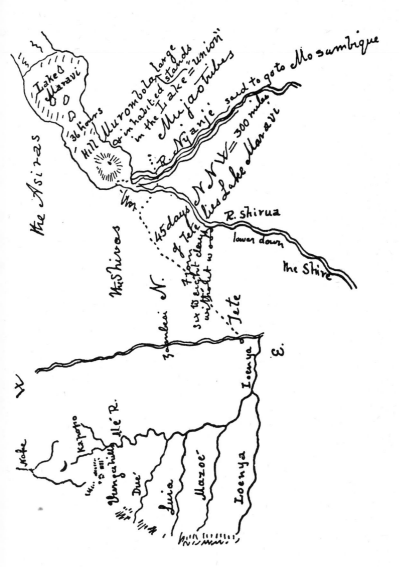

Livingstone's annotated copy of Cardoso's sketch map of Lake Nyasa.

nearer parts of the Marawi territory, who use them as store houses and places of refuge in time of war. The sea has evidently formed them," Livingstone added, "as well as round holes used as cisterns which we have seen."

Livingstone recounted the information he had obtained from Cardoso in letters to several friends, and repeated it at length in his book, *Missionary Travels*.[1]

Cardoso was apparently thrilled by his new friend, the famous explorer, as indeed were all the people who had the chance of meeting him through Major Sicard. Like Sicard, Cardoso did everything he could to make Livingstone's stay comfortable; they saw a good deal of each other, and Cardoso was convinced that Livingstone had become his friend for life.

Candido José da Costa Cardoso was born in Tete around 1800, the son of Antonio Cardoso and a local woman of Goan origin. His father had come from Lisbon to south-east Africa at the end of the 18th century; he served in the Tete Military Command, and then took up trade. The probability is that, like other Portuguese officials, he received his salary irregularly, if at all. Trading in ivory and slaves was not so much a choice as a necessity. His wife, who is believed to have had some Arab blood, brought him a considerable dowry.

The Cardoso family lived in the type of house illustrated opposite p. 164;[2] built in bricks, with a tiled roof, and slim columns decorating the front; it had several spacious rooms with an earth floor but sizeable windows. Work about the house was performed by slaves, whose position, however, was more like that of medieval retainers. In some households the plight of slaves was miserable as can be gauged from the following description of Portuguese slave-owners by a celebrated Governor of Moçambique, Francisco Maria de Lacerda e Almeida, who wrote of them: "The Portuguese community was mostly made up of former retainers of the viceroys and governors, and soldiers exiled as criminals to the colonies. Marrying into the local families and suddenly finding themselves affluent, these convicts allowed their old habits to flourish with an unrestrained luxuriance. The first concern of the newcomer to the Zambezi world was to show what a great person he was by his brutality towards his slaves, by his malice to all and sundry, by his pride and disobedience to the government. . . . These men kept their own private prisons in which they tortured and killed their prisoners."[3]

This did not apply to the Cardoso household, for which the best proof is Candido's friendly relations with the house slaves and with other Africans, thanks to whom he was completely familiar with their way of life. Livingstone heard from "Mr Candido" – as he referred to him – about the Africans' beliefs, and noted in his diary in April, 1856: "The natives known to the Portuguese have universally the clear idea of a Supreme God, the Maker and Governor of all things. He is named Morimo, Molungo, Reza and Mpambe[4] in different dialects; the Barotse name him Nyámpi, and the Balonda Zambi. All promptly acknowledge him as the ruler over all. When undergoing the ordeal, they hold up their hands to the Ruler of Heaven, as if appealing to him to assert their innocence. When they escape, or recover from sickness, or are delivered from any danger, they offer a sacrifice of fowl or sheep, pouring out the blood as a libation to the soul of a departed relative. They believe in the transmigration of souls, and also that while persons are still living, they may enter into lions and alligators, and then return again to their own bodies."[5]

It is odd that Cardoso did not tell Livingstone about the spirit mediums, who had such an enormous influence among the Zambezi tribes. If he did, for some reason Livingstone did not make a note of it. But he recorded the rest of what Cardoso had said: "If a man marries and does not pay the principal man of his wife's family, the children begotten belong to the family, and enter into the heritage of the mother. They are those of the grandmother. If he pays, they enter into the heritage and family of their own father. On this side of the river, the sons are said to inherit the chieftainship, but on the other side, as Maravi, Babisa, etc. etc. children of a sister alone, and not those of the chief himself, occupy the chieftainship. Mr Candido never saw nor heard of any ancient inscriptions in this country, nor yet fossils nor shells. Yet a young man from Sennà declares that inscriptions do exist at Gorongosa; on the way to Manica, and says they are on large slabs of stone lying flat on the top of a hill."[6]

Cardoso went to Tete School, the only one where local Portuguese children could learn to read and write, and where two "gentlemen of colour", doctors of Dogmatic Theology and Moral Philosophy, taught religion. The school founded by the Jesuits, closed when the Order was dissolved in 1759, was not restored in Tete when the ban on the Jesuits was lifted in 1814. Antonio Cardoso sent his two sons, Candido and Joao, to Goa for higher education, as did other Portuguese of sufficient means. Cardoso picked up African dialects easily

– by the time he was twenty he spoke four of them fluently.[7] He was a tall, attractive youth with fair hair and very blue eyes. He showed no trace of his Indian and Arab blood. But it could not have been his looks alone that decided the powerful Dombo Dombo – Gonçalo Caetano Pereira – to marry his daughter Francisca to him.[8] Candido must have given proof of ability and the kind of courage that was needed for a man to hold his own in the lawless world of Zambezia. Through his marriage Cardoso became a member of the most powerful clan in the country – his father-in-law, Dombo Dombo, and his grandson, Chisaka (Pedro Caetano Pereira) dominated the entire south bank of the Zambezi area from Tete to the unbounded north. Moreover, Candido also became connected with Zambezia's most experienced trading organisation, for the Pereiras traded even with Kazembe, the famous ruler of the Lunda.[9]

Cardoso was well liked by his father-in-law, and the rest of the Pereiras; with his wife, Francisca, he often visited them in their strongholds. The Marquess Sà de Bandeira, who in 1836 became Prime Minister of Portugal, and did a great deal to develop the colonies and abolish slavery, wrote that Major Monteiro, on his way from Tete to the Kazembe, met Cardoso on June 3, 1831. The meeting took place at the *prazo* of Soche, on the southern side of the Zambezi. Cardoso, he said, was "a relation of the Pereira family and stayed in the living house in Luane".[10]

Although his wife eventually received the *prazo* of Soche, Cardoso took up trading. With the unique connections of his in-laws, it was not difficult to establish himself, and he proved very successful. It was during his extensive trading expeditions that in 1846 he visited Lake Nyasa. From Tete he went to the *prazo* of Soche, and from there along a track joining the Luanwe; then down the escarpment to the shores of the lake.[11] Cardoso told his friends that he made an exhaustive exploration by canoe of Nyanja Grande, also called Mangune. As in 1846, Ngoni warriors were ravaging the area in which the direct overland route from Tete lay, and as the Shire river at that time was believed to be impassable, he had to take a round-about way, which he covered in 45 days.[12]

Five years later, he was living in Tete, in a large house in Fumbe, now called Tenente Primo Caulhao Street. (The house was pulled down a few years ago.) From January 1851 onwards he exercised the functions of Acting *Captain Mor* of the Crownlands of Tete Township. *Captain Mor*, in exact translation captain-major, in 19th century Moçambique meant commander of a military district. According to the *Archivo Historico de Moçambique* in Lourenço Marques, Cardoso's appointment was confirmed by the Governor's decree only on March 6, 1861, and by Order No 22 from Lisbon on March 18, 1861. In 1853, Cardoso was also President of the Tete Municipal Chamber.

A year and a half after he met Livingstone, on October 28, 1857, Cardoso was appointed President of a Commission of Mines. The Acting Military Commander of Tete, Joao de Sousa Nunes Andrade, asked him to prepare a report about the gold, iron and coal deposits of the Tete region for the Governor of Quelimane and Rios da Sena. As his in-laws had built up their vast fortune on gold prospecting, it was taken for granted that Cardoso was acquainted with the mineral deposits north of Tete. His report earned high praise from Portuguese officials, including the Governor of Moçambique.

Two days after his appointment to the Commission of Mines, Cardoso and other Tete citizens were requested by Circular No 85, to place at the disposal of the Acting Commander of Tete Township, Senor Andrade, a number of canoes with the requisite number of oars "to transport a force from Tete to provide aid to the force in Sena."[13] Cardoso was the moving spirit of this operation, which was well carried out. It may be mentioned at this point that the Zambezi Wars, which lasted 48 years, and which completely transformed the situation in Moçambique, had already started. Of this more later on.

Cardoso was by now going from strength to strength. On February 2, 1858, he became *Juiz Privativo dos Milandos Cafriaes* – a lay magistrate who dealt with breaches of customary law by "Cafirs" [Africans]. In his Despatch No 23, Senor Andrade reported to the Governor that Cardoso had been duly installed.

And then his friend, Dr Livingstone returned. On June 20, 1858, the Governor of Quelimane and Rios de Sena instructed the Acting Military Commander, Senor Andrade, to give all assistance within the Tete District to the traveller "Dr Levingstone [sic] and his party."[14]

Livingstone arrived in Tete in his specially constructed steam-launch, the *Ma-Robert* on November 2, 1858. The *Ma-Robert* had already made several trips to Tete, carrying equipment for the expedition to Cabora Bassa. By now Livingstone was HM Consul of Quelimane on the eastern coast of Africa. He wore an impressive gold braided cap, and had eight Englishmen working for him. He was delighted to be re-united with the Makololo, who thanks to Major Sicard had not only grown their own food, but had participated in trading operations. They seemed to enjoy their life "with the decadent Portuguese" and to Livingstone's horror, some suggested that they did not want to go back to Sekeletu.

But Livingstone did not call on his old friend Cardoso – to the latter's chagrin. It soon became evident to Cardoso, as well as to other Portuguese observers, that there were differences of opinion within the Livingstone party, and that there was trouble with the unusual ship. The *Ma-Robert* consumed immense amounts of wood, including expensive hardwood like ebony and *lignum vitae*. The Portuguese did not know that her feed pipes often became choked, and the cylinders and boilers also gave trouble. Then Cardoso heard that the doctor had sent home an important man, Commander Norman Bedingfeld, who left in an obvious huff.

On November 8, 1858, Livingstone and two of his companions went to "Kabrabassa" to see for themselves what the jutting-out rocks were like. Five days later they were back in Tete; again the doctor did not go near Cardoso. On November 22 he and his whole party went further up and at last it became clear to all of them that the rapids were completely impassable.

News of the Englishmen's disappointment flashed about Tete in no time; it also became known that Livingstone intended to sail up the Shire and find "Lake Nganja" (Lake Malawi), as the Portuguese called it. And still he did not visit Cardoso, who longed to hear about Livingstone's plans for visiting "his lake". Dr John Kirk at least called on him twice, on October 31, 1859 and on February 13, 1860, and Cardoso told him in great detail all he could recollect about his own trip in 1846. Eventually, on May 1, 1860, Livingstone did get in touch with Cardoso – because he wanted to buy his donkey for the journey up the Shire. Ever-forbearing, Cardoso would not sell, but loaned him his donkey,[15] as Livingstone noted in his *Journal* that day. Three weeks later, Livingstone wrote to Cardoso in his capacity as Commander of the Tete District, "desiring him to count the goods returned and deliver them to Rowe." William Rowe, the *Ma-Robert*'s leading stoker, was left behind in Tete because he was ill. Cardoso once more obliged Livingstone.[16]

Richard Thornton, Livingstone's practical mining geologist, also provides a few glimpses of Cardoso. In his diary he describes him quite inaccurately as Major Sicard's agent; more accurately he said

House similar to that in which Cardoso lived in Tete. This one has the now common corrugated-iron roof.

The *Ma Robert* (*Mansell Collection*)

that in 1857–59 he "wrote mineral reports", and correctly that he was *Capitao-Mor da Coroa, Villa Tete* – military-commander of the Crownlands of Tete Township;[17] then Thornton noted that on July 5, 1859, he visited "a small neat village named Mattema owned by Sr Candido";[18] a year later, on August 4, 1860, Thornton wrote in his diary: "Soon we arrived at cultivated ground, then at a village of Candido, whose native name is Pindouka"; the village formed part of an estate – a *prazo* – called Missonga. On August 5 Thornton noted: "A little beyond the first came another hut, still on the land of Missonga of Candido. . . . About 1.30 reached the village of Mittore of Candido", which was at the junction of the Imhambea (Nhambia) and the Revubué rivers, and the last of the Crownlands of Tete. "Opposite: land of Chisaka – Makanga." Had Thornton known of Cardoso's connections, it would not have surprised him that his property was close to that of his first wife's nephew. By then both were dead. Chisaka had died in 1858; Francisca in 1856. On August 6, 1860, Thornton entered in his diary: "Called at two other villages of Candido's. . . . Arrived at the first village of Tsoche [Soche] about noon. Here were two half-caste sons of Candido." These were Francisca's sons, who lived on her *prazo* of Soche; in 1857 Cardoso re-married; his second wife, Helena Nunes Heget, was a woman of Goan origin, although according to her name, Heget, she might have been an Anglo-Indian. Their first child, a son called Leandru, was born in 1858 and lived until 1963 – to the age of 105.

Cardoso's disappointment over Livingstone's behaviour reached its highest pitch when the doctor returned from his expedition to Lake Nganja and did not call on him to exchange impressions about their respective experiences on the journey to the lake. And worse of all, Cardoso learnt in due course that the doctor accused him of having misled him – in fact, of not having been to the lake at all.[19]

By then many of the Portuguese in Tete were up in arms against Livingstone – they had heard what he had said and written about them. On April 24, 1860, Livingstone noted in his journal: "Generoso[20] has made a false translation of some parts of my book" [*Missionary Travels*]. This was possible, but the doctor's articles published in the Cape Town papers, and his lectures in Britain, abounded with insults about the Portuguese, so this would not have mattered very much. The people of Tete were particularly unhappy as they had done their best to entertain Livingstone and to help him in every possible way. Cardoso felt deeply hurt, as he had poured out all his knowledge to satisfy the doctor's curiosity. When news came that the Protestant missionaries were struggling with difficulties, that they were practically at war with the Africans, and that many of them – including a bishop – had died, the Portuguese of Tete felt little sympathy.[21]

Cardoso never got over the disappointment Livingstone had caused him. But his career continued successfully. On June 27, 1863, in recognition of the services he had rendered to the Portuguese crown, King Dom Luis made him a Knight of the Order of Christ. This was a great honour, as the Order of Christ was the successor of the Order of the Templars, and its members ranked high even in Portugal.

Meanwhile the Zambezi Wars, which lasted 48 years and influenced events all over south-east Africa, had grown more serious. They began as a private war between Chisaka (Pedro Caetano Pereira) and Coimbra[22] (Antonio José da Cruz). In the next phase two younger *prazo* holders fought each other, and in it African chieftains already took sides. In the late 1860's, the Portuguese government tried, unsuccessfully, to suppress the da Cruz's. Meanwhile the African chiefs split into two groups and they too fought each other. In the last phase of the Zambezi Wars a new character emerged, Joaquim Carlos Paiva de Andrade, at the time described as the Portuguese Rhodes – only without Cecil Rhodes's money. Manuel Antonio de Sousa – nicknamed Gouveia, after whom Vila Gouveia is named – in 1874 strengthened his hand by marrying the daughter of the reigning Macombe Paramount Chief, and then made common cause with Andrade. Between them, they decided to capture the goldfields of Mashonaland. At this point the Africans staged their first nationalist uprising at Massingire, which de Sousa – at Portuguese request – crushed and then reached the Ruo river. But instead of occupying the Shire area, which was completely defenceless, he turned back in order to gain control of the Mashona goldfields. During a truce Andrade and de Sousa had negotiated with the Mashona, they were captured by Cecil Rhodes's British South Africa Company troops, and spent nearly a year in prison in Cape Town. For a long time their families had no idea what had happened to them.

In 1887, for the first time, the powerful African chiefs – Mtoko, Barue, Rupire, the da Cruz and the Mwene Mutapa – formed an alliance against de Sousa, Andrade and the Portuguese, who in the end defeated them. But – remarkably – *muzongos*, members of the old *prazo* families, were fighting on both sides.

Now back to Sr Candido. In 1868 the Governor of Moçambique requested him to mediate between the Pereira and the da Cruz factions. He did his best, but with both Dombo Dombo and Chisaka dead, he had no real chance of interceding in the rivalry of the two clans; only brute force could have achieved that, and this did not exist, certainly not in the hands of the Portuguese authorities.

Yet Candido must have shown diplomatic ability, for a few years later the Governor entrusted him with the task of making an alliance with the chiefs of the Shire valley. He knew the area up to the Lake, and he was acquainted with the chiefs. At first it seemed as though he would be successful, but then Sir Harry Johnston, with Cecil Rhodes's backing, outbid him, acquiring for Britain the areas that form today's Malawi.[23]

The Zambezi Wars ended in 1888; two years later Candido José da Costa Cardoso lay buried in the Tete cemetery.

## CHAPTER SIXTEEN

# Livingstone breaks the Shire blockade

David Livingstone's discovery that the Cabora Bassa rocks made navigation of the Zambezi impossible was a shattering experience. It meant he had to give up his dream that Christianity and trade, sailing up and down God's Highway, would exterminate slavery. His descriptions in England of healthy areas for mission stations, fertile land for growing cotton, markets among Africans for British industry, were all dependent on the Zambezi. When it proved to be unnavigable, all his plans lost any basis of reality. Livingstone was stunned and looked it, but his strength of character enabled him to pull himself together, and to concentrate on finding a substitute for the Zambezi and for the Batoka Plateau.

His state of mind, when his reputation and his position were at stake, perhaps explains the ruthless manner in which he proceeded up the Shire – which was to replace the Zambezi: he destroyed the blockade maintained by four chiefs to keep the slave trade out of the Lower Shire without even realising the damage he was doing. The disasters that followed were consequences of his own stubborn ambitions and his lack of knowledge of local conditions. He knew as little about the Shire blockade as he knew about Cardoso's influential connections.

The tremendous reception Livingstone was given in England in 1856 after he had crossed the African continent, is well known. Few have received as much adulation and been fêted as enthusiastically as he was. It seemed that everyone, from Queen Victoria to the humblest factory hand, wanted to cheer the great explorer. Among the many honours that he received were the freedoms of London, Glasgow and Edinburgh. At a time when serious criticism was being levelled against the injustices of Victorian society, and businessmen and industrialists were becoming targets of hostile comments, here was Dr Livingstone, a missionary, telling the young to go out and preach the Word of the Lord to the benighted heathen, and at the same time telling the traders that by taking their wares to Africa they would undermine the slavers. The traders were only too glad to have moral justification for the large profits they were making. The saving of souls, going hand in hand with the export of English goods, was an exploit which conveniently appealed to piety and commercial enterprise alike.

Away from the public eye, Livingstone's activities were less commendable – his treatment of the London Missionary society was shabby. He confided only to Sir Roderick Murchison, President of

Part of a letter from Livingstone to Sir Roderick Murchison

the Royal Geographical Society, that he had made up his mind to leave the LMS, provided he could get government employment at a salary that enabled him to have his children educated. By May 1857, thanks to Sir Roderick's intervention, the Foreign Secretary, Lord Clarendon, was prepared to offer Livingstone a position.[1] Yet at the LMS General Meeting on May 14, when it was resolved that a new mission was to be set up in Makololo land under Livingstone's leadership, he did not say one word to indicate that he might not be available. Then for five months he did not communicate with Dr Tidman; he was writing his book, *Missionary Travels And Researches In South Africa*, while Dr Tidman was waiting for funds to be collected for the new missions – a second one was to be set up in Matabeleland under Dr Robert Moffat. Only in October 1857 did Livingstone inform Dr Tidman that he would no longer work for the Society. Dr Tidman had never felt confident in the success of the Makololo mission; now that Livingstone had let the Society down, he wanted quietly to drop the project. But he reckoned without Livingstone, who pressurised the Society to go through with it, on the grounds that funds for it had been raised. This was true, in fact £6,400 had come in instead of the £5,000 originally demanded. "I should be glad to be assured that the intentions of friends in subscribing so liberally are likely soon to be realised," Livingstone wrote to Dr Tidman in February 1858. The implication was clear. If the money were used for paying off the Society's overdraft instead of devoting it to the purpose for which it had been donated, the Directors would have to answer awkward questions, and face difficulties when next they tried to raise funds. So arrangements for sending out three missionaries with their families went ahead.

Meanwhile Livingstone had the satisfaction of being appointed HM Consul for Quelimane for the eastern coast and the Independent Districts of the Interior and Commander of an Expedition for Exploring Eastern and Central Africa. Lord Clarendon had, originally, wanted him to be consul for Moçambique as a whole, but the Portuguese refused to countenance this. On the grounds that Quelimane was open for foreign trade while Sena and Tete were not, their *exequatur* was valid only for the Zambezi delta.[2] This by itself proved (if proof were still needed) that the Portuguese had no intention of making the Zambezi an international river, least of all in cooperation with Dr Livingstone who had abused them in print and by word of mouth. Lord Clarendon was aware of this, but he was too much taken up with the Indian Mutiny to think about Livingstone's trading prospects. He had given him employment and agreed to provide, through the Treasury, £5,000 for his expedition. Clarendon was almost forced to do this, as Livingstone, through his addresses, had created such enthusiasm among businessmen, scholars and students. Businessmen wanted to know about conditions, mineral deposits, transport possibilities; these could only be ascertained by a team of experts. Livingstone had to collect men able to do this – his list was ready so quickly that he probably prepared for this development.

By this time Livingstone, who in his early days in Africa had shown much understanding for African beliefs and traditions, and advocated slow, gentle methods in the work of conversion, had changed his attitude, and had grown convinced that organised colonisation was the essential prelude to Christian success. But colonists would only come if they and their sponsors were convinced that central Africa would prove profitable and relatively accessible. This is what he had to prove; once he had done it, he believed the British government would bring pressure to bear on Portugal to throw the Zambezi open to international trade, or eventually oust Portugal altogether,[3] which is what would have suited Livingstone best of all.

The story of the disastrous Zambezi expedition has been told many times – first and foremost by its members. Livingstone's party consisted of Commander Norman Bedingfeld, RN, Dr John Kirk, botanist and doctor of medicine; Richard Thornton, geologist; Thomas Baines, artist who was to act as storekeeper; George Rae, engineer; and Charles Livingstone, the Doctor's brother, "the moral agent" of the expedition who knew about photography and cotton.

The expedition was unlucky from the word go. HMS *Pearl*, which brought the party out from England, arrived at Quelimane on May 14, 1858; it took her nearly four weeks to find the Kongone, the largest channel leading into the Zambezi. By June 16 it was clear that the *Pearl* could go no further in the shallow river, blocked by sandbanks and mudflats. So the supplies as well as the seven members of the party had to be transferred to the *Ma-Robert*, which Rae had quickly put together. Overcrowding on this small steam launch in the intense heat would have taxed the nerves of any group of men. Livingstone's companions had all read *Missionary Travels*, from which he had left out virtually all the unpleasant features of African exploration. They were prepared for adventure, danger, rough living, but not for debilitating hardships in a temperature always over 100° F, tropical rain which soaked but did not cool them, mosquitoes, ticks, tropical ulcers, unfamiliar diet, and, every day, hours spent in dragging the *Ma-Robert* by ropes and winches when she got stuck. And then came malaria – which Livingstone had described in England as no worse than a common cold. The men suffered from giddiness, delirium and vomiting, and they resented Livingstone's

The *Ma Robert* on the Zambezi (*Mansell Collection*)

aloofness over their "trivial ailments" when they felt very ill indeed. Obviously there were arguments and rows. The worst was between Commander Bedingfeld and Captain Duncan, a Merchant Navy man, which Livingstone handled very undiplomatically, siding openly with Duncan. Bedingfeld, who was after all a commander in the Royal Navy, left for Cape Town offended, and his reports did much damage to Livingstone's reputation. The main trouble, however, was caused by Charles Livingstone, an inveterate gossip, who intrigued freely and worked little.

Livingstone knew that it would take weeks to get the supplies up to Tete. The *Ma-Robert* was entirely unsuited to the Zambezi; she consumed an enormous quantity of wood, especially hard wood, which took a long time to chop. A day and a half's wood cutting would keep her going only for one day. Throughout July, August and September the *Ma-Robert* did a slow series of painful trips, and the last of the supplies arrived in Tete finally by November 2.

At this point Livingstone's main concern was to investigate the Cabora Bassa rapids, of which he had made light in England. On November 8 he set out with Kirk and Rae to see for himself. Soon the Zambezi's bed narrowed to twenty yards, and the current became so strong that the *Ma-Robert* was damaged on a rock, fortunately above the water line. On the following day Livingstone and Kirk continued on foot and came to a point where the Zambezi divided into several branches. Livingstone scrambled over the rocks bordering one, Kirk over those along another, and both came to what Livingstone called a cascade. Kirk said in his diary that when he looked down at the water over a ledge "at a considerable angle I saw a mass of broken water at the bottom." He did not believe that even at flood time ships could negotiate these rapids; for his part Livingstone wrote in his diary, "I believe that, when the river rises about six feet, the cascades may be safely passed. If not at flood, when the water is spread over all the dell."[4]

Five days later they were back in Tete, and now Livingstone began to question the locals about Cabora Bassa. He did not look up Cardoso – he was in no mood for a comfortable chat. Instead, he talked to a trader by the name of José St Anna, who had recently been to Cabora Bassa, and traded in that area. St Anna's descriptions really alarmed Livingstone; on November 20 he recorded in his diary: "Things look dark for our enterprise. This Kebrabasa is what I never expected. No hint of its nature ever reached my ears. St Anna de-

scribes it fearful when in flood. . . . The Governor[5] sent down two
negroes in a canoe and neither they nor the canoe was ever seen
again. Then a canoe alone and that was smashed to pieces. What we
shall do if this is the end of the navigation I cannot now divine, but I
am trusting Him who never made ashamed those who did so." To his
companions he talked very differently – he insisted that when the
water was high, all would be well. To make quite sure of the situation, on November 22 he took his whole party to Cabora Bassa.

The climb over the rocks was very tiring, but during the first four
days the rapids they saw were no worse than the ones Livingstone
and Kirk had explored on their first trip. Livingstone was getting
quite cheerful, as he believed that the rocks they had seen *might* be
blasted away, and that a powerful steamer *might* get through at flood
time. He had already decided to return to Tete, when Masakasa, one
of the Makololo crew, told him – according to his *Journal*[6] "that the
same persons[7] informed him that there was a waterfall as high as a
tree and, though perishing with thirst, it was so difficult of access a
man would retire in fear of it." Livingstone listened in stunned
silence[8], then became very angry with the Makololo for having kept
such crucial information from him. He shouted at them, then at the
rest of the party that they could stay, or go, do as they liked, he would
complete his investigation. Kirk volunteered to go with him, and the
Makololo, who had been on the verge of mutiny, followed Livingstone. This was an illustration of his personality and influence over
them.

Progress along the Zambezi was terrible. The black glazed rocks
were burning hot, hands blistered if left for even a short while on
them. To cover any distance, a hard climb down into a gully, and
then another one up a slippery granite hill was necessary. Even
Livingstone said that this was the hardest work he had ever done.
And then, at a sudden bend of the river, he and Kirk saw the waterfall
Masakasa had been talking about. The Africans called it "Morumb-
wa". It was a magnificent sight – though smaller, it was similar to the
Jellala waterfall Magyar had seen on the Zaire.

For a while Livingstone could say nothing. Then like a drowning
man grasping at a straw, he suggested to Kirk that if the water rose
eighty feet after the rains, even this waterfall might not prove an insuperable obstacle! In his *Journal* he gave a factual, almost clinical,
description of the waterfall: "It was about 30 feet high, but inclined
at an angle about 30°. There are two large stones on one side of it,

and on the north-west bank a ridge of rocks is thrust out and causes irregular flow of water. . . . Both banks consist of high perpendicular slippery porphyric rock. We tried to get nearer, but deep furrowed gullies prevented us."[9]

This was the end of Dr Livingstone's plans for using the Zambezi to build up trade with the Batoka Plateau. True to himself, on the way back to Tete he was already planning another trip – up the Shire, which was to replace the Zambezi. To Dr Kirk's amazement, in his letter of December 17, 1858, to the new Foreign Secretary, Lord Malmesbury, Dr Livingstone wrote, "We are all of the opinion that a steamer of light draught would pass the river without difficulty when the river is in full flood." And what is more, Livingstone considered this a good moment to ask the Foreign Office for a replacement for the already rusting *Ma-Robert*.

Livingstone wrote similar optimistic letters to others – for instance to Sir Thomas Maclear in Cape Town: "I have not the smallest doubt but a steamer of good power could pass up easily in flood." This was a typical Livingstone tactic to make sure that his report to Lord Malmesbury would be borne out by his friends. But in his heart he knew that he was beaten – that his only chance was to play for time, and come up with a sensational result in some part of Africa, thus to retrieve his own position. Obviously, it could not be in central Africa, but it might be along the Shire – in the high lands he had heard about – even if they were 400 miles from the sea. If he knew nothing of their geographical condition, he had even less idea of the power-game that was being played out there, in which he had to take a part – and as it turned out, a fatal one.

For an understanding of Livingstone's journeys in the Shire country and around Lake Nyasa, the political situation of the area must be explained. It was complicated. By the time Livingstone arrived, the Shire valley (or Mang'anja country) was divided into four areas. Owing to their past, in all four Phiri-Marawi immigrants of the 15th century held the higher echelons of power, while the original inhabitants, the Chi-Chewa speakers (also called Mang'anja) who had settled there in the 12th century, had retained control of the village organisations up to village headmen. In the course of time this political duality was matched by differences in religion, ritual and social organisation. Between the middle of the 16th and the 17th centuries, the Marawi rulers expanded their territory, and split it into two kingdoms, the one in the north-west under Undi, and the other

Cabrabassa rapids (from a picture by T. Baines)

one in the south-east, under Lundu. These were not personal names, but names of rulers.

From the end of the 18th century onwards, these two kingdoms had to face threats from several directions. In the north there was a separatist movement led by powerful chiefs; there were massive ethnic movements; *prazeiros* and rebels from neighbouring Zambezia occupied tribal lands and started trading – in ivory and slaves – directly with the local population, without the intermediary of the chiefs.

Resistance to all these pressures differed from one area to another. By the time Livingstone arrived, the Mang'anja country was divided into four areas, two ruled by strong chiefs determined above all to keep out the slavers; two by weak men whose territories were disintegrating, but who were protected – up to a point – by the blockade maintained by the two strong chiefs. They were Chief Tengani, who ruled the south-eastern area, and Chief Mgundo-Kaphviti, who ruled the north-west, thus holding the heartland of the former Undi and Lundu kingdoms. They had been able to keep their headmen under control; they had kept out Portuguese intruders as well as African and Arab slave traders. The two weak chiefs ruled the south-western area and the eastern highland areas. The leading chief of the south-west was Kapichi, whose area had shrunk to almost half of its original size. He had had to come to terms with Goanese and Portuguese rebels from Zambezia, who had established themselves on the north bank of the Shire and from there raided northwards for slaves. Owing to the Zambezi Wars in Moçambique, this was much safer than operating in their old haunts. In Kapichi's realm Mang'anja middlemen – Africans – were also operating, as agents for the Tete merchants, but they also dealt with the rebels. Among the Mang'anja middlemen the most important was Chibisa, who was to play a crucial role in Livingstone's story.

Chibisa's original home was at Mikolongo, where he was related to the local chiefs. He served in the household of a Tete merchant until after 1840, then he managed to insinuate himself as the heir of Kapichi, the weak ruler of the south-western area. Chibisa gradually extended his influence towards the Zambezi, where twice he suffered defeat, once at the hands of Chisaka, Pedro Caetano Pereira, and once at those of his grandfather Dombo-Dombo, Gonçalo Caetano Pereira. Eventually Chibisa settled with his followers at Chikwawa, a village situated on the major trade route from Tete to the highlands, almost exactly in the geographical centre of Mang'anja territory. Chibisa's ambition was to rally the scattered Mang'anja forces around his person. But the divisions among the chiefs were too deep to be overcome by negotiation, however shrewdly conducted; what was needed was force. Chibisa had insufficient force; he wanted to use Livingstone to provide him with the guns to achieve his aim.

Monkhokve was the most outstanding among the weak and divided chiefs of the fourth area, the eastern highlands, which were threatened by the Ajawa slavers who acted on behalf of the Quelimane merchants on the one hand, and by the Chikunda traders who acted for the Tete people on the other. Inter-village raiding for slaves had begun; headmen wanted to make profits and shake off the hold of the chiefs. However, traditional authority was still acknowledged, although it was on the verge of collapse. The chiefs were looking among themselves for a person to give their loose federation new life, check the abuses of the slave trade and stop the threatening incursions of the Yao, the most dangerous slavers of all.

Their first choice wás Mankhokbe but he proved both unable and unwilling to give determined leadership. This was probably due to his reading of the political situation: he concentrated on the defence of his own area and refrained from allying himself with anyone – unless forced to do so, as ultimately happened.

This was the situation in the Shire country when on December 20, 1858, Livingstone, Kirk and Rae left Tete on the *Ma-Robert*. 200 miles lower down the Shire river flows into the Zambezi. This point is a hundred miles from the sea, and 300 from Lake Nyasa, the Shire's source. Livingstone came, as said above, determined to find a substitute for the fertile Batoka Plateau, but he also came, as was clear from the statement of the Chancellor of the Exchequer when he justified the Government's £5,000 contribution to the Livingstone expedition, to induce the natives to grow cotton. He had repeatedly said that African cotton would be much cheaper than the cotton the American South could provide. Livingstone instructed the members of his team to explore the mineral and agricultural resources of east and central Africa, and to engage the inhabitants to exploit these resources with a view of exporting raw materials to England and by so doing, help to end the slave trade. This implied setting up a permanent base station, where experiments on crops could be carried out for the benefit of the population.

Privately Livingstone visualised Englishmen as colonisers and civilisers of central Africa; he also believed that influential chiefs could be won over to these ideas, and instructed the members of his expedition to treat leading men of villages with great respect. Peaceful persuasion and non-interference were to be the major guidelines of his policy. But he assumed, without any prior investigation, that his industrial and colonial propositions would be acceptable to the chiefs and the ordinary people. In view of his failure over the Zambezi, he was determined to succeed – at any price. The test came as soon as he entered the Shire and reached Chief Tengani's village.

This is how Father Schoffeleers describes what followed:

"Tengani was one of the most powerful Mang'anja chiefs who had been able to retain firm control over his area.[10] This he had managed by rigorously keeping out all Portuguese traders who had proved to be the main disruptive elements elsewhere. Not long before Livingstone's arrival his armed men had managed to turn back a Portuguese ship. Livingstone heard the story at Sena, and he knew that he would be far from welcome. His party was hailed by a band of warriors whom Kirk estimated at between 400 and 500 and whose weapons were superior to anything they had seen on the Zambezi. Peaceful persuasion was of little help, for Tengani's people were not prepared to make a distinction between English and Portuguese, had they been able to. Confronted with their continuing threats Livingstone finally reacted by having his party's arms loaded and showing them to the chief's trembling deputy with the announcement that if Tengani's people were ready to fight, so was he. Permission to proceed was reluctantly given, and the ship continued its course with an unhappy and morose Livingstone aboard. . . . He realised very well that he had broken a carefully maintained blockade but he thought it was his good right to do so since Tengani had no business to halt rightful trade or peaceful exploration. Only much later did it dawn on him and Kirk[11] among others that much more was involved and that by forcing their way in they had inadvertently opened the door to the slave traders who began everywhere treading in their footsteps."[12]

As we will see in the next chapter, Livingstone did not meet Tengani on his first trip, and, on his second, owing to an inefficient interpreter, he could not explain his plans to him. Yet this is what Livingstone wrote on p. 76 of the *Narrative*: "At the village of a chief named Tingane, at least five hundred natives collected and ordered us to stop. Dr Livingstone went ashore; and on his explaining that we were English and had come neither to take slaves nor to fight, but only to open a path by which our countrymen might follow to purchase cotton or whatever else they might have to sell, except slaves, Tingane became at once quite friendly. The presence of the steamer, which showed that they had an entirely new people to deal with, probably contributed to this result, for Tingane was notorious for being the barrier to all intercourse between the Portuguese black traders and the natives further inland; none were allowed to pass him either way."

Livingstone's diary, written contemporaneously, indicates hardly any difficulties with Tengani, in contrast to Kirk's diary, in which he admits to feelings of worry and discomfort about the situation.

Yet Livingstone knew what he had done: "The bearing of the Mang'anja at this time was very independent; a striking contrast to the cringing attitude they afterwards assumed, when the cruel scourge of slave hunting passed over their country."[13] Whatever one may think about David Livingstone's ambivalence, and about his deceit and lies to cover up the fact that only armed threat had enabled him to steam up the Shire, his horror of slavery and the activities of the slavers was absolutely genuine. Breaking the Shire blockade, and allowing in the slavers south of Lake Nyasa, from where they had been kept out by the four chiefs, led by Tengani, must have prayed on his mind in the last years of his wanderings, when he was ill, devoid of medicines, and often dependent on Arab slavers.

## CHAPTER SEVENTEEN

# Forestalled at Lake Nyasa

Having forced his way through the Shire blockade, Livingstone withdrew into himself and spoke little to anyone. He was in the grip of a deep depression; Kirk and Rae were left entirely to their own devices. On both sides of the Shire, hostile Africans made it all too clear that the doctor and his companions were unwelcome. They shouted at the *Ma-Robert* to stop and pay dues for passage; when she did not stop, they threw stones or shot poisoned arrows from the river bank, and Livingstone had to ask Kirk to fire warning shots in reply. He would rather risk poisoned arrows than set a precedent that the local Africans could prevent travellers from passing.

Livingstone sailed past Mankhokve's village, unaware of the Paramount Chief's identity and importance. On January 12, 1859, the cataracts he named after Sir Roderick Murchison, forced him to turn back. Three days later he was again on the Zambezi, and had to admit that the first trip up the Shire had achieved little. Apart from one friendly message from a chief called Chibisa, he had met only with hostility.

The next two months Livingstone spent between Sena and Shupanga, still depressed, still not communicating, not even with his brother Charles. On March 14, 1859, he set out on his second Shire visit with Kirk; Rae pronounced the *Ma-Robert* unfit because of the many leaks, so he was left behind. This time Livingstone met Chief Tengani. But bad luck again dogged him; having a very poor interpreter, who mixed up cotton with Christianity, he could not explain the purpose of his journey. Not that Tengani cared; even when the man told him that according to The Book he would have to grow cotton and sell it to the English, he just looked blank. His worries concerned the growing pressure from the slave traders, to whom Livingstone had opened the way when he broke the blockade. Tengani felt not only resentment against the doctor, but he was deeply suspicious of him. It was their first and last meeting, and it was not a success.

Livingstone also spent a night at Mankhokve's village. Next morning he was asked to wait a little for the chief to appear; petulant

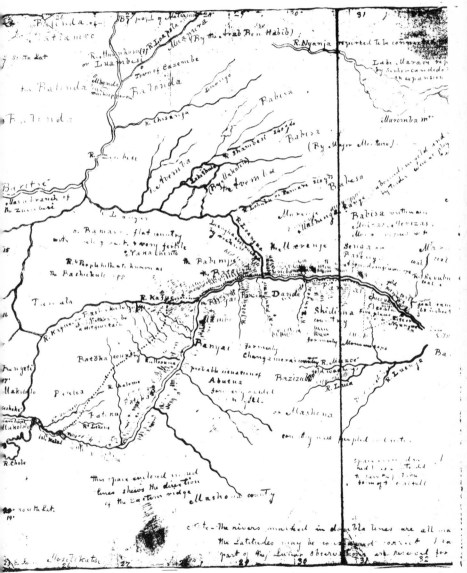

Part of Livingstone's map of the Zambezi area

and impatient over what he called Mankhokve's showing off, he left declaring that this would teach "Mankhokve the great chief" a good lesson – perhaps that he could not treat Englishmen as though they were Portuguese. Thus he turned another important man into an enemy, and on the next occasion Mankhokve refused to receive Livingstone. Yet Mankhokve could certainly have smoothed the way of the missionaries or settlers who, in Livingstone's dreams, were to grow cotton, rice and sugar in this fertile land. Livingstone would not believe that he was the Paramount Chief of the northern Mang'anja; yet, to his annoyance, every chief whom he met and asked assured him that this Mankhokve indeed was. They referred to one more important person, "the true ruler of all the Mang'anja," but never mentioned his name. Father Schoffeleers is certain that they meant Lundu – old, blind, powerless – who would see no strangers, and whom therefore Livingstone never met.

Livingstone was again depressed, and Kirk spent much of his time in his cabin, which he shared with hundreds of cockroaches. It was an immense relief to the doctor when at least one chief, Chibisa, gave him a friendly reception. His heart warmed to the lack of formalities, the absence of suspicion, and the ready answers to all his questions, although some of the information turned out to be far from accurate. Chibisa assured Livingstone that all the bad tribes lived downstream, and that by now he had already passed them. The people in the highlands, he was assured, were quite different; they were civil, like children.

Livingstone realised fairly soon that Chibisa wanted to use him in his ambitious plans to establish his authority in his predecessor's area.[1] In fact, on the fourth day of Livingstone's visit, Chibisa said openly that he urgently needed guns and military backing from the English. He pleaded for assistance in his punitive action against Mang'anja headmen from across the river, who had attacked him.[2] Yet Livingstone discovered that the first village they travelled through had been laid waste by Chibisa himself, and to add to his dismay, he learnt that Chibisa's representatives told the natives that the Englishman had been sent by their master in order to claim all the country he went through.

The Highland population – in stark contrast to what Chibisa had told him – was just as hostile as the people in the Lowlands, with the difference that in their respective areas, Chiefs Tengani and Mankhokve were in full control, while Chibisa was only trying to assert his authority. To quote Father Schoffeleers once more: "From all appearances what counted was the right of the strongest. Going toward Lake Shirwa (the aim of this second expedition) hostility was, if anything, increasing. Signals were transmitted from village to village and cries of defiance and intimidation were shouted in their ears. Kirk even mentions that the local people made an attempt to drown them in the lake."[3]

In spite of Chibisa's deceit, Livingstone did not drop him. He was his only influential ally in an otherwise hostile region – Livingstone still did not know how equivocal Chibisa's position was; and what was perhaps even more important, Chibisa's village lay at a strategic position for his launch to anchor, and for the setting up of a base camp, from which to explore the Highlands.

From the Murchison cataracts, Livingstone and Kirk went on foot to find a smaller lake which, they had been told, was only some forty miles away. This area was inhabited by the Ajawa, who acted as middlemen for Arab slave traders operating further north. They were just as hostile as the Mang'anja, although in one village the chief, who had stopped all trade, was prepared to have dealings with the Englishmen at a good price. According to Kirk, "One man has attached himself to us. He is rather mad, but seems very willing to go on. He speaks of a hill called Dzomba from which when young he saw a great lake with a river running to the east and what he thought the Shire, coming from it and going south. . . . The people fall upon our madman guide and abuse him for going to shew us the way, so that he goes off and we hear no more of him."[4]

After some three weeks' trouble with the Ajawa, whose chiefs and headmen tried to swindle or extract money from Livingstone, they found Lake Shirwa. First they caught glimpses of it, and then on April 18, at 10 a.m. they stood by its shore, and watched its shimmering water. Livingstone made only one entry in his journal: "Reach Lake Shirua." Kirk wrote a detailed description, ending, "To the North it was open and nothing but a blue water horizon meeting the sky was to be seen, with the tops of two mountains beyond it. These were said to be islands."

After a few days' rest, they returned to the *Ma-Robert*, and the Zambezi, for now Livingstone was sure that the big lake so many people had talked about was what he was looking for. The Ajawa told him that north of Lake Shirwa "you pass over a flat no more than we passed this morning, and then begins Lake Ninyessi, or the

Avoiding cataracts

Lake of Storms, called also Musingogwa, or Nanja Noghulu, which goes on so far north that they never heard of anyone who reached the end of it. The River Shire comes from it."[5] Livingstone wanted the whole expedition to be present at this important discovery, so they returned to Tete to fetch his companions and more supplies.

It was late August 1859, when Livingstone and his party set out north from the Murchison cataracts. It took them three weeks to cover the first hundred miles of the two hundred mile journey to Lake Nyasa. By the time they started climbing into the Highlands, they were tired and irritable. Livingstone himself was deeply upset; it had now dawned on him that slavers were operating freely in this fertile and healthy land. No wonder villagers were terrified of strangers; he and his companions had seen a party of slaves being led by Arabs, and at many points of the path they were following, they stumbled over piles of sticks, with forked ends, for securing the slaves' necks. In midst of such conditions, how were English colonists to create cotton-fields and sugar plantations, and administer entire areas? Livingstone knew that there would be serious difficulties, and that he would be blamed if things went seriously wrong. But he had no alternative – if he failed to bring missionaries and settlers to the Shire Highlands, his work in Africa would have been wasted, as there was no other place that he knew of along a navigable river that ran into the sea. Without such communications, missions and settlements had no chance.

With all these worries besetting him, when he reached the magnificent Lake Nyasa, the second largest in Africa, Livingstone merely noted in his *Journal*: "17th Sept. Reached Lake Nyassa from which the Shire emerges."[6]

Apart from slavery, the very important question weighing on Livingstone's mind was whether he was the first European to discover the Lake? He had no idea that a 22 year old German, Albrecht Roscher, travelling as an Arab, was also advancing towards the lake. The exiled king of Bavaria had commissioned him to investigate the rumours about the inland seas in the centre of Africa. Roscher was inexperienced, he operated on a minute budget and wasted much time in Zanzibar trying to engage porters. He decided to join an Arab caravan setting out for the interior to hunt slaves. The Arabs robbed and maltreated him, and he was continuously ill with fever. Yet he struggled on, and when he came to the village of Nusewa – the modern Lusefa – he had the supreme satisfaction of seeing the blue waters of Lake Nyasa. Roscher remained by the lake to explore its eastern shore – and heard accidentally that a party of white men had arrived before him at the southern end. Livingstone had beaten him by 72 days. Poor, forgotten Roscher. In March 1860, he began the long march back to the coast, leaving behind his heavier load and personal journals, which have never been recovered. Three days later he was murdered for the sake of his scanty possessions near the lake at Kisoon-goonie.

If Livingstone was not in a position to worry about Roscher, he was plagued with anxiety lest Cardoso had forestalled him. Cardoso had told him of the large lake he had visited in 1846; Livingstone had relayed the information to friends, and reported it in *Missionary Travels*. Yet Livingstone's own subsequent writings clearly demonstrate that he was determined to prove that he was the first European to visit the lake and had no intention of giving Cardoso credit for the useful information he had provided, as that would have meant admitting that Cardoso had been there before him.[7] In view of his earlier recognition of Cardoso in what he had written in *Missionary Travels*, the only course Livingstone could adopt was to discredit the man by proving that his account, in which there were discrepancies, was a tissue of lies, and that on the most charitable interpretation, the Portuguese had visited a different lake altogether. The trouble was that he could not put a name to this other lake.

Livingstone's case was that Cardoso had said that canoes were punted across a "broad and shallow lake" with "a strong current" from which "two rivers issue forth", in whose centre there was a hilly island called Murombola, and "which lay 45 days N.N.W. of Tete." He, Livingstone, could testify on the basis of having seen for himself that every one of these statements was wrong. Lake Nyasa, to which he and his party had been, was narrow and far too deep for punting; it had no current; it was drained by a single river; the mountain called Morumbala – which clearly Cardoso meant – lay not in the lake but two hundred miles away, near the confluence of the Shire and the Zambezi – as anyone who went there could see. Finally instead of being "45 days to the N.N.W. of Tete", Lake Nyasa was north-east and only 150 miles away.

In the uncritical atmosphere of hero worship which surrounded the name of Livingstone, the world was only too willing to believe the doctor – there were after all several Englishmen in his party to bear witness to him. In any event, no one had ever heard about this unknown Portuguese. John Kirk's diary might have given food for thought to some of Livingstone's biographers, but it was only published in 1965. And none of David Livingstone's admirers took the trouble to go to Tete to find out whether Cardoso had been in a position to go to Lake Nyasa, and what the local inhabitants knew about the whole affair.

Oliver Ransford, who spent years in Nyasaland, was the first to make a thorough topographical study of Lake Nyasa, Lake Shirwa and Lake Malombe. He drew attention to three facts: Livingstone was not fluent in Portuguese and may have misinterpreted some of Cardoso's statements. There had been an unusual number of earthquakes between 1846 when Cardoso visited the Lake, and 1859, when Livingstone went there, added to which cyclical variations in the water level may have altered the appearance of Lake Nyasa and its appendage, Lake Malombe.[8] Cardoso – like the Africans of today – regarded Nyanja Grande as a single unit made up of Lake Nyasa, Lake Malombe, and the Shire river, while Livingstone, and the geographers who followed him, saw them as three separate entities.

This is the conclusion Ransford reached: "The only part which conforms to Candido's description of his crossing place as being surrounded by 'level plains covered with grass' is that shallow portion we now call Lake Malombe and which he considered to be an integral part of the 'Nyanja Grande': this can easily be punted across, and in it there is an appreciable current. Thus Livingstone's most damaging piece of criticism is disposed of at once."[9]

Then there was Cardoso's statement about a hilly island in the centre of the lower end of the lake. We know on Sir Harry Johnston's authority that an island once stood in the centre of Lake Malombe, exactly where Cardoso had drawn it. Livingstone said, on the basis of a conversation carried on in Portuguese, without anyone else present, that when Cardoso spoke of an island called Murombola, he clearly meant a mountain called Morumbola, which was 200 miles away, and consequently assumed that the elephant marsh at the mountain's foot would be Lake Nyasa. According to Mr Ransford, this assumption "was prompted by the name Morombala (so similar to Morumbala) which Livingstone had written beside the island on Candido's sketch map. But in his account of the meeting, Livingstone notes that the island is also called Murombo, while Kirk wrote of it as Marumbo after questioning Candido on the subject. The likelihood is that Candido was speaking of Malombe, which Bocarro had called Moromba."[10]

Cardoso's apparent error in saying that Lake Nyasa was drained by two rivers, was also based on a misunderstanding. When talking to Kirk he said, "No river flows out of it, it [meaning the lake] is merely expanded." Ransford goes on: "Nothing could have been much closer to the facts. This still leaves Candido's misleading information about the distance and direction of the lake from Tete to be explained. But he never seems to have told how he reached Lake Nyasa."[11]

Livingstone never asked Cardoso – as we know, he did not have another talk with him – so Cardoso never told him. In view of the roundabout route the Portuguese followed,[12] it may well have been 500 miles and 45 days. Ransford's final argument is that on his map Cardoso correctly named the Shire as the outlet of the lake, and precisely identified the Cewa (Shiva) and the Yao inhabiting its opposite shores.

Livingstone got away with his contention that he was the first European to have seen Lake Nyasa. But in view of the considerable evidence the Portuguese provided for him, it is certain that others had been there before him. To Silva Porto Livingstone showed a Portuguese map, which shows that he was well aware that the Portuguese had visited central Africa. In other words, Livingstone must have known that his claim was untrue. What he did not know was that Cardoso was a half-caste.

The light this story throws on Livingstone's character is a different matter. It is on a par with his refusal to recognise Cotton Oswell's explorations, with his lies about Silva Porto being a half-caste slave trader, and about the non-existence of László Magyar. Oswell was such a generous personality that he did not care; Silva Porto published an indignant rebuttal when he heard of Livingstone's slanders; Magyar, totally unknown in the west, would have been very unhappy had he found out that Livingstone, his hero, pretended never to have heard of him. Cardoso knew of Livingstone's untrue statements, and never got over the fact that his friend should have betrayed him.

Livingstone's pathological determination to be "the first" in whatever part of Africa he explored – regardless of truth, other peoples' feelings or reputations – was one of his greatest faults. For nearly a hundred years his reputation of being the most eminent Africa explorer, went unchallenged. Oliver Ransford, as described above, was the first writer to query the Cardoso story; Tim Jeal in his book

*Livingstone* placed the doctor's record under very detailed analysis, and thoroughly reassessed his character. One of Livingstone's gravest shortcomings was his obstinate belief that he knew best where missionaries should go – ignoring not only advice, but discounting risks. At the time of the Shire expeditions, a tragedy was taking place which illustrated the consequences of his stubborn conceit. Livingstone only came to hear about it a year later.

## CHAPTER EIGHTEEN

# Disastrous missions

It will be recalled that, earlier, David Livingstone had pressurised Dr Tidman and the LMS to send a mission to the Makololo.[1] Tidman had little confidence in the project, especially when Livingstone opted out of it; Dr Moffat, when he heard about it, called it sheer lunacy. But under the threat of adverse publicity the mission was duly sent out, and arrived in Cape Town at the end of 1858. Then it headed post haste towards Linyanti so as not to miss Livingstone. How the misunderstanding ever arose that he was waiting for the missionaries in the Makololo capital, will probably never be known. Livingstone had certainly not promised that he would be there in February 1859. On March 6, 1858, he had written to Tidman: "Should they (the missionaries) come through Mosilikatze's country to the Zambezi to a point below the Victoria Falls where our steam-launch will be of any service to them, my companions will readily lend their aid in crossing the river."

The Mission was led by Holloway Helmore, accompanied by his wife and four children; Robert Price with his wife and baby; John Mackenzie, the third missionary, had to stay behind as his pregnant wife fell seriously ill. Helmore knew that February was the worst possible month for "the fever", but he was also aware of the importance of Livingstone introducing them to the Makololo. The party reached Linyanti on February 19, and had a very unfriendly reception from Sekeletu, who had no use for a group of tired people who spoke of God, and did not even know of Livingstone's movements. Sekeletu's only concern was that he wanted a member of Robert Moffat's family to live with him as a protection against attack by Mzilikazi. Besides, Livingstone had promised to bring back his men within a year, and now four years had passed, and they still had not returned. He had promised him trade and wealth, and Sekeletu had turned away several traders from the south, waiting for Livingstone's

traders to paddle up the Zambezi. Sekeletu vented his displeasure on
the missionaries who were quite unprepared for the treatment that
was to be meted out to them by the Makololo.

Livingstone depicted writing his Journals

In his writings, Livingstone had passed in silence over the tribe's
less attractive characteristics. When the missionaries asked
Sekeletu's permission to move to a healthier area from the fever
infested valley, Sekeletu took away Helmore's wagon, and his men
robbed the missionaries of most of their possessions. Malaria did the
rest – within two months Mr and Mrs Helmore, Mrs Price and three
out of the five children were dead. Roger Price and the two Helmore

orphans had to start on a thousand mile return journey with few provisions, and no means to pay the toll that was demanded of them at every drift[2] they came to. But for their meeting with John Mackenzie, the missionary who stayed behind with his sick wife, Price himself would not have lived to tell his terrible tale.

Livingstone heard the story when he brought back twenty of the Makololo to Linyanti in the autumn of 1860.[3] What passed between him and Sekeletu is not known; but that he must have found out most of the facts can be deduced from a letter his brother Charles wrote to a friend in 1862: "I have no doubt that he [Sekeletu] treated the mission body badly. . . . I suspected at the time that he stole from Mr Price. . . . Mr Price was no doubt very much frightened, and they seeing this, took advantage and plundered him. I believe they would have treated us the same way had we been afraid of them."[4]

Livingstone was aware that he would be blamed for the disaster. His first letter to Tidman contained one unfortunate passage. After a few words of condolences he went on: "At the very time when our friends were helplessly perishing, we were at a lower and a much more unhealthy part of the river, and curing the complaint so quickly that in very severe cases the patient was able to resume march on foot a day or so after the operation of the remedy." When in reply Tidman enquired why Livingstone had not told him of this efficacious medicine, the doctor retorted that he had mentioned it in *Missionary Travels* (in one sentence towards the end), and it was contrary to medical etiquette to advertise a medicine before it had been properly tested.

But worse was Livingstone's attitude to Roger Price. The doctor made out that the Makololo had taken very kindly to Helmore – who was not alive to comment or contradict. "They wished to get acquainted with him," wrote Livingstone, "a very natural desire before removing to the Highlands, and hence the delay that ended so fatally."[5] Livingstone went on to say that the Makololo had resented Price who had antagonised them – on one occasion he had kicked a man, on another he had tied a Makololo to a wheel of his wagon, and even threatened people with his revolver. Livingstone never produced any proof that Price had done any of these things; he ended his letter by telling the Directors he hoped they would not be cowardly enough to leave the field because of an initial setback. "Judicious missionaries" could set up a flourishing mission.[6]

Price's amazement that Livingstone accepted Sekeletu's version of what had occurred can be imagined. On top of everything he had had the horrifying experience of seeing the Makololo dig out his wife's body, cut off her head, put it on a pole and take it to Sekeletu. And now Livingstone was saying that missionary activity would suffer because a handful of "stupid and culpably negligent men had allowed themselves to die." Livingstone even said – and this was untrue – that Helmore had not written to him because he had wanted to do everything on his own. "A precious mull they made of it."[7] By this time Livingstone knew that Helmore had rushed to Linyanti during a month dangerous from a fever point of view specifically in order to see him; and he surely remembered his own letter to Tidman, in which he said that there was no point in his meeting Helmore, as he had nothing to tell him.

In his *Narrative of an Expedition to the Zambezi* Livingstone condensed his account of the tragedy into two pages, which cannot be read without embarrassment. He did not name Price – referring to him as Helmore's missionary associate; he mentioned a party of nine Europeans, which sounded better than two missionaries, two wives and five children. Livingstone implied that the missionaries arrived already ill, which was not true and he must have known it. He never mentioned that he had had any connection with the sending of the mission, or that he had refused to be its leader. The theft of the missionaries' goods was omitted; he even implied that Price had given Helmore's wagon to Sekeletu, with no consideration for Helmore's orphans. Livingstone even blamed Tidman for not sending a doctor, and not providing the missionaries with adequate medicines. When Price said in Cape Town that Livingstone had known that without river communications no mission could survive in Barotseland, Livingstone accused him of lying and cowardice.

Tim Jeal has summed up Livingstone's role in most clear terms: "Livingstone had deliberately maligned innocent people for whose deaths he had been partially responsible, in order to escape the slur of having misrepresented the true situation in Barotseland. He never showed regret for his behaviour nor did he ever exhibit any trace of remorse for having maliciously maligned and slandered Roger Price, a man who had just suffered the horrifying tragedy of losing his wife and only child – a baby. There are other blots on Livingstone's reputation, but none would be greater than his response to the Makololo disaster."[8]

In England there was no national outcry over the tragic fate of the missionaries. The news trickled through gradually; many people neither grasped the details, nor even the number of the dead – least of all did they know that three of them were small children. But there was to be a very different reaction to the fate of the University Mission to Central Africa, UMCA, led by the Anglican Bishop, Charles Frederick Mackenzie. The UMCA was formed in direct response to Livingstone's appeal to the students at Oxford and other universities and it left England in a blaze of publicity. When the tragedy struck, fate presented a far higher bill to Livingstone than he received for the Makololo mission.

When Livingstone and his party arrived back in Tete from Linyanti, there was mail and news. The Foreign Secretary turned down Livingstone's suggestion for establishing a colony, but he extended the period of the mission for another three years. The replacement Livingstone had requested for the *Ma-Robert* was on the way, but there would be no contribution to a ship for Lake Nyasa, for which Livingstone would have to pay from what was left of the royalties of *Missionary Travels*. Finally – and this was most exciting – the UMCA mission under Bishop Mackenzie was due to arrive in January 1861. Livingstone understood the political significance of an Anglican Bishop being sent; a bishopric created in an area not in British possession, was a quasi claim to the area. Indeed, it was for this reason that Lord John Russell had opposed Mackenzie's consecration; he wanted no show-down with the Portuguese – after all, the UMCA Mission, as well as Livingstone and his party, were operating in territory claimed by Portugal, even if the Shire country had never been occupied, let alone administered, by the Portuguese.

Livingstone was very much aware of the disintegrating forces at work in the Shire Lowlands and Highlands. He had seen the slave traders in action; he knew that Portuguese and Arab slavers were stepping up their operations, and that the Mang'anja and the Ajawa were fighting a tribal war against each other. What he did not know was that the social order was also breaking up and a social revolution was taking place, in which the Chewa speaking Mang'anja were in the process of shaking off their Phiri-Marawi overlords, the chiefly aristocracy that had ruled them for five centuries.[9] Tengani and Mankhokve could have explained this to Livingstone – they were resisting their own headmen on the one hand, and the slavers on the other. However, personal animosity ruled out the possibility of frank discussion between Livingstone and these two traditional chiefs. Cardoso also knew what was happening in the Shire country.

Slave raids, civil war, social revolution – hardly the Arcadian situation Livingstone had described in his lectures in England. Had he subsequently admitted that the situation had changed, the UMCA mission would not have come, let alone English colonists, and all his work in Africa would have been in vain. Yet owing to the misleadingly optimistic pictures he had painted, matters went wrong, and an Anglican Bishop, a dignitary of the Established Church, came to grief. Livingstone wrote to the Secretary of the UMCA, to warn the missionaries against the difficulties they would have to face, but he put all dangers down to the slave traders' activities.

Bishop Mackenzie and his party arrived on February 7, 1861, at the Kongone mouth of the Zambezi, where Livingstone, his brother Charles and Dr Kirk were waiting for them. All three took immediately to the Bishop, a brilliant scholar and athlete, who had done missionary work among the Zulu in Natal. Mackenzie was lively and easy-going, but even he was taken aback when Livingstone informed him that he would have to wait three months before starting his missionary work. The doctor, worried over the possibility that the antagonistic Portuguese might close the Zambezi and Shire rivers to transport, wanted to find out whether the Rowuma river had its source in Lake Nyasa, and could serve as an alternate route to the sea. Captain Crauford of HMS *Sidon* (on which the Bishop had come out) told him that the Rowuma was navigable for only 45 miles, and in low water for 30 miles. But Livingstone wanted to see for himself.

It was April by the time the *Pioneer* – the replacement for the *Ma-Robert* – which the *Sidon* had brought out in tow, was loaded with supplies, and 48 men had been squeezed into quarters intended for twenty. The *Pioneer* started up the Zambezi on May 1, 1861; soon she was stuck on sandbanks and mudflats, and had to be dragged with ropes and winches. It was the *Ma-Robert* story all over again. The missionaries were struck down with fever, and experienced the difference between malaria and a common cold. On July 8, 1861, they sighted the Murchison Cataracts; on July 15 Livingstone set out with the Bishop and his party on a 70 mile trek to Magomero, the village he had selected as the centre for their work.

There was a little trouble when the African porters dawdled, and the Bishop, unused to this hazard of African travel at that time, poked them with his crozier. But the next day – July 16 – they came up against a party of 84 slaves, their heads held in forked slave-sticks. The slave drivers ran away; Mackenzie and the others felt greatly elated as they watched the poor wretches being freed from their shackles, and heard, through an interpreter, of their dreadful experiences. Only Livingstone knew that the Ajawa would not take this lying down – moreover, the 84 liberated slaves would have to be fed. By the time they arrived at Magomero, the Bishop's party had 150 people on its hands.

Then there was the question of arms. Livingstone advised the missionaries to carry guns, which he regarded as the best means of deterring attack. Mackenzie hated the idea of holding a crozier in one hand, and a gun in the other. In Magomero, Livingstone received ample information that the Ajawa were preparing to attack a Mang'anja village ten miles away. Now he had to tell the Bishop of the tribal war that was going on. On July 22 they decided to go and watch the Ajawa raid. Having passed several burning villages, suddenly they saw a long line of Ajawa warriors, herding numerous captives. The Ajawa pelted them with poisoned arrows – thereupon Livingstone gave the order to fire – the Bishop handed him his rifle, and the doctor blasted away. They routed the Ajawa, at least six of whom were killed. Then Livingstone led them into the Ajawa town and set it on fire.

Three days later Livingstone called a meeting of Mang'anja chiefs, and Mackenzie believed that he pledged himself and the Mission to give them protection. The Bishop had already decided that when it came to liberating slaves, or protecting villages, the use of firearms was justified. The thin dividing line between offensive and defensive use of arms was not fully elucidated when Livingstone left for Lake Nyasa. On his return in November he heard that the Bishop had twice led an attack on the Ajawa, without even waiting for them to attack. Livingstone had a very good idea of what the British public would think of missionaries "coming out to convert people shooting them."[10] He asked the Bishop "to say as little as possible about it at home." But the Bishop had already sent a full, detailed account, and Henry Rowley, the Bishop's deacon, had published an article in a Cape Town newspaper, saying that the attacks had been in response to Dr Livingstone's first fight against the Ajawa.

So Livingstone also wrote a number of letters, dissociating himself from the Bishop, whom he blamed for the fighting. Moreover he would not accept the Bishop's contention that in a situation of chaos the Mission could not function. As there was no one to restore order, he had taken it upon himself to do this. To make his own disapproval

Surprising a slaver

Notes and sketch map from Livingstone's diary of the area around Lakes Bengweolo and Moero.

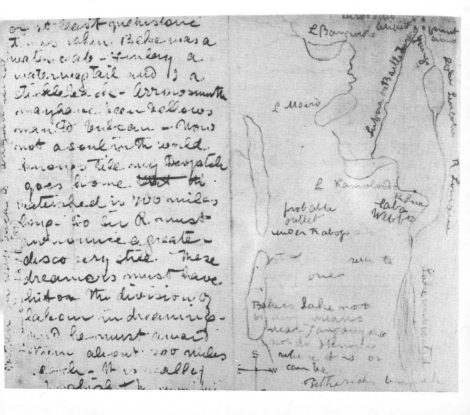

even more pointed, Livingstone refused to let the Mission use the *Pioneer* any longer, telling the Bishop that his men would have to find an overland route to the Ruo river.

Letter from Livingstone to Sir Roderick Murchison

And then came news that Mary Livingstone, the Bishop's sister and Henry Burrup's bride[11] were coming out on the next ship, soon due at Kongone. Livingstone sailed down the Shire and the Zambezi to meet them. The Bishop would have liked to come with him, but

Livingstone persuaded him that in such an explosive situation it was his duty to remain in Magomero.

The two members of the Mission, Lovell Procter and H. C. Scudamore, whom the Bishop sent to open a suitable path to the Ruo, were attacked, robbed and their followers captured. They were lucky to escape with their lives. The Bishop organised a punitive expedition, which was not really successful – all the tribes having, by now, become antagonistic to the Mission. A path to the Ruo was, therefore, out of the question. The Bishop decided to go, with Henry Burrup, to wait for Livingstone at the confluence of the Ruo and the Shire. The two men were already ill when they left Magomero; then their canoe was upset, they got soaked and they lost their medicines. Without medicines or decent food, their health deteriorated, and on January 31 the first Bishop of Central Africa drew his last breath. Burrup managed to drag himself back to Magomero, to die there on February 14, 1862.

Meanwhile HMS *Hetty Ellen* arrived at the Kongone, with the three ladies, their maids, and the *Lady Nyasa*, Livingstone's ship for the Lake, in pieces. She was to be assembled in Shupanga, sailed to the Murchison cataracts, taken apart and carried to the Upper Shire, there to be re-assembled. The journey to Shupanga was far from happy – Mrs Livingstone was very different from the placid, submissive woman her husband had known in the past. She had few kind words for missionaries; she was full of concern over her children, especially her son Thomas. Livingstone feared that she had lost her faith. Actually, he should have worried more about her heavy drinking. Miss Mackenzie was an invalid, and had to be assisted at every move she made.[12] Mrs Burrup was sweet but bewildered by it all. When they reached the Ruo there was no sign of the Bishop, or of anyone else from Magomero; only on March 3 did Livingstone discover that the Bishop had died. Poor Mrs Burrup had to endure another week of uncertainty. Kirk and Wilson took the two ladies back to Shupanga, from where eventually they made their way home.

Livingstone's letters to the Foreign Secretary and various friends were as insensitive about the Bishop's "responsibility for his own death" as they had been about Roger Price. Only when Livingstone heard, belatedly, that Dr Pusey[13] attacked him and the missionaries for having denied themselves a martyr's death by using firearms, did he change his attitude, and began to pay glowing tribute to the noble bishop.

Eventually Livingstone took the bereaved women to the Zambezi delta himself, and then went on to Shupanga, where his wife caught the fever. She did not respond to any treatment; she was given so much quinine that she became deaf. For eight days Livingstone did not move from her bedside, and watched her getting steadily worse. When he realised that she was going to die, he was utterly broken and wept like a child. Taking her into his arms, he choked: "My dearie, my dearie, you are going to leave me. . . . Are you resting on Jesus?" The thought of her dying without believing in God agonised him. This time he admitted that he had not given her a home for ten years and had not helped her with the education of the children.

Mary Livingstone died on April 27, 1862, and was buried under a large baobab tree, now on the sugar estate of the Hornung family. She was 41 years old. James Stewart[14] conducted the service. No sooner was it over than Livingstone went on with his work. In two months the *Lady Nyasa* was assembled, and in tow to the *Pioneer* she was on her way to the Shire. But the expedition was disintegrating. Only George Rae had stayed on. At the mission station in Magomero H. C. Scudamore and John Dickinson, the doctor, both died of the fever.

Bishop William George Tozer was sent out to replace Bishop Mackenzie, and he was convinced that the mission would have to be withdrawn. When he learnt of the death of Scudamore and Dickinson, he wanted to speed up the process. To avoid the accusation of cowardice, he decided to give the mission a final trial further south, on Mount Morambala, at the junction of the Shire and the Zambezi. It was an unsuitable place, although Livingstone had, in 1859, described it as "ideal for a sanatorium and possibly a college" which the Portuguese had been mad not to utilise.[15] But when Tozer took the mission there, Livingstone had something completely different to say: "A mountain 4,000 feet high, where clouds rest perpetually at some season and the condensed vapour drips constantly through the roofs of huts."[16] This was a much more accurate description than what he had said in 1859, although, when Tozer asked Livingstone's opinion, he had said that while not as good as the Shire Highlands, it was not a bad choice.

When, in June 1863, Tozer eventually decided to withdraw the Mission altogether (he moved it to Zanzibar), Livingstone flew into a rage. Apart from the libellous letters he wrote about Tozer to the Foreign Office and to friends, he said in *A Narrative Of An Expedi-*

*tion To The Zambezi*: "The Mission in fleeing from Morambala to an island in the Indian Ocean acted as though St Augustine would have done had he located himself on one of the Channel Islands when sent to christianise the inhabitants of Central England."[17]

Livingstone would have liked to leave at once when he got the Foreign Office orders of recall on July 3, 1863, although they had been signed on February 4 of that year. But he had to wait until the end of 1863, when the water would rise again. To pass the time, and to show that he was no idler, although emaciated and looking deadly ill, in September and October 1863, he walked seven hundred miles along the western shore of Lake Nyasa, a remarkable feat for a man in his state of health. And when he reached the Zambezi delta, he sent the *Pioneer* to Cape Town, but he sailed the *Lady Nyasa* to Zanzibar – one thousand miles away. As he could not get a fair price for her there, he sailed her another 2,800 miles to Bombay,[18] from where he returned to England.

As Livingstone brought the Makololo to Tete, and later settled sixteen, who had come with him from Linyanti in 1860, in the heart of the Shire country, the end of their story should be briefly told. Only twenty of the original 114 elected to return to Linyanti. They were the unlucky ones for in 1865 the oppressed Lozi and allied tribes rose against their Makololo rulers, and massacred them. Those who had remained in Tete, Livingstone later settled in Chibisa's village of Chikwawa.

Here the Makololo became headmen in their own right, and lived luxuriously on the produce of their lush river gardens during the 1862 famine, which decimated the Mang'anja population. Because of their lack of discipline, Livingstone and the UMCA missionaries disowned the Makololo. When they had all left, chaos threatened to engulf everything. Then the Makololo faced the same decision as Bishop Mackenzie had: either they restored order, or they would be engulfed themselves. They decided to do the former, in their own way. In the words of Father Schoffeleers: "In a series of swift strokes and aided by Yao gunmen and Mang'anja retainers, they first secured the defences to the south and west and then proceeded to the systematic extermination of the Mang'anja chiefs. Kapichi, Mgundo Kaphviti and Lundu were among the first victims; soon it was the turn of Chibisa and Tengani.[19] Only Mankhokve proved unconquerable for a number of years, but finally he too was defeated. . . . The Makololo destroyed the aristocratic leadership, together with their shrines, but they spared the senior headmen. . . . Their absolute rule lasted only a quarter of a century, but this was long enough to see the English return and the country of the Mang'anja become a British Protectorate."[20]

Thus the Makololo saved the Mang'anja, for without them they would have been wiped out. In the last resort it was Livingstone who had provided the ruthless force needed to unite the Mang'anja to survive until the day when they could again rule themselves.

# Part Four

## CHAPTER NINETEEN

# Disappointments and disillusions

The last eight years of David Livingstone's life were a series of disappointments and disillusions. Owing to a shortcut in his journey across Africa, he by-passed the Cabora Bassa cataracts, and failed to discover that the Zambezi could not become God's Highway. Yet all his great plans depended on its navigability and the promises and possibilities he propounded in England were thus completely misleading.

In 1858, when he was back with an official expedition, Livingstone realised his mistake. Had he then been frank with the Foreign Office, or at least with Sir Roderick Murchison who was devoted to him, something might have been worked out. Unhappily, pride prevented frankness. Livingstone had to succeed; he had to find a substitute for the Batoka Plateau. The Shire Highlands were a reasonable substitute – but not under the then prevailing conditions. If Lord John Russell, or Sir Roderick Murchison, had had any idea of the slave trade which Livingstone himself had promoted by breaking the blockade of the four chiefs, of the tribal wars, and the social fragmentation that was taking place, they would not have allowed a single missionary, let alone a settler, to go out. Livingstone had to keep these unpleasant facts from them.

There was a grim fatalism about all this: one mistake, for which Livingstone could not be blamed, destroyed his chief aim in Africa. With his character, in order to save his life's work, he was bound to prevaricate, and lie. His determination, his endurance, his courage – all his great qualities – were used for a false purpose.

When he returned to England in July 1864, the general public ignored him. Thanks to Sir Roderick Murchison he was, however, taken up by high society and clearly enjoyed it. Within a few hours of his arrival in London, Livingstone noted in his diary: "Sir Roderick took me off with him, just as I was, to Lady Palmerston's reception.

My Lady was very gracious. Spoke to Duke and Duchess of Somer-
set. All say very polite things, and all wonderfully considerate." On
the next day he wrote: "Got a dress suit at Nicol & Co. and dined
with Lord and Lady Dunmore, very clever and intelligent man, and
lady very sprightly. Thence to Duchess of Wellington's reception. A
grand company – magnificent rooms. ... Ladies wonderfully
beautiful – rich and rare were the gems they wore." On the third day:
"See Lord Russell – his manner is very cold as all the Russells are.
[This he must have heard from Sir Roderick Murchison, he could not
have known it.] Received invitation from the Lord Mayor to dine
with her Majesty's Ministers."

And more of this until he went to Scotland, where the ordinary
people had not forgotten him, and resentment over the death of
Bishop Mackenzie was not as great as in Anglican England.
Livingstone's almost childish enjoyment of aristocratic circles in
London is partly explained by the sense of inferiority that had stayed
with him throughout his life. Yet he was very conscious of the position he had achieved – in his letters to his children, especially when
castigating Thomas, he often said that all Thomas wanted to do was
to bask in his father's glory as a famous explorer. Poor Thomas had
in fact changed his name so as not to bring shame on his famous
father, enlisted in the Federal Army in the American Civil War and
died of his wounds.

Livingstone was immensely proud of the long way he had gone
from the Blantyre textile factory. It is sad that on his second return,
when he had such a success with the high and mighty, he did not find
time for months to see either Dr Kirk or Rae.

The Foreign Secretary, Lord John Russell, had received him, but
he only appointed Livingstone "Consul to 25 Independent Chiefs"
without salary or pension rights. Murchison's intercession did not
help until much later – two months after Livingstone's death, on
June 19, 1873, he was granted a pension of £300 a year.

The Royal Geographical Society commissioned him to find the
sources of the Nile, but they only gave him a miserly £500 (the same
amount the Government had offered him) and set conditions Livingstone regarded as humiliating, such as handing over, on his return,
all his notes to the Society. Had it not been for the generosity of
James Young, the inventor of paraffin, whom he first met as a student in Glasgow, and who gave him £1,000, he could not even have
gone back to Africa. Yet he could not have stayed in England either;

he could not bear to be a failure, and he knew that the Foreign Office regarded him as such. Moreover *The Times* had written harshly about the Zambezi and Shire expeditions: "We were promised cotton, sugar and indigo . . . and of course we got none. We were promised trade; and there is no trade. . . . We were promised converts and not one has been made. In a word the thousands contributed by the Government have been productive only of the most fatal results."[1] Some were suggesting that the famous doctor should marry a rich widow and live on the laurels of his *traversa*.

And there were further humiliations. Livingstone had to promise Lord John Russell to keep away from any territory owned or claimed by the Portuguese; not to make promises to chiefs that might embarrass the government; not to allow himself to be made prisoner, since if the government could not rescue him, other explorers might be put in jeopardy. Livingstone was deeply offended by the terms of his appointment: to the end of his life they outraged him, and in his letters he repeatedly referred to "the most exuberant impertinence that ever issued from the Foreign Office."[2]

As he had broken with the LMS, Livingstone could not go to Africa as a missionary, although he still felt himself to be an instrument of The Lord. He did not want to be just another explorer, so he determined to investigate thoroughly the slave trade and force the government to take more action, if not on the seas then on land. This was another failure to face up to reality, as Livingstone understood perfectly that British foreign policy made a distinction between slavery along Africa's West Coast, where Europeans, and Englishmen in numbers, had been involved; and on the east coast, where the trade was entirely in Arab and Indian hands, with African cooperation. Lord John Russell told Livingstone that if Britain leaned too heavily on the Sultan of Zanzibar, this would only benefit the French and the Germans. Nonetheless, Livingstone intended to force the government to take action on the mainland against the East African slave trade.

To retrieve his own reputation, he would find the sources of the Nile. He hated Richard Burton[3] – not surprisingly as their views and principles were diametrically opposed. For John Speke he had great respect; corresponded with him and anticipated meeting him. Yet he would not go to any part of Africa in which these two men had operated. His reasoning, that the source of the Nile had to be much further south than where Burton and Speke had looked for it, was not illogical. But again a mistake ruined his chances. He refused to accept Sir Roderick Murchison's advice to ascertain first of all whether a river did flow out of Lake Tanganyika into Lake Albert, and from Lake Albert into Lake Victoria. He took it for granted that this river existed, and had its source somewhere near a lake he had heard mentioned by the natives, called "Bemba" or "Bengweolo". This river did not exist.

On August 13, 1865, Livingstone left England for the last time and sailed to Bombay. He stayed for three months with the Governor, Sir Bartle Frere, a good friend, strongly opposed to slavery. He was very much in official society, which he obviously enjoyed. He looked stouter, better and healthier than a year before. The *Lady Nyasa* had still not been disposed of; when she was eventually sold, the money was put into a bank that failed and Livingstone never saw a penny. With nine liberated slaves educated at Nassick, thirteen Sepoys of the Bombay Marine Battalion, Susi, Amoda, Chuma and Wikatani, he arrived in Zanzibar to purchase supplies and engaged ten Johanna men.[4] On March 19, 1866, HMS *Penguin* landed him at Mikindani, a port just north of the Rowuma. From then on nothing was to go right.

First, because of the Ngoni wars, Livingstone could not obtain the additional porters he needed; sixty-two porters was a minimum requirement; most explorers would not set out without ninety. Local Africans would not sign up because they were afraid of being captured and killed or sold into slavery. Second, he happened to have struck a part of what is today Tanzania covered in thick jungle, and a way had to be hacked not only for his men, but for his three buffalos and a calf, six camels, four donkeys and two mules. He wanted to know how these animals would react to the tse-tse fly. But the Sepoys treated them so brutally that when they did die, Livingstone could not tell whether this was due to their festering wounds, or to tse-tse bites.

Two hundred miles inland, he ran into almost famine conditions, partly owing to the drought, partly to Ngoni marauders. The Sepoys dawdled and pilfered, and ate one of the buffaloes. Livingstone could not establish his authority. The Sepoys were eventually sent back.

When Livingstone reached Lake Nyasa, the local Arabs refused to let him have a dhow, and he had to walk around its northern shore. This was too much for some of the remaining Africans, who deserted, leaving Livingstone with only eleven men. Then he fell ill with severe diarrhoea and fever. Yet more blows were in store. The porter who carried his precious chronometers, on which he relied for establishing his position, fell and the chronometers were damaged. As a result, his observations for longitude were twenty miles too far east. Later, due to an earthquake, his chronometers were again affected, and from then on his longitudes erred fifty miles to the west. Even more serious was the desertion of the man who carried the medicine chest. Ill and weak, Livingstone was left without any medication.

Another traveller would either have retraced his steps, or sent someone to Kilwa at least for quinine and waited for his return. Not so Livingstone. He went on, to find Lake Bangweulu. The winter rains had started, and progress was unimaginably difficult. In his *Journal* Livingstone described how they battled along, showing no bitterness: "The rains as usual made us halt early. . . . We roast a little grain and boil it, to make believe it is coffee. . . . Ground all sloppy; oozes full and overflowing – feet constantly wet. Rivulets rush strongly with clear water. . . . Rivulets can only be crossed by felling a tree on the bank and letting it fall across. . . . Nothing but famine and famine prices; the people living on mushrooms and leaves. We get some elephants' meat from the people but high is no name for its condition. It is very bitter, but we used it as a relish to the maëre porridge; . . . the gravy in which we dip our porridge is like an aqueous solution of aloes, but it prevents the heartburn which the maëre causes when taken alone; . . . the want of salt makes the gnawing sensation worse."[5]

At the end of 1867 Livingstone crossed the Chambezi, but at that time he did not know that it flowed from Lake Bangweulu into Lake Mweru. He was again very ill, and the country was almost totally flooded.[6] In his desperate situation the first ray of light was his meeting with an Arab caravan, which gave him food and supplies, but more important, agreed to take letters to the coast. And these letters did arrive – one was written to Mr Seward, Consul in Zanzibar, whom Livingstone asked to send him supplies and medicines to Ujiji, a thriving Arab town on the eastern shore of Lake Tanganyika. Somehow Livingstone reached the western shore of Lake Tanganyika, which he wanted to explore and to find the river that connected it (that in his mind *had* to connect it) with Lake Albert.[7] But once more his way was blocked. There were tribal wars, and fighting between Arabs and Africans, so he had to go south. In his appalling condition of health his only chance to save himself was to take refuge at the nearest Arab settlement. This he did on May 20, 1868, and remained until August, when he joined the caravan of Tippoo Tip, a well known figure among Arab slavers, who was on his way to Lake Mweru. Livingstone was quite interested to see it, but as the Governor of Moçambique, Lacerda e Almeida, had died in Casembe in 1799,[8] and since then three expeditions from Tete had

Canoe

passed by it, there was no chance of being "the first" to discover it. Yet here Livingstone made two very important discoveries – surprisingly, he did not publicise them in a report to the Royal Geographical Society. He established that the Luapula river links Lake Bangweulu with Lake Mweru; and that from the north-western corner of Mweru a very powerful river flows northward. Livingstone was convinced that this was the Nile; he may have wanted more proof – by following its course – before presenting his great achievement to the world. But again he was thwarted: penniless, without medicines, his supplies almost exhausted, he could not set out on his exploratory journey that would have revealed to him (and to the world) that the Lualaba was the Zaire. He had to continue with

Tippoo Tip's caravan to Casembe, one of the largest trading centres in central Africa. Tippoo was to have taken him to Ujiji, but after a month he changed his mind and went on to Katanga. So Livingstone joined another Arab slaver, Muhammad bin Salim, who had to go to Ujiji. But the rains caught up with them, and with the entire country one mass of slush and mud, so deep in some places that animals could disappear in it, they made up their minds to sit it out in a village. Then suddenly Livingstone took a fantastic decision – in spite of rain, mud, poor health, and lack of supplies – he decided to go with his few remaining followers to Lake Bangweulu. Muhammad bin Salim thought him mad, implored him to stay; yet he went, and incredibly, reached Casembe in 27 days. There he joined yet another Arab, Muhammad Bogharib,[9] who was on his way to Bangweulu. Bogharib stopped ten miles from the lake; Livingstone did the last stretch on his own.

Once more Livingstone's plans were frustrated: when he reached the lake, he managed to get a canoe, but not for long enough to establish the size and shape of the lake. He thought four days would be sufficient; but the canoe was a stolen one, and after two days the Africans refused to go on. Because of the exceptionally high water level and a tree covered island that cut his vision, Livingstone misjudged both its size and shape. Had he paddled on two more hours, he would have realised his mistake.

On August 1, 1868, he rejoined Bogharib; on their way to Ujiji they passed through the village where Livingstone had left Muhammad bin Salim. Here five of Livingstone's deserters asked to be forgiven and taken back. Gently, he agreed. Bogharib and bin Salim joined caravans to go to Manyuema, which suited Livingstone very well. Soon however the Arabs were drawn into fights with Africans; they feared that this might lead to a full scale war and therefore decided to take their valuable cargo of a thousand slaves and a mountain of ivory to Ujiji. But they moved slowly and the rains set in. Exhausted by his exertions at Lake Bangweulu, Livingstone fell seriously ill. On January 7, 1869, he wrote in his *Journal*, "Cannot walk. Pneumonia of right lung, and I cough all day and all night. Spute rust of iron and bloody; distressing weakness." Then he was no longer able to write and became delirious; but for Bogharib's devoted care, he would have died.

But Bogharib was a trader and had to get to Ujiji; he had a wooden litter constructed for Livingstone, and instructed his men to carry him with utmost care. On that rough ground, however, with the best will they could not prevent jolting him from side to side; when conscious, this caused Livingstone excruciating pain. At last they reached Ujiji, and Livingstone hoped that his worst tribulations were over.

But only disappointment awaited him. Most of the supplies Seward sent had been pilfered; worst of all, his letters and medicines had disappeared. All Livingstone could do was to write to Kirk to send him more supplies, and for once, he had a lucky break. Of the 44 letters he entrusted to an Arab caravan, this one alone appears to have been delivered. Kirk complied with his request, and the stores duly reached Ujiji, although not Livingstone.

While convalescing in Ujiji, Livingstone questioned every Arab trader who passed through about the Lualaba, and they all said that it flowed north, then west; therefore it was more likely to be the Zaire than the Nile. This did not suit Livingstone's thinking; so he tried to persuade himself that the Lualaba being such a big river, somewhere further north it divided into two branches, one flowing into the Nile, the other into the Zaire; therefore the Lualaba was both the Nile and the Zaire. He still believed that Lakes Tanganyika and Albert were connected by a river he had to find.

At the end of July 1869, Livingstone set out as Bogharib's guest for the Lualaba, to plot its course. Once more a luckless chance played against him. He crossed Lake Tanganyika twenty miles north of a river called Lukuga, which flowed *out* of its western shore. Had he seen it, he would have realised that if there was a river in the north, it was likely to flow *into* Lake Tanganyika, not out of it.

This journey proved extremely slow and painful – it took a whole year for Livingstone to reach the town of Babarre, 150 miles west of Lake Tanganyika, exactly half-way between the lake and the Lualaba. The pneumonia had affected him badly, and he had difficulty in breathing; he found even three hours' walking on dry, level ground exhausting; his resistance to fever had lessened; he had dysentery and heavy anal bleeding because of his piles; finally, painful ulcers developed on his feet, and from July to October 1870, he could not move at all. He wrote in his *Journal*:[10] "If the foot were put to the ground, a discharge of bloody ichor flowed, and the same discharge happened every night with considerable pain, that prevented sleep."

But even when he got better, he could not continue his journey. Manyuema had become an ivory boom area, with Arab traders coming and going, with constant rows over prices; when Africans held out for what they considered right, the Arabs often murdered them, or set their villages on fire. When Bogharib went off trading, Livingstone was completely helpless with only three Africans – Susi,[11] Chuma and a Nassick boy, Gardner – to look after him. He was extremely unhappy to discover that the Manyuema tribesmen were apparently cannibals, who had eaten one of his own deserters, a Nassick boy called James.

As usual, Livingstone used his enforced leisure to collect information. He questioned every Arab and African about the source of the Lualaba. He did also much day-dreaming, and imagined that Moses had been in that area. He confided these thoughts to his *Journal*, and on October 25, 1870, he wrote: "I had a strong presentiment during the first three years that I should never live through the enterprise, but it weakened as I came near to the end of the journey, and an eager desire to discover any evidence of the great Moses having visited these parts bound me, spell bound me, I may say, for if I could bring to light anything to confirm the Sacred Oracles, I should not grudge one whit all the labour expended."[12]

To confirm the Sacred Oracles became a new obsession. Before leaving London, Livingstone had read all the ancient writings on the Nile, and was fascinated by Herodotus and Ptolemy. Then two Arab traders, Josut and Moenepembe by name, told him that south-west of Lake Bangweulu two sources which supplied an unnamed river (Livingstone immediately called it the Lualaba West) and flowed through an unvisited lake, joined the Lualaba several hundred miles north of Lake Mweru. To the south of these two sources were two more sources, from which flowed the Upper Zambezi and its main tributary, the Kafue. This information was correct, but unfortunately Livingstone equated it with the four fountains Herodotus had written about. Herodotus said that the scribe of the sacred city of Athene had told him that at a point midway between two hills with conical tops "are the fountains of the Nile, fountains which it is impossible to fathom: half the water runs northward into Egypt; half to the South."[13]

Ptolemy in his *Geography* said that the source of the Nile consisted of two springs situated in a range of hills which he called the Mountains of the Moon. Livingstone thought that Ptolemy had made a mistake and mentioned two sources instead of four. Now he knew that he had to visit these four sources. But how? For all practical purposes he was a captive of the Arabs. Then the unexpected happened: on February 4, 1871, ten men arrived who had been sent from the coast to Ujiji, and from there directed to join Livingstone in Manyuema. The supplies they brought were less than a quarter Livingstone had asked for; but at least he had quinine, tea, sugar, coffee, a few fathoms of cloth, and he could go on to the Lualaba on his own. At first the men refused; they demanded higher wages and were mutinous, but when he threatened to shoot their two leaders, they became amenable. On February 16, 1871, they marched north; six weeks later, at a town called Nyangwe, they reached the Lualaba.

Livingstone was much disturbed to discover that the river flowed at the same altitude as Sir Samuel Baker had given to Lake Albert, which meant that it was most unlikely that it could flow into this lake. But maybe it did join the Nile some few hundred miles further north? Local people and Arab traders assured him that the river bore north, then west; he did not wish to listen when the same answer was given again and again. But his reaction was very different when he heard that there was a fourth river, the Lomani, which flowed parallel with the Lualaba, eventually emptying into it. Here was proof – in Livingstone's mind – of the four rivers Herodotus had described: the Zambezi and the Kafue flowing south, the Lualaba and the Lomani north. He wanted to cross the Lualaba, determine its course and then go in search of the four fountains.

This time Fate stepped in, in the shape of the local Africans' irrational refusal to let him go across. The Arabs – Bogharib was away – were not helpful either. After three months' waiting, in near despair, he offered the leading Arab of Nyangwe, Dugumbe, £400 and all his stores[14] in Ujiji for one good canoe. While Dugumbe was still pondering his offer, the Nyangwe massacre took place. Livingstone's own despatch to the Foreign Office was published after his death, and his biographers have reported it in detail. Here let it suffice to say that at least 400 Africans were murdered, and as many drowned in the Lualaba trying to escape. The screams, the howls, the confusion, the terror, it was as near hell on earth as could be imagined. Sick with disgust and choked with rage against the perpetrators, Livingstone felt that he could not accept even a canoe from an Arab, and returned to Ujiji.

This time his supplies had been stolen by a rich, powerful Arab called Sherif Bosher,[15] who had invested the proceeds in ivory that was safely locked away. Bosher bribed the three principal men in the

"Dr Livingstone, I presume." Note Livingstone's left arm, injured years earlier by a lion.

Magomero

city not to give Livingstone the key, so he could not get at his rightful property. Unless Kirk helped once more, he knew that he would be dependent on Arab charity. He could not return to the coast – even had he wanted to – because around Unyanyembe there was heavy fighting, and he had no chance of getting through.[16]

In this situation, without hope, he heard shots one day.[17] News flashed through Ujiji that they meant the arrival of a caravan headed by a European in a beautifully pressed white suit, wearing a topi, and a flag being carried by his side. Every man, woman and child gathered to see this strange European march into Ujiji. Livingstone, in his shabby clothes, holding his tattered consul's cap, standing in front of a semi-circle of Arabs, received him. None of the onlookers understood the four immortal words, "Dr Livingstone, I presume?", but they saw the joy in the face of both men.

## CHAPTER TWENTY

# Livingstone's death

Stanley was the first European Livingstone could talk to in six years, and he brought him news of events such as the Franco-Prussian war, the opening of the Suez Canal, the first transatlantic telephone, the pacific Railroad, and so on. He also handed him letters he had picked up in Zanzibar and Unyanyembe, and the information that the Government had voted Livingstone another £1,000. The story of their friendship needs no re-telling; Stanley provided Livingstone with as much comfort as he could, and divided all his supplies with him. He even cooked for him and watched him regain strength. Finally they explored the north of Lake Tanganyika together, and established that only one river, the Lusize, flowed *into* it, and none *out* of it – therefore no connection existed between Lakes Tanganyika and Albert. This meant that everything – as far as Livingstone was concerned – depended on the Lualaba.

On March 15, 1872, Livingstone and Stanley set out for Unyanyembe; Stanley to go home and write the articles and books that were to make him famous and rich, and to create the Livingstone legend that lasted a century. Stanley tried to persuade Livingstone to come home with him, but he was adamant in his refusal. Livingstone did not want to go to England before he had found the source of the Nile, and thus been able to force his detractors (the Foreign Office, the Royal Geographical Society and all) to apologise for the mean, unjust manner in which they had treated him. In England he would either receive a hero's welcome or nothing. But what finally made up Livingstone's mind was Stanley's account of Kirk's behaviour.

A warm, close relationship – almost like one between father and son – had developed between Livingstone and Stanley. During their five months together, the two men told each other not only their life histories, but Livingstone poured out all his grievances, his disappointments and his hurt feelings. When Stanley reciprocated and

Livingstone and Stanley catching up on the news (*Mansell Collection*)

among other things related how Dr Kirk, by now assistant consul in Zanzibar, had not been at all keen to help him to find Livingstone, the doctor interpreted this as part of a conspiracy to lure him home to lay hands on his notes, so as to spoil his chances of restoring his reputation. It did not make sense; nor was Stanley's statement accurate, for Kirk had only tried to warn him that Livingstone did not like to travel with other Europeans, and resented journalists in particular – especially since the severe criticism he had experienced from the Press after the death of Bishop Mackenzie.

Stanley gave Livingstone all the supplies he could spare, and promised to send him from the coast a first class caravan with ample supplies so that Livingstone could start on his Lualaba expedition – the most arduous task he had ever undertaken – well provided for his physical needs. Their parting at Unyanyembe was sad and emotional. By then Stanley must have read Livingstone's character and known that he was neither saintly, nor forgiving.[1] But at that moment he saw only the remarkable, intrepid, fantastically courageous old man, whom nothing could deter from his self-imposed mission.

Livingstone had to wait six months in Unyanyembe for Stanley's caravan to arrive. During this time he heard that a relief expedition had also been sent from England to look for him, with his son Oswell a member of it. When this party learnt that Stanley had found Livingstone, it dissolved itself and to Livingstone's great sorrow, Oswell returned with the others to England. Here was the fruit of his treatment, of his children. Livingstone gave vent to his feelings in two angry, hurt letters to Oswell, but soon his mind concentrated on the task before him. He had two aims: to find the source of the Nile, and to bring slavery to an end in east Africa.

For achieving the first, he had to skirt Lake Bangweulu, find the Lomani river, follow it to the Lualaba, and then to into Katanga to locate the four fountains. Livingstone did worry whether the Lualaba was the Nile or the Zaire? He confided his doubts to his *Journal*. On May 21, 1872, he wrote, "I am oppressed with the apprehension that after all it may turn out that I have been following the Congo . . .". On May 31: "In reference of this Nile source I have been kept in perpetual doubt and perplexity. I know too much to be positive. Great Lualaba, or Lualubba, as Manyuema say, may turn out to be the Congo . . .". On June 24: "I am even now not 'cock sure' that I have not been following what may after all be the

Congo . . .". In an unpublished despatch to Lord Granville, there is a cry from the heart: "The Lualaba, the enormous wresting it made caused me at times to feel as if knocking my head against a stone wall. It might be the Congo and . . ."[2]

Nor was he more confident that he could achieve his other aim, to stamp out slavery in east Africa. He wrote dispatches and letters; his reports on the Nyangwe massacre he hoped would have their effects; his letters to the *New York Herald* he trusted would enlist American support. It was in one of his depressed moods that he wrote in his *Journal*[3] the words that are engraved on a tablet near his tomb in Westminster Abbey: "All I can add in my loneliness is, may Heaven's rich blessing come down on everyone, American, English, or Turk, who will help to heal the open sore of the world."

At last on August 9, 1872, Stanley's men arrived; they had been carefully chosen, and each one had a two year contract, with a pay of the equivalent $20 or $25 a year and his keep. Some old friends were with Livingstone: he had engaged Chuma and Amoda in 1864; Mabruk and Gardner, both Nassick boys, in 1866. As far as stores were concerned, the ones Stanley sent were the best Livingstone had ever had.

And yet disaster was still in store for him: a large chest of dried milk, on which Livingstone depended whenever he suffered from dysentery, was the only one left behind when the expedition set out on August 15, 1872. The rains were approaching and he knew that the good weather had passed while he waited in Unyanyembe. Just before the rains, the heat was intense, the terrain difficult, and the advance slow. The difficulties eased up when they reached Lake Tanganyika – Livingstone was determined to map its southern border. His health was again poor – he could hardly bring himself to move. On November 9 he wrote in his *Journal*: "I too was ill, and became better only by marching on foot. Riding exposes one to the bad influence of the sun, while by walking the perspiration modifies beneficially the excessive heat."

Beyond Lake Tanganyika, Livingstone and his party ran into a famine area; from the thinly scattered population no food could be obtained. So they bore south, approaching Lake Bangweulu from the west. The rains had turned the country into a swamp; sometimes it took days to induce the local Africans to lend them a canoe to cross the rivers and rivulets.

Then he had another piece of bad luck. When the guide told him

Susi and Chuma

". . . the main stream came up to Susi's mouth and wetted my seat and legs."

that they had reached the west shore of Lake Bangweulu, Livingstone refused to believe him. Basing himself on his faulty calculations of 1868, when his chronometers had been damaged, he thought that he was on the north-east end of the lake, not on its west side. Yet had he gone on another two hours, he would have recognised where he was – for it was the very point where he had reached Bangweulu in 1868. He took the fatal decision of going south-west, thinking that the lake was 125 miles long – in fact it was only 25 miles long. Instead of reaching the expected sheet of water, Livingstone floundered in marsh and mud. Because of the rain, he could make out no landmarks – swamps and reed covered over a hundred miles.

This was the last blow fate struck at him; the rest was done by his stubborn, wilful character. Early in February 1873, when the weather cleared a little, he took new bearings with the instruments Stanley had sent him. They proved the guide to have been right, which Livingstone would not accept; so he insisted, fatally as it turned out, on continuing on his course. Since January his health had been very poor; he was constantly losing blood; it was wet and cold; he had no milk, no decent food, and not even at night could he gather strength by a little warmth. He waded through oozing mud and overflowing streams. His progress was at the rate of one, or one and a half, miles a day. In spite of these terrible conditions, few of his men deserted; they had developed an amazing loyalty to this extraordinary old man; they wanted to help him, although few had even the vaguest idea of what he was trying to achieve. On January 24, 1873, he noted in his *Journal*, "Carrying me across one of the broad, deep, sedgy rivers is really a difficult task. . . . The first part, the main stream, came up to Susi's mouth, and wetted my seat and legs. One held up my pistol behind, then one after another took a turn, and when he sank into a deep elephant's footprint, he required two to lift him, so as to gain a footing on the level which was over waist deep." His descriptions of how the women folk managed to carry on are the more painful to read for the stark hopelessness of the record. "The water was cold, and so was the wind, but no leeches plague us. . . . Our progress is distressingly slow. Wet, wet, wet, sloppy weather, truly, and no observations that the land near the Lake being very level, the rivers spread into broad friths and sponges." In fact Livingstone was lost – his calculations were inaccurate – the scouts he sent out brought misleading reports.

Not only was Livingstone lost; he was also bleeding to death. He

Livingstone soon before his death (*Mansell Collection*)

was semi-delirious; in his waking dreams he still clung to the Herodotus theory of the four fountains; when he could sit up, he drafted
dispatches he was to send to the Foreign Office, announcing his success in finding the source of the Nile, with only the dates to be written
in. And yet, he was still haunted by the fear that the Lualaba might
turn out to be the Zaire instead of the Nile. By April 10 he was so ill
that even he admitted his weakness. Two hours' walk tired him so
much that he had to lie down; finally he had to be carried. Yet he
went on observing, making notes, watching nature. Seventeen days
before his death he wrote in his *Journal*: "Here, after the turtle doves
and cocks give out their warning calls to the watchful, the fish-eagle
lifts up his remarkable voice. It is pitched in a high falsetto key, very
loud, and seems as if he were calling to someone in the other world.
Once heard, his weird unearthly voice can never be forgotten. It
sticks to one through life."[4]

At last he and his party were passing round the southern end of
Bangweulu – but they were doing it in April instead of in November,
as Livingstone had originally intended.

On April 20 he made his last precise entry into his diary. "Sunday.
Service. Cross over the sponge, Moenda, for food and to be near the
headman of these parts, Moansambamba. I am excessively weak.
Village on Moenda sponge. 7 a.m. Cross Lokulu in canoe. The river
is about thirty yards broad, very deep, and flowing in marshes two
knots from S.S.E. to N.N.W. into Lake." From then on he was not
strong enough even to ride the donkey. The chief of the village
assigned him a hut, where Livingstone spent the night, while Chuma
and Susi made a litter to carry him. Next day he noted in his *Journal*,
"Carried on *kitanda*[5] over Buga S.W. $2\frac{1}{4}$," (which meant two hours
and a quarter in a south-westerly direction). The next three days were
slow, painful progress – Susi and Chuma knew by now that Livingstone was dying. On April 25 they reached a village; while his men
were busy making a hut for him, he asked the villagers, who came to
sit around him, what they knew of a hill on which four rivers took
their rise. The village spokesman shook his head and said they had no
knowledge of it; they were not travellers; all those who used to go on
trading expeditions were by now dead.

By the next morning Livingstone must have realised that the end
was near, for he instructed Susi how to divide up his supplies, to
enable each one of his men to reach the coast.

On April 27, 1873, Livingstone made the last entry of all:

Livingstone's last diary entries

"Knocked up quite, and remain – recovery – sent to buy milch goats. We are on the banks of the Molilamo." As he could not walk to the *kitanda*, he told his men to knock down the walls of the hut and bring the litter to his bed. On April 29 the party pressed on, although Susi and the rest knew that Livingstone would never reach the Lualaba. They crossed a substantial river, and came to the village of Ilala. Chitambo, the local chief, assigned them a hut. Next day he came to call on Livingstone, but the doctor was too ill to see him. He could hardly speak any more. But in the evening, he suddenly asked Susi; "Is this the Luapula?" When Susi said it was not, he asked, "How far is it?" Susi replied, "I think it is three days, Master." "Oh dear, dear," murmured Livingstone and fell asleep. Later he asked Susi to boil some water, and with great effort took some calomel from his medicine chest, mixed it and drank it.

After dark, Susi left a young man called Majawara to watch over the doctor in the hut. But Majwara fell asleep; when he woke at about 4 am (it was May 1, 1873), he saw something that alarmed him and he ran to wake Susi with the words, "Come to *Bwana*, I'm afraid. I don't know if he is alive." Susi woke Chuma and Matthew, and two others. The six Africans walked quickly to Livingstone's hut. A candle stuck to the top of a box in its own wax was still burning.

They stood still in a tight group – looking at their master for a sign of life. Livingstone was not in his bed; with superhuman effort he had crawled to a kneeling position, and appeared engaged in prayer, his body stretching forward, his head buried in his hands upon the pillow.

Hut in which Livingstone died

Pointing at him, Majawara whispered, "When I lay down, he was just as he is now, and it is because I find that he does not move that I fear he is dead." Also in a whisper Susi asked him how long he had slept? Majawara was not sure, but it must have been some time. The men drew nearer and listened. He did not stir; there was no sign of breathing. Finally Matthew advanced softly and placed his hands on Livingstone's cold cheeks.

Aged sixty years and 42 days, David Livingstone was dead.

The remarkable story of how Susi and Chuma embalmed[6] Livingstone's body and packed it in canvas, covered with bark, painted with tar, and carried it for five months to Unyanyembe, is well known. There they met a relief party sent to look for Livingstone, commanded by Lt V. Lovett Cameron. He advised the Africans to bury the body, but Susi and Chuma believed that their master would have wanted to be buried in England. It is possible that they were also anxious that no shade of suspicion should fall on them on the grounds that they had murdered Livingstone. They knew that young Albert Roscher had been killed by Arabs on his way back to the coast, and the murderers were apprehended a year later and

View of Bagomoyo

Livingstone's body being carried back to the coast

A wrecked slave dhow

hanged in Zanzibar. Having brought Livingstone's body as far as Unyanyembe, they could have carried out Lt Cameron's instructions, and buried him there. It seems from the notes of Horace Waller, who questioned Susi and Chuma at length and described Livingstone's last days and death on the basis of their account, that they were greatly impressed by the mighty country their master came from, and were determined to get him back, to his home, for burial. They continued their journey, arriving in Bagamoyo in February 1874.

Susi sent Chuma to Zanzibar; Kirk was on leave, and Captain Prideaux, who stood in for him, was shy and inexperienced. He went himself to fetch Livingstone's remains, but he did not dare to take Livingstone's faithful servants with him to Zanzibar, from where the body was to be conveyed to England. He paid them from his own pocket, and was not refunded for three years.

This is why none of those who had been closest to Livingstone during the last eight years of his life, were present at Westminster Abbey at his grand funeral. But Horace Waller, who edited David Livingstone's *Last Journals*, needed help in reconstructing the record of the last days of Livingstone's life. James "Paraffin" Young paid for Susi and Chuma to come to London, where their clear memories of the smallest details enabled Horace Waller to complete his task.

## CHAPTER TWENTY-ONE

# The creation of the Livingstone legend

The Livingstone legend was in part conceived in 1869 by an imaginative American newspaper proprietor, James Gordon Bennett, Jr. He believed that the American public – indeed the world public – would be thrilled to read about a dedicated explorer who had been lost "somewhere in Africa", and whom a reporter of the *New York Herald* had found and interviewed. That Livingstone had been adulated, but later, on account of the disastrous UMCA Mission, execrated, and that in 1868 an unfounded report of his alleged death had rated only a few factual obituaries, Bennett coolly discounted. He knew his public, and its exceedingly short memory. An extraordinary story, a moving account, and the *New York Herald* would boast one of its biggest scoops for years.

Bennett had on his staff a reporter who, he was equally certain, just fitted the job. Henry Morton Stanley, the adopted son of a New Orleans wholesale merchant, had led an adventurous life and ended up in the American Civil War as ship's writer in the Federal Navy. From there he went into journalism; his colourful reports soon landed him a job on the *New York Herald*. Bennett was confident that Stanley, with his toughness and initiative, would if at all possible find the lost explorer. On October 28, 1869, he gave him *carte blanche* to spend what he liked, as long as he tracked down Livingstone and reported what had happened to him during the six years he had not been seen.

The unexpected news that a letter from Livingstone had reached Zanzibar did not suit Bennett at all. He wanted Stanley to find an explorer who had been lost, good and proper. So he sent him to report on the situation in Egypt, in the Holy Land and Turkey, in Persia, finally in Bombay. By then – Bennett once more guessed correctly – Livingstone had vanished again, and when Stanley reached Zanzibar in January 1871, there had been no news of him for over a year.

Stanley spent £4,000[1] to equip one of the most elaborate expeditions ever seen; he took with him, in addition to 192 porters, two Englishmen – W. L. Farquar and J. W. Shaw – neither of whom survived the journey.[2] After five months spent with Livingstone, he went to London and unfolded his tale.

Stanley was a highly intelligent man and his assignment was not to write a balanced account of a single-minded man, in poor health, full of rancours and resentments, yet also blessed with courage, tenacity and remarkable gifts of observation. Bennett wanted Livingstone portrayed as a saint, who had dedicated his life to a cause and was continuing – despite illness and advancing years – to carry out his self-imposed task. This is the story Stanley told, and he told it well. Some of Livingstone's dispatches, including the one about the Nyangwe massacre, were published and helped to build up the picture of a man burning with righteous indignation over evil, especially the evil of slavery. By the time Stanley concluded his series of articles, he had become almost as famous as his subject. Bennett had proved right: no questions were asked, no memories revived. The legend was created, and, unforeseen even by Bennett, it lasted for a century.

The British public were given a new hero at a time when heroes were scarce. Some members of the Foreign Office and the Colonial Office knew better, but they kept their peace. With the growing demand for colonial possessions, which developed a decade later into the Scramble for Africa, Livingstone became a useful symbol, and later on his ideas influenced the shape British colonial rule was to take.

It is, however, odd that, until Tim Jeal's book was published in 1973, Livingstone's many biographers did not examine some of the obvious questions. Jeal's research was limited to Livingstone's own writings, including some letters which had only just come to light, and writings about him, official and private, published and unpublished. Jeal did not go to Africa to try to find out what was remembered about Livingstone – what the descendants of some of the people who knew him had heard their elders tell. However, Dr Bridglal Pachai and his team, whose essays were also published in 1973,[3] have done that, and have shown that even at this late date, much can still be accomplished. It is sad to think how much evidence could have been collected, and what a remarkable portrait of David Livingstone could have been drawn from African sources, had this been done sooner.

A second reason why the Livingstone legend could live on for a whole century unchallenged was the character and the conditions of some of the men who played a decisive role in his life: William Cotton Oswell, László Magyar, Candido José da Costa Cardoso, and Muhamad Baghrib.

Of these four men Cotton Oswell, who gave Livingstone his first chance, was the only one who had a real relationship with him. Their friendship endured to the end of the doctor's life. There were special reasons for this. Cotton Oswell, as we have seen, was a rare personality, completely devoid of both ambition and vanity. After his African wanderings (as he called them) he settled in Sussex to enjoy life, surrounded by a loving family, popular with friends and neighbours, without financial worries or any other frustrations.

Cotton Oswell did not seem to resent the fact that Livingstone would not give him credit for his explorations, nor admit that without him he could not have got to Lake Ngami, and that Oswell had contributed more to the discovery of the lake than Livingstone. Oswell was aware of Livingstone's all-pervading ambition, but he helped him where ever he could. When his family and friends remonstrated that his contributions had not been recognised, Oswell laughed; when the Royal Geographical Society begged him to write an account of the Ngami expedition so that they could give him their gold medal, Oswell refused. Shortly after this Oswell was struck down with a severe attack of fever, and fearing that during coma, or in the event of his death, publication of his papers and maps might be attempted, he ordered his note-books to be brought to his bedside, and himself cut out every page of importance, and had them burnt in his presence. Livingstone got to hear about this self-effacing incident, yet remained stubbornly silent about Oswell's share in the discovery of Lake Ngami.

But even Oswell must have had some reservations about Livingstone's attitude, for he refused to go to Newstead Abbey, where Livingstone stayed with Mr and Mrs William Webb from September 1864, until April 1865, writing his book on the Zambezi and Shire expeditions. Oswell also refused to edit Livingstone's *Last Journals*; but he never said a word to prick the legend.

With László Magyar, it was a completely one-sided relationship, as Livingstone pretended on the two occasions when asked, never to have heard of the Hungarian. Perhaps if Father Jácint Rónay, the Benedictine monk who asked for news about Magyar, had worded his question differently, and said, "What do you know about *'Ngana Komo?*" Livingstone might have given a different answer?

Livingstone had an extraordinary fascination for Magyar. He was not influenced by his writings (which he had not read), or by his oratory (which he had not heard). To Magyar Livingstone represented the brave, single-minded, successful explorer whom the world acclaimed, and whom his countrymen greeted as a hero. Livingstone was the personification of everything Magyar wanted to be.

In order to meet Livingstone, Magyar broke up his home, sent his African wife and children back to Bihé; interrupted his explorations of the Kasai river, and at great sacrifice went with a handful of followers to Linyanti, where Livingstone would not even speak to him. As Magyar's diaries of this period, and his 32 page outline for the second volume of his book (which might have described his dealings with Livingstone) were lost, we will never know for certain what happened. What we do know is based on memory, which is fallible, and on hearsay.

Magyar's failure to meet Livingstone haunted him all his life, and he referred to it again and again. On August 20, 1856, he wrote to his father, "I am especially anxious to obtain the travel reports of the English Dr David Livingstone, who is at present travelling with me, and which have probably been already published in his English homeland. This brave traveller spent some twenty days in my neighbourhood, in the country of the Zsenzse kaffers.[4] When I went to see him at the place where he was staying, which took me six days of travel, on arrival I learnt sadly that he had left on a journey some ten days earlier. For almost two years we have been circling around each other without either he or I being able to know about each other. The Moors[5] are calling him everywhere by the name of *Munari*, therefore it is very difficult here to know which country a traveller belongs to. It is to be believed that he too must often have heard of *'Ngana Komo*, but how could he have guessed that an orphaned Hungarian is roaming around the boiling hot African plains?"

In his address to the Hungarian Academy of Sciences, when he had been elected a corresponding member, and which was read on his behalf on October 10, 1859, Magyar began by saying, "Dr David Livingstone can be rightly counted among those successful African travellers who in recent years have, with remarkable determination,

made wonderful discoveries, and in this manner, by their thorough
scientific knowledge, have considerably extended the horizon of the
geographic world. The merits and results of Livingstone's travels are
better known in Europe than they are to me; therefore I do not intend
to discuss them any further. I only want to give you a brief report of
those areas of the Moropuu (or Moluva) and the Lobal countries,
where Livingstone's path touched mine. This is an extract of the
second volume of my book; from it the mistakes of the worthy English traveller regarding the geographical position, the proper name
and direction of the rivers of the above named countries will best
emerge." Magyar added to this in a footnote: " 'Lunda' or 'Ba-
Lunda' are not real geographical definitions; they are mainly used by
the people of the Kimbunda and Pungo-Adungo caravans, who
travel there from abroad. Correctly translated, they mean: *a very
large country filled with many uninhabited deserts*. This is indeed a
good characterisation of the Moluva empire, where populous areas
are often divided from each other by uninhabited deserts of many
days' journey."

That Professor János Hunfalvy, Magyar's friend and adviser, did
not cut out the passage referring to Livingstone, indicates that he too
felt that Magyar had a justified grievance against the doctor. With
Magyar, Livingstone's slight rankled to the end of his days, yet he
tried to explain it away; he admired the doctor immensely, but
among the explorers of his generation he came nearest to pointing
out the flaws in Livingstone's work.

Two questions must be asked in establishing the contribution
Magyar made: first, what did he himself achieve as an explorer?
Second, in what way did he render himself useful to Livingstone?

Magyar's contribution to African exploration falls under four
main headings. In 1848, he wrote a description of the Zaire Delta,
which is superior to H. M. Stanley's written 29 years later. In
1850–51 he explored Moropoaland and the Kasai and Kuango
rivers; his account of them is unique – but written in Hungarian. In
the summer of 1878, a Portuguese expedition, led by Capello Brito
and Ivens Robert established the course of the Kuango, and they
figure as the discoverers of its origin. Twenty eight years earlier
Magyar had already done it.

During the same period Magyar discovered the greatest watershed in south-west Africa, known by Africans as the Mother of All
the Waters. He gave the first description of the Cassaquer Bushmen,

27 years before Alexander de Serpa Pinto claimed this honour. Finally, he explored and mapped the Kunene river. In addition to all this, he portrayed the customs, political organisation, religions and superstitions of innumerable African tribes, not through interpreters and at second hand, but by sharing their lives as a friend and a relation. He also spoke eight African languages.

Magyar erred in some of his geographical definitions, as W. D. Cooley pointed out, but his main conclusions stand up even today. And he did all this without ever receiving one penny from a Hungarian, or any other source. The only person who helped him financially was His Black Majesty, Dalaber Almanzor de Trudodat, who rewarded him for services rendered.

Richard Burton was one of the handful of authorities on Africa who realised the importance of Magyar's explorations. In 1858, in a lecture at the Royal Geographical Society, he said: "Modern travellers like Magyar, Grace, Livingstone, met with the same exuberant vegetation."[6] Burton also recalled that all three had described "the rapid streams discharging into the Atlantic", which cut across stony ridges and grass-covered uplands. Not only did Burton mention Magyar before Livingstone, but he expressed the view that Magyar had, as much as Livingstone, established that the heart of Africa was in parts lush and fertile territory. While Consul in Fernando Po, Burton went in July and August 1863, to Loanda and made a trip into the interior of Angola. He realised the difficulties which had beset Magyar and sent him a considerable sum of money to Moçamedes, but Magyar had been dead a whole year when it was delivered in Ponto de Cujo.

With hindsight it is easy to realise the remarkable work László Magyar achieved in south-west Africa. In addition to lack of funds he laboured under additional disadvantages. W. D. Cooley, who in commenting appreciatively on Magyar's reports read out at the Royal Geographical Society meeting on February 14, 1853, also said of him: "His siting of geographical positions was not merely discordant, but wholly erroneous and unfounded. His estimate of distances was tolerably correct."[7] Magyar was well aware of this, and in his letters to József Antunovics, he often lamented his lack of proper training in the use of scientific instruments. Yet, it must also be said, that in view of his inability to establish correctly his geographical positions, he and Pakasero between them had a remarkable sense of location.

Livingstone scored heavily over Magyar on two points. He had a cause – the conversion of the Sons of Ham to the Christian faith, and the suppression of the slave trade by opening up Africa to Christian traders. Even though Livingstone made only one African convert and he lapsed, he attended to sick Africans (and Europeans in Portuguese territory) effecting many successful cures.

Magyar had no cause – except his wish to further the development of science, and to bring glory to Hungary by publishing his reports and books in Hungarian. His writings were lively and informative, but he was not an evangelist set on reforming the thinking of his age.

. The greatest advantage Livingstone had over Magyar was that he was a child of his time, while Magyar did not belong either socially, or intellectually to his generation of Hungarians. Livingstone was an evangelist, in the tradition of William Wilberforce, Hannah Moore and their friends; what is more, by his writing he exemplified and, in his own way, led the contemporary stirrings in the character of the English people – their sometimes sanctimonious but usually earnest striving after Christian principles and moral rectitude. Livingstone certainly believed that "righteousness exalteth a nation" and that reverence for the Almighty would make the English the superior to all other races.

Magyar had little information of what was going on in his native land, let alone the chance, or the inclination, to influence the moral values of the Hungarian people. In one sense only were his aims similar to those of Livingstone: both vowed, using almost identical words, that they would either explore the unknown parts of the Dark Continent, or perish. But beyond that, László Magyar merely wanted to enrich science and widen the horizon of learned geographers. The notion of Christian trade and Christian religion sailing, hand in hand, up the un-navigable African rivers, never entered Magyar's head – he knew African topography too well for that.

Now we can attempt an assessment of Magyar's contributions to Livingstone's 1,800 mile trek from Linyanti to Loanda. First, by his visit to the Makololo, Magyar demonstrated that the journey from Benguela via Bihé to the Zambezi could be made by one white man travelling with only a few Africans. If Magyar had been able to overcome the obstacles on the way, this was proof to Livingstone that his difficulties would not be insurmountable.

Secondly, in his conversations with Sekeletu, Magyar explained the shortest route to Bihé – of course he spoke in terms of so many

days' journeying – up the Leeambyé, as the Zambezi north of Linyanti was then called, until the point where the Leeba flowed into it.
There the traveller had to follow the Leeba – also called the Lumegi,
or Luamegi – until its confluence with another river, bearing west
along this one until Lake Dilolo. From there Magyar indicated the
route to Bihé's capital, Kombala an Bihé, the starting point for caravans to Benguela on the coast.

This proved immensely useful to Livingstone, who during his own
journey was racked by fever and diarrhoea, sometimes being so weak
that he had to rest for several days. As his aim was to reach Loanda,
which he knew to be north of Benguela, from Lake Dilolo he bore
north-west along the Lotembwa river to the Kasai,[8] and then west
until he reached Ambaco, where the Portuguese resident received
him and sent him on to Loanda. On his way back Livingstone also
followed the route Magyar had indicated to Sekeletu. He must have
been aware of the debt he owed to *'Ngana Komo*, even if he did not
know his European name. As practically no one in the west had
heard of the Hungarian explorer, Livingstone's claim to have been
the first European to travel through Barotseland and Angola to the
south-west coast of Africa, was accepted without question.[9]

Livingstone's relations with Candido José da Costa Cardoso were
superficial and also one-sided. There was never any doubt about
their having met; Livingstone wrote to several friends about the well
informed Portuguese whom he had befriended in 1856, and who told
him about the big lake to the north he had visited ten years earlier. He
also described him in his book, *Missionary Travels*. This was at a time
when he still thought that the Zambezi was navigable, and the
Batoka Plateau would provide homes for missionaries and settlers in
central Africa. When he returned to Tete in 1856, for unexplained
reasons he did not look up Cardoso, who could have told him what
to expect at "Kabrabassa". When Livingstone realised that these terrible rocks put an end to his central African plans, he had to find a
substitute for the Batoka Plateau, and he could see none other than
the Shire country. But if British missions and colonial settlements
were to go there, he wanted to be the explorer who had discovered
Lake Nyasa. Therefore he had to wipe out his own evidence that Cardoso was a reliable and honourable man. We know how he maligned
him on top of ignoring him. Cardoso's reactions can only be guessed.

Thus the Livingstone–Cardoso friendship foundered on the

doctor's high-handed and unfair treatment, with the Portuguese first humiliated, and later indignant over "Livingstone's lies". But the real loser was Livingstone himself. Had he made some enquiries about Cardoso, he would have discovered, firstly, that he was a mulatto, and, in any case, that he, Livingstone, was not the first European to see Lake Nyasa. But he gave the man a wide berth when he thought Cardoso might be regarded as the discoverer of the lake; yet when it suited him, Livingstone asked him to take care of his stores and even accepted the loan of a donkey from him.

Secondly, with a little investigation, Livingstone would have found out who Cardoso's first wife had been and through her, who his influential relatives were, with whom Cardoso was on excellent terms. Livingstone realised Chisaka's power; on November 15, 1858, he noted in his *Journal*, "Sent presents to Chisaka – 1 railway rug, 2 imitation native cloths; 2 scizzors [sic], 2 knives, needles several packets; thread and two pieces of cloth to buy grain to bring back to Makololo." It would have been to Livingstone's advantage had Cardoso taken him to see his father-in-law, Dombo Dombo, and his grandson, Chisaka, and he could have drawn on their knowledge of conditions and people.

Livingstone's greatest mistake was not to question Cardoso about conditions in the Shire country through a good interpreter, as his own knowledge of Portuguese was limited. Cardoso could have told him not only who was involved in the slave trade, but explained the causes of the inter-tribal fighting and of the social strife then going on between the Marawi rulers and Chewa subjects. Had Livingstone seen the Shire situation as a whole, and had he – for he certainly was thorough – gone with Cardoso to consult Chisaka and Dombo Dombo, he would have had a completely different grasp of the dangers involved.

It is still improbable that even with such knowledge at his disposal Livingstone would have informed the Foreign Office, but he could have chosen one of two alternatives. He could have taken Sir Roderick Murchison into his confidence – although he is not likely to have done this. Or, when the UMCA Mission arrived, he could have stayed with it and not let Bishop Mackenzie out of his sight. Duly warned, this is probably what Livingstone would have done – in order to protect his own reputation, already tarnished by the tragic deaths of the Makololo Mission. Had Livingstone remained at Magomero, the story of the UMCA Mission would have been com-

An established UMCA mission

pletely different. Bishop Mackenzie would not have attacked the Ajawa – Livingstone and his Makololo would have seen to that; the health of the Mission would have been better for Livingstone had not only much experience, but real talent for treating fever. Had Mackenzie and Livingstone acted in unison, the bishop would probably not have died. Nor – though this is a minor matter – would he have written the letters describing his fight against the slavers that caused indignation among High Churchmen. Mackenzie had not been sent out to wage war against the Africans who caught slaves for the Arabs; his task was to spread the Word of the Lord, but under the then prevailing conditions, this was impossible. Livingstone's presence would have stopped the Bishop from taking upon himself the task of restoring order.

Perhaps Cardoso was the greatest influence on Livingstone's life. He provided an alternative for the Batoka Plateau; with proper handling, he could have helped to prevent the tragedies that beset the UMCA Mission, and undermined Livingstone's reputation.

Livingstone's friendship with a number of Arab traders had a greater influence on his life than is generally realised. In view of his hatred of the slave trade, it has puzzled generations of Livingstone admirers that he spent almost three years in the company of slavers; accepted their hospitality and enjoyed the comforts of travelling with them. Yet there are three valid reasons for this.

The first is that Livingstone differentiated between Arabs as individuals, and Arabs as slave traders. During his visits to Zanzibar, he
had seen how the Arabs treated their domestic slaves – more like servants or retainers, if not as lesser members of the family. This treatment bore no resemblance to what was being done to slaves in the
American South. It was an individual relationship which Livingstone knew from Africa, where in certain remote regions domestic
slavery is still in existence.

Living and travelling with the Arab slavers, Livingstone had occasion to observe at close quarters their methods of treating the
slaves they bought, who had to carry ivory, copper, and other goods
to the coast. On June 24, 1867, he noted in his *Journal*, "These Zanzibari men are very different from the slavers of the Waijau country."
In a despatch to the Earl of Clarendon, written at the end of
December 1867, he said: "I am glad that I was witness to their mode
of trading in ivory and slaves. It formed a complete contrast to the
atrocious dealings of the Kilwa traders, who are supposed to be, but
are not, the subjects of the same Sultan (of Zanzibar). If one wished
to depict the same slave trade in its most attractive, or rather least
objectionable, form, he would accompany these gentlemen subjects
of the Sultan of Zanzibar." Livingstone also described how slaves
frequently managed to escape; the concessions made to pretty
women slaves, who invariably got away and could never be re-
caught. All this was, according to Livingstone, a far cry from the
"disgusting phases" followed by the Kilwa traders or the Portuguese
half-castes from Tete.

The second reason for Livingstone's friendship with the Arab traders was that without their help, he could not have survived physically. He was without supplies of any kind; he had no cloth or beads
left to buy food; no medicines to relieve his illness. In 1868, on an occasion when he was very hungry because no food was obtainable in a
drought stricken area, "an Arab, Sef Rupia or Rubea, head of a large
body of slaves, on his way to the coast, most kindly came forward
and presented an ox, bag of flour, and some cooked meat, all of
which were extremely welcome to half-famished men, or indeed
under any circumstances."[10] Four months later he met another
slaver, Mohamed Bogharib,[11] with whom he was to travel for
months. The Arab told him his life history, and it emerged that
Livingstone's letter from the Sultan of Zanzibar had been instrumen-
tal in effecting Bogharib's release from Kazembe, one of the most

powerful rulers of central Africa, who had held him imprisoned for ten months.

When Livingstone fell ill, Bogharib nursed him personally; the fever developed into pneumonia and delirium, and this saved Livingstone's life. Without Bogharib, Stanley could not have written the articles and books that created the Livingstone legend. Bogharib was, therefore, as much responsible for Livingstone's fame as Bennett and Stanley.

The third reason for Livingstone's friendship with the Arab traders was humanly the most understandable: they were the only people with whom he could talk during the six years he had vanished in Africa. For instance, on February 24, 1868, he noted in his diary: "Mahamad bin Saleh is very intelligent, and takes an interest in all that happens, and his father was equally interested in his country's affairs." Of course, neither Mahamad bin Saleh, nor the other traders had any information about Europe, but they knew Africa intimately, and received news from Zanzibar as their caravans constantly went to the coast and back. From these Arabs Livingstone learnt a good deal about African political affairs and trading possibilities which, he hoped, would one day be carried on by Christians.

Livingstone also met "Tipo Tipo" – as he called him. Tippoo Tip was a nickname which meant "gatherer of wealth". On July 29, 1867, he entered in his *Journal*, "Tipo gave me a goat, a piece of white calico, and four big bunches of beads, also a bag of Holcus sorghum, and apologised because it was so little." They talked at length, and did so again on August 30.[12] From his Arab friends, Livingstone heard the story of this impressive young man of about 25.

His real name was Hamed bin Muhamad. His grandfather, Juma bin Rajab, had founded a great commercial enterprise, which his son, Muhamad bin Juma, expanded and strengthened by marrying two daughters of the Nyamwezi Paramount Chief.[13] Tippoo had African blood, although his mother was the daughter of another wealthy Arab trader. Livingstone was dead by the time Tippoo became the ruler of a commercial and political empire north and west of Lake Tanganyika, and was far more powerful than Sultan Barghash of Zanzibar, his nominal over-lord. Tippoo's power was eventually broken by King Leopold of the Belgians, and he ended his days in 1905 in Zanzibar, a wealthy man who liked to entertain Europeans, but would answer few of their questions.

It can be imagined what it meant to Livingstone, who was without any contact with the outside world, to have discussions with men of the stature of Tippoo Tip, and even with lesser men like Bogharib, bin Saleh and many others. The Arabs knew of Livingstone's efforts to destroy the slave trade, their livelihood, yet they held him in high esteem, and treated him – to quote Livingstone's own words, "with great kindness." They often acceded to his requests for clemency. Without his Arab slaver friends, Livingstone could not have survived.

The stories of the men who played parts in David Livingstone's life reveal a good deal about his character, his successes and his failures. Once the curtain of the Livingstone legend had been drawn aside, there appears not a saintly, dedicated missionary-explorer, but a single-minded, courageous man, whose ruthless ambition was to open Africa and be the first to do so. It also emerges that Livingstone was neither a good missionary, nor an effective explorer. How has all this affected his place in history?

Moral and physical courage were outstanding traits from the day he decided to get out of the Blantyre textile mill, until the day – when at death's door – he still continued with his efforts to find the sources of the Nile. However difficult, however dangerous a situation, Livingstone never faltered.

Tenacity, endurance, initiative – these are virtues all the 19th century African explorers had to possess. But none of them – with the possible exception of László Magyar – possessed them to the same degree as Livingstone. His all pervasive ambition drove him forward, yet it contained an ugly streak. When the situation turned against him, he was prepared to deceive and to lie; to drop friends and to destroy reputations. The greatest sufferers were the members of his immediate family, whom he deserted, and then criticised for not being more devoted to him. The darkest blot on his record is his attitude to the men, women and children of the Makololo and the UMCA Missions, for whose deaths he was partly responsible, but whom he blamed for incompetence – because by dying they disproved the feasibility of the plans he had thought out.

The David Livingstone who remains is a complex personality, who when dealing with Europeans, with whom he could never get on, had to be first in any enterprise, or he would opt out. It may be countered that he had many friends, as demonstrated by his voluminous correspondence. But they were friends at a distance, who admired him and gave him the praise and recognition that his ambition – and also his self-esteem – required. Against this Livingstone was usually gentle, patient and understanding when dealing with Africans. Here is another similarity with Magyar: Livingstone defended the Makololo even when their record was indefensible – as after their dreadful treatment of the Holloway Helmore Mission.

But if Livingstone was a modest explorer – Lake Bangweulu being his only undisputed discovery, and a poor missionary – his only convert having soon lapsed, how could the Livingstone legend have survived so long? The explanation lies in David Livingstone's greatest attribute: he could and did communicate with his friends in England; in his books he described what he had seen and observed in a manner that made his readers the world over feel they had been there, and had participated in his experiences. David Livingstone was one of the great journalists of his day. It was his letters, his diaries and his books with their accurate maps and fine drawings that made the Livingstone legend credible. No explorer (and few others) came anywhere near David Livingstone in his power to convey the things he had observed in Africa. Thus it was that Livingstone did what he had set out to do: to open up the Dark Continent.

However, this is not all. During his lifetime, as a result of the Zambezi not being navigable, and the Shire country not being habitable, Livingstone's aims seemed to have collapsed, and to have been a failure. Yet within three years of his death, the missionaries were back in Nyasaland; Scottish industrialists and shipping magnates formed the Livingstonia Central African Company, later to become the African Lakes Company, and began to trade with the Africans. A steamer was brought out, carried over the Murchison cataracts, and then launched on Lake Nyasa, just as Livingstone had planned. Because of several Arab attacks on the missionaries and members of the African Lakes Company, the British Government had to intervene, and in 1891 Nyasaland became a British colony. In 1894 Uganda followed as a British protectorate, and in 1895 Kenya became a British Protected Territory, while Cecil Rhodes planted the British flag in areas that are today Zambia and Rhodesia–Zimbabwe; in 1898 Nigeria and the Sudan came under British rule – just as Livingstone had prayed should happen.

Livingstone's idea of a handful of Englishmen ruling millions of Africans by administering them from a few centres, also came to be.

He may have acquired the idea in Bombay from the manner in which India had been ruled since the days of Clive; in Africa, under Lord Lugard, this became known as Indirect Rule.

Taking all this into consideration, Livingstone's influence in Africa was of long-term and historic importance. Livingstone, the man, who can now be seen as intensely human, with great strength of character and equally great faults, had – more than any other explorer – left his mark on British colonial developments.

David Livingstone achieved his place in history as a thinker and a writer – not as an explorer, certainly not as a missionary – who blazed the spiritual trail for the British Empire in Africa.

# Postscript

Having, in the course of writing this book, thought for so long about David Livingstone, and the men who played a part in his life, I felt I should visit his tomb in Westminster Abbey, and read the tablet bearing the words that had so deeply affected his Victorian contemporaries. It is a large, black marble slab, in the middle of the knave, in line with the grave of the Unknown Warrior, and beyond it lies the bright green slab boldly carved with the name: WINSTON CHURCHILL. On the black marble slab inscribed in golden letters is the name "David Livingstone", the date and place of his birth and of his death, and then: "For thirty years his life was spent in an unwearied effort to evangelise the native races – To explore the undiscovered secrets – To abolish the desolating slave trade of CENTRAL AFRICA, where with his last words he wrote" and there follows the famous quotation: "All I can add in my solitude is, may heaven's rich blessing come down on everyone, American, English, or Turk, who will help to heal this open sore of the world".

In fact, these were not the last words that Livingstone wrote; those were written on April 27, 1873: "Knocked up quite, and remain – recovery – sent to buy milch goats. We are on the banks of the Molilamo." Somehow it was appropriate that even on his tomb there should be an inaccuracy which heightened his reputation.

As I stood looking at it, I reflected that David Livingstone's reputation might have been very different if more documentary records of those who had helped him had been preserved.

It occurred to me that, even at this late stage, I might myself perhaps find out what had become of the descendants of Livingstone's helpers. One of Cotton Oswell's grandsons now lives near Wolverhampton in Staffordshire with his family. But what has become of László Magyar's African family? Are any of Cardoso's descendants alive, and if so, where? I decided to go to Angola and Moçambique in search of them.

At the end of February 1973, I was due in Malawi, from where I could make my way to Tete. I knew it would not be easy, on account of guerilla activities and the mines placed by them on the road from Blantyre to Tete.

I was lucky. On March 7, 1973, I was flown by private plane to Beira, and from there in Senhor Jorge Jardim's private aeroplane, with his two beautiful daughters Kanysha and Xenica as my interpreters, to Tete. I visited the tremendous Cabora Bassa dam, built into the rocks that had ruined Livingstone's plans; I saw where the immense lake would be that would reach the Rhodesian border. Now, for the first time, it would be possible for ships to sail from the Indian Ocean to the heart of Africa – and thus bring to life Livingstone's dream.

Back in Tete I tried to get in touch with a Jesuit Father who was said to be a great authority on Moçambique. Unfortunately he was in retreat, and refused to break it to see me. On the advice of Mrs Peggy Aires, whom I met at Government House, my two interpreters arranged an interview for me with Antonio Martins Pires de Carvalho, a mining engineer who has lived in Tete for over twenty years, and has made a close study of its history. On March 8, 1973, he came to see me at the Zambeze Hotel. We talked in the bar, used almost exclusively by soldiers (Tete is the headquarters of the war against what the Portuguese call the terrorists, and the independent African states to the north the freedom fighters). Not only did officers and other ranks drink side by side, but white, black and coloured men mixed on equal terms. This is when I realised that about sixty per cent of the Moçambique Forces are made up of Africans.

Senhor Carvalho had never heard of Candido José da Costa Cardoso, but promised to consult someone who would know, and to return to see me next morning. "It will not be early," he said, "for I must do some research. If the man you are interested in was *Capitan Mor* and *Juiz Privativo*, there must be traces of him at the Town Hall and at the Law Courts."

Next morning Senhor Carvalho arrived with a young man who was probably three-quarters African: he had crinkly, though not woolly hair; dark African eyes but European features. Judging by the colour of his skin, he must have had European as well as Indian or Arab blood. He was the Chief Clerk of the Tete Law Courts. His name was Alvaro Nunes Marques dos Santos. He told me that the best way to find out about Senhor Cardoso was to consult the elders.

Stanley

Engineer Pines de Carvalho, Kanysha Jardim, the author and Senhor Marques dos Santos

First we went to see a very old man, nearly 100 years old, who could have known Cardoso. Unfortunately he had lost his memory, and seemed only interested in the bath that was being prepared for him. So we went to see another old man, Senor José Antonio de Abreu, at his house in Rua de Circunvalação. Born in Tete in 1893, he was entirely African; he received us sitting in a comfortable chair in a semi-dark room into which you walked straight from the street. Senhor de Abreu's house is in the poorer quarter of Tete. He thought for a while after Senhor dos Santos had told him what I wanted to know; then he asked that I should come back the next day as he wanted to consult some of his friends before he made any statement about Senhor Cardoso.

Later that afternoon, Senhor dos Santos drove three of Senhor de Abreu's friends to his house: José Manuel do Rosario, born in 1890; Antonio da Costa Xavier, born in 1893; and José da Costa Xavier, born in 1894. Apparently they had a three hour discussion, in which the past was thoroughly explored.

About 7.30 Senhor dos Santos came to the Hotel Zambeze, and told me that Senhor de Abreu and his friends indeed remembered having heard about Candido José da Costa Cardoso, who had drawn a map of Lake Nganja for Dr Livingstone. He had been tall, fair, with very blue eyes – the "Cardoso eyes" – as the members of his family called them. He had been *Capitan Mor* of Tete and the Lower Shire area; because of this he had occasion to visit the lake many times. Senhor de Abreu said that the Portuguese had known for a very long time about the lake, as in 1624 Father Mariano, a Portuguese Jesuit, had sent a description of it to his Superiors in Goa. It was very accurate.[1] The four Africans believed that Livingstone knew this, for he met the Jesuits while he was in Tete, and as they were proud of Father Mariano they would probably have boasted of him to the doctor.

At the meeting the four men agreed that Senhor Cardoso's father, Antonio Cardoso, had arrived from Portugal in the late 18th century, and that he had married a coloured woman, with English, African and probably Indian blood. But their son, Candido José, looked completely European, and was taken for a Portuguese by Livingstone.

From his first marriage to Francisca Pereira, Candido Cardoso had two sons; from his second marriage to Helena Nunes Heget, three children – Leandru, Balbina and Rosario. Rosario died young, but Leandru lived to the age of 105, and died in 1963; his sister Balbina lived to the age of 92, and died in 1953. Leandru, who had married Julia Carvalho Heget, had eleven children: Candido, Francisca, Manuel, Custodio, Francisca, Trindade, João Nunes, Cativa, Ana, Silva, and Pedro. Their surname was Nunes Cardoso. Of the eleven, Francisca, Trindade, Cativa and Pedro were alive in March 1973.

Sr dos Santos told me with more puzzlement than excitement: "I always knew that Trindade Nunes Cardoso was my great-grandmother – she had a daughter called Joaquina, whose daughter, also called Joaquina, is my mother. When I heard that Trindade Nunes Cardoso had been the daughter of Leandru Cardoso, I exclaimed: 'But then I must be the great-great-grandson of Candido Cardoso!' Mr de Abreu looked at me and laughed. 'Of course you are, I always knew it.' Isn't it amazing? I thought I was helping you to establish Senhor Cardoso's genealogy, and now I have established my own."

Meanwhile Senhor Carvalho ascertained that Candido Cardoso had participated in the 48 year war that ended in 1888; that he had been sent back to the Shire to sign up chiefs to accept Portuguese protection: "This was at the time of the Scramble for Africa, when Portugal tried to retain her Moçambique possessions. Dr Livingstone and Dr Kirk had made the first moves to secure Lake Nyasa for Britain, so as to prevent Angola and Moçambique from linking up. Cecil Rhodes and his money did the rest," Senhor Carvalho said with some bitterness.

On the morning of March 10, Kanysha, Xenica, Senhor Carvalho, Senhor dos Santos, and myself went back to Senhor de Abreu and there I met two African women – no different from thousands of African peasant women, except for their bright blue eyes – "the Cardoso eyes", as Senhor dos Santos told me.

They were Leandru's daughters, Cativa and the younger Francisca. I asked Cativa about her family – she replied that she had never married as she had been the mistress of a Governor, and after that she was not going to marry just anyone. Francisca had a large family, with many children and grandchildren. She was in very high spirits, and for good reason. When it was realised that Senhor dos Santos was the great-nephew of Cativa and Francisca, they held a family reunion. This ceremony begins by the relatives standing in a tight group, and what ever liquid they are drinking, being sprinkled around them in a wide circle. Senhor dos Santos provided beer for

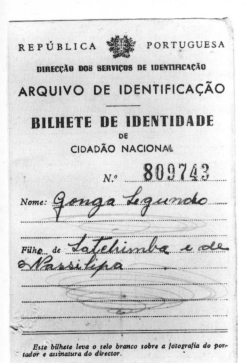

REPÚBLICA PORTUGUESA

DIRECÇÃO DOS SERVIÇOS DE IDENTIFICAÇÃO

ARQUIVO DE IDENTIFICAÇÃO

BILHETE DE IDENTIDADE
DE
CIDADÃO NACIONAL

N.º 809743

Nome: *Gonga Segundo*

Filho de *Satetimba e de*
*Nassitipa*

Este bilhete leva o selo branco sobre a fotografia do portador e assinatura do director.

Natural de *Cuimbale*
*Huambo — Angola*
Data do nascimento: *1914 mil no-*
*vecentos e catorze*
Estado civil: *Solteiro*

Residência: *Dombe Grande*
*Benguela — Angola*

Impressão do *indicador direito*

Gonga Segundo

Francisca and Cativa Nunes Cardoso

this family reunion, and Francisca had partaken liberally from it.

Senhor dos Santos was a little embarrassed by this, and he told me in a mixture of French and English: "In all families some do well, while others go down in the world. My great-aunts have gone down, while my father is a respected citizen, and I am the Clerk of the Tete Law Courts, where I work very hard." Senhor dos Santos lives in a European-style house; his wife is well educated, as are their children. She is also of mixed blood and has the same pale skin as her husband.

The Cardoso descendants and the old men of Tete all know about the positions Candido held. Senhor de Abreu said, "He was afraid of nothing – he was a very brave man indeed." Another one said, "He was very clever and his judgements were right." "He was a fighter, and a good one," said a third. There was no doubt whatsoever in their minds that he had been many times to the lake – "so many people went there at that time" – and they were also certain that he had drawn a map of the lake for Dr Livingstone. "If there were mistakes in the map, that was because of the long route he took, or maybe because he lacked geographical training," Senhor de Abreu concluded.

In this generation, the Cardoso fortune is only a memory. The *prazo* of Missonga no longer belongs to Candido's descendants, and some of them have indeed gone down in the world. But the blue "Cardoso eyes" are the pride of his grandchildren.

My research revived interest in Candido José da Costa Cardoso, and his achievement in having been to Lake Malawi – as it is now called – before the famous English explorer, from whom he earned nothing but scorn, although he had generously presented him with all the information he himself had of the great lake to the north.

From Tete, Kanysha Jardim flew me to Salisbury, and from there in due course I continued by a scheduled flight to Loanda, the capital of Angola. 109 years had passed since László Magyar's death, yet I hoped I would at least be able to establish whether or not he is remembered by the people among whom he spent seventeen years of his life. Besides his five children by Princess Ozoro, he had a number of offspring by his concubines. There was a remote chance that someone might have heard of these descendants and of their European great-grandfather.

From Loanda I flew to Lobito, Angola's thriving port, through which every month some 31,000 tons of Zambian copper have been reaching the outside world. On the Benguela Railway I travelled first to Benguela, and from there, skirting the Katumbela river, as Magyar had done, up to the Bihé plateau. At a leisurely speed of thirty miles an hour, I made the overnight journey to Silva Porto, the pretty town which has grown up close to the place where Kombala an Bihé had been in Magyar's day. With his caravan, he had taken forty-one days to cover the same distance.

While having breakfast in the dining car, I talked with a young woman who spoke good French and turned out to be a teacher at a Nova Lisboa secondary school. To show how many primary and secondary schools exist in Angola she produced a thick volume, listing all schools in Angola. Turning the pages idly, my eye caught sight of the following entry: *Vila Nova: Escola Primaria No 44, de "Americo Magyar" – I. lugar.* In a different print it added that the school had been founded in 1922, and named after a Hungarian explorer of the 19th century, who had done valiant work in southern Angola.

On my way back to Benguela, I had the good fortune to be driven part of the way by car to Vila Nova, a small town with handsome villas surrounded by gardens. In the centre of the town stands an old primary school – built in brick, with a smart tiled roof, painted regency green with bright yellow shutters and doors. Unfortunately, March is a holiday period, and both the director and the teacher were away on leave. I could not ascertain whether Americo – a poor translation of the Hungarian name Imre – was a reference to László Magyar's middle name, which he adopted in honour of his father, or had the school been founded in memory of Imre Magyar? None the less, to the people of Vila Nova, the school is undoubtedly a memorial of an explorer of southern Angola, although they are not certain where the man had come from. "Some distant country, probably in Europe," one woman told me. "It all happened a long time ago."

In Silva Porto, the President of the Friends of the Silva Porto Society took me to the restored house of the great Portuguese *sertanejo* – settler–explorer. Belmonte, as he called the house, consists of three rooms, with thick brick walls, a straw roof, and a narrow verandah on the entrance side. The austere iron bed is the one Porto slept in. A strange monument, the shape of a giant urn, stands in the garden, on the spot where Silva Porto committed suicide in 1890. Wrapped in a Portuguese flag, he blew himself up.

The President explained that Porto took his life because a group of chiefs accused him of lying when he assured them that the Portuguese had no intention of occupying the interior. Alas, from Silva Porto's diary and correspondence it is evident that this was indeed the policy he had recommended for years, so as to prevent encroachment either by the British, or by the South Africans. It is a fact that one of the chiefs was highly disrespectful, and pulled Silva Porto's beard. Porto, a very proud man, was deeply mortified by such behaviour on the part of Africans he considered his friends – especially as his own government had done nothing to realise a policy he considered vital and urgent. In his despair he decided to take his life in this dramatic manner. The result was equally dramatic. The Portuguese government began a systematic expansion of its rule, and by 1914, Portugal's hold on Angola was complete. Yet to this day many Africans visit Silva Porto's house and the giant urn, some praying at its foot.

The significance of Silva Porto for the present narrative became apparent to me from the leaflet which is given to all visitors to Belmonte, entitled: *Consagracão Ao Sertanejo Silva Porto.* On the first

View of the exterior of the village of Belmonte in Bihe

page are listed Porto's three closest friends. One of them was "Ladyslau Magyar". The President of the Friends of the Silva Porto Society was not sure where Magyar had lived, except that it had been fairly near, he said, otherwise he could not have been such a frequent visitor. Actually, Magyar's *libata* stood on the shores of the little

Kuitu river, which flows five kilometres south of Belmonte. Next day
I went there with Senhor José Martins Lopes, the indefatigable
Public Relations Director of the Benguela Railway, and Senhor
Estanislau Ivanhoe Matos de Fonseca, the Administrator of the
Silva Porto Railway Station.

Recently a modern settlement has been created in the area László
Magyar described so affectionately as the beautiful sight he had
chosen for his *libata*. A primary school and a surgery, several houses
in which African families live, all built in brick, form the spotless
centre of the settlement. Men and women were working in the fields.
Senhor Fonseca, who had been to Msisi before, asked to see the old
men – hoping that they would remember the European who had lived
there and married the daughter of a king – King Kaiaia Kajangula –
who in 1857 was deposed and murdered by his nephew, Mu-Kinda.
Unfortunately, within the last two years, the last of the very old men
had died, and their sons and relations did not seem to remember. Yet
gradually a conversation got going, a few bottles of beer loosened
tongues, and it seemed that Senhor Fonseca was eliciting some information.

Two women then joined the group, and they advised the men: "Do
not tell him anything, you do not know why he asks so many questions. Be wise, do not answer." The men heeded this irritating advice,
and the talk dried up. They made only one concession: they pointed
in the direction where "a great chief" is buried. I asked whether they
meant Kaiaia Kajangula. The Africans, who belong to the Mbundu
tribe, shrugged their shoulders, and repeated sullenly: "A great chief,
yes, a great chief."

With Senhor Fonseca, Senhor Martins Lopes, and Mena Coelho
who interpreted for me, I set out in the direction of the tall trees,
behind which was said to be the tomb of the great chief. Senhor Fonseca knew from previous visits that these beautiful trees are regarded
by the Africans as symbols of power. They are planted only close to
the house, or to the tomb, of great chiefs.

For some Africans a chief's tomb is an enclosed space, surrounded by tall trees or rocks, with the chief's tin mug, wooden or
metal plate, and his knife, spoon and fork placed in its centre. A Bihé
chief – as was Kaiaia Kajangula – had a very grand burial ground; a
small house – almost like a children's playground toy-house – built of
bricks, with a slate roof: inside was an enamel mug and plate, but the
knife and spoon were missing. The house must have been built more

recently than 1857, when Kaiaia Kajangula was murdered by Mu-Kinda. But a nearby village is called Kajungula, which indicates that his memory still lives, even if present generation Africans say that they have only a hazy idea of who the man was.

So far, my explorations had not produced any evidence of descendants, or even of personal memories either of László Magyar, or of his wife, Ina Kullo (Princess) Ozoro. It was on our way back to Silva Porto that Senhor Fonseca sent for an old railway worker, whose father had been an authority on Bihé's tribal customs. The African was asked whether he had ever heard of László Magyar, or – to use his local name – of '*Ngana Komo*? He shook his head. "My father may have known, I do not. He did not tell me . . ." Senhor Fonseca then asked whether he had ever heard of a European who had lived in Bihé. The African's face brightened. "Yes, I have," he replied cheerfully. "My father told me that once upon a time, a very long time ago, a white man came from a far away country – a cold country. He was an excellent shot, who killed a hundred lion. And he sent for a wife to Kajungula; she was an African and bore him many children. That is all I remember."

So the legend, somewhat garbled, was there, but alas not the facts. Back in Benguela, it was the Catholic Bishop, Mgr Armondo dos Santos Amaral, himself a coloured man, who suggested that I should go to Dombe Grande. "That is where Ladislau lived out his last years in poverty, that is where he died, that is where he must be buried. I believe you will find some of Ladislau's descendants there."

Mgr Amaral always referred to Magyar as Ladislau – this seemed to be his popular name in Angola.

Thanks to Senhor Martins Lopes, the Compania de Asugar de Angola – the CAA – was approached, as the old cemetery of Dombe Grande forms part of their sugar cane estate. The management very kindly provided a Landrover and a guide to search for the ancient cemetery, which lies fairly close to Ponto de Cujo, where László Magyar died on November 9, 1864.

From Benguela to Dombe Grande the distance is less than 200 miles, and until Bahia Farte (the Bay of Farte) the road is excellent. But from there on it is an earth track, full of large potholes. After a good three hours of bumping, we reached the headquarters of the CAA, an attractive group of buildings, dating back to 1886. The Director, Engineer José Baptista Serra, received us graciously, and providing yet another guide, made arrangements that our party should be able to cross the Coporolo river – in Magyar's day it was called the Kimbangululu. A narrow, single railway track, mounted on a few iron girders, renders service for all cross-river transport. A stool, fixed onto two wheels, and pushed by an African, carried me and my interpreter across the river. It was an uncomfortably lonely place from which to look into the swirling Coporolo, alive with crocodiles.

By an ingenious device, the Landrover was fixed onto a platform with four wheels, each pair the width of the rails. It too was pushed across the river, and we set out on the last lap of our journey. Twenty minutes later we stopped in an arid, sandy place, outside an ancient iron gate, leading into a walled-in cemetery. For once the word ancient was apposite, for no one had been buried in this cemetery for many decades. None of the graves bore an inscription; most of them had been reduced by time, and wind-swept sand, to little mounds; some had hand-made iron crosses lying on them. But one grave bore a marble slab, and on the slab a Maltese cross, carved by a practised hand. "Here lies the Ungaro," the local guide said, pointing to the Maltese cross. "This is his cross, not ours."

There is no name on the slab, crumbling at the edges; a rough iron cross adorns the head of the tomb, also without any identification. The guide had no idea who had paid for the tomb; or who had made it. He got bored with the questions, shrugged his shoulders, and repeated, "Here lies the Ungaro." Later, while I was taking photographs, he volunteered, "There is another graveyard near the Bahia dos Elephantos (the Elephant Bay), more than 100 kilometres south of here. Another Ungaro is buried there. Perhaps you want to see that grave too? But he did not live at Ponto de Cujo." But Ponto de Cujo is the place where Magyar spent the last two years of his life.

Who commissioned the marble slab on the grave? Who paid for it? Perhaps Senhor Joao Estevas de Aranjo, in whose care Magyar's papers and maps had been placed and whose house was alleged to have been burnt down, with all its contents. And if it was not Magyar's grave, if he lies under one of the anonymous mounds, why do the local people firmly believe that it is the resting place of the eccentric Ungaro?

We wanted to be back in Benguela before nightfall, and we were already standing by the Landrover, back at the CAA offices, when I asked Engineer Serra, whether among his employees he had a man called Gonga?

Cemetry in which Magyar is buried

Magyar's grave

The personnel manager was sent for, and fortunately turned out to be a Goanese, Natalicio Pais, who spoke fluent English. "Did you ever hear of a man called Gonga, probably a carpenter, among the Company workers?" I asked him.

"Yes," Mr Pais replied, "but that was long before my time. I believe he died in 1949."

"Has he any children or grandchildren?" I asked.

"I believe he has," replied Mr Pais, "If you will be good enough to wait, I think I know where one of them is."

Mr Pais returned with a tall, grey-haired African, with handsome un-African features except that his skin was dark, and his hair crinkly. But his skull had a definitely European shape. He would not answer any questions – he would not even give his name. Whether he was frightened of the Director, or of us foreign visitors, or just in no mood to talk, I never discovered. When I was becoming quite desperate with curiosity, Mr Pais said to the man in his own tongue, "You are Gonga?" to which he nodded. As he would not say where he was born, I asked whether any records were being kept. Gonga had an identity card, which after some persuasion he handed to Mr Pais. On it his name was spelt clearly: "Gonga Segundo." Mr Pais shook his head. "I have never seen this description of a man before – funny that I had not noticed it. This is a royal description. He must come from an African ruling house." As for his birthplace, on the identity card it said: Huambo, the modern version of Hamboland, where Donna Isabella lived in Magyar's time, and where in 1857 she saved his life by protecting him from Mu-Kinda's thugs. And it is not many miles from Bihé's border. Gonga's father's name is Latehimba, his mother's Nassilipa; he was born in 1914. At last I realised I had made a positive discovery.

Gonga Segundo must be the grandson of Gonga I, that is László Magyar's great-grandson.

Back in Benguela, through the good offices of Bishop Amaral, I learnt that Gonga has a relation, a mulatto, who also works at Dombe Grande, called – Alfonzo Magyar. Unfortunately he was on holiday.

In the final analysis I am satisfied that László Magyar's descendants are alive – members of the Angolan working class – and that Alfonzo Magyar is a clerk in the CAA office. Neither he nor Gonga can have any doubt of their European blood.

László Magyar at one time wrote that he was proud to have

planted his Hungarian seed in Africa; he might be glad to know that his blood flows in African veins.

| | DAVID LIVINGSTONE | WILLIAM COTTON OSWELL |
|---|---|---|
| 1805 | | |
| 1813 | Born | |
| 1818 | | Born |
| 1826 | | |
| 1831 | | |
| 1837 | | Sails to India |
| 1840 | Ordained | |
| 1841 | Arrives in Africa | |
| 1842 | | |
| 1843 | | |
| 1844 | | Sails to South Africa |
| 1845 | Marries Mary Moffat | Meets DL at Kuruman; 1st expdn. |
| 1846 | | 2nd expdn. |
| 1847 | Colobeng | |
| 1848 | | |
| 1849 | Lake Ngami with W.C.Oswell | 3rd expdn; Lake Ngami with DL |
| 1850 | Fame; Zambezi trip fails | 4th expdn. |
| 1851 | Zambezi trip with WCO succeeds | 5th expdn.; reaches Zambezi with DL |
| 1852 | Wife, children to England | Returns to England |
| 1853 | Reaches Linyanti | |
| 1854 | Sets out to Loanda | Sails for Crimea |
| 1855 | Reaches Loanda | Returns England; goes to S. America |
| 1856 | Reaches Tete, meets Cardoso; gets to Quelimane; London | |
| 1857 | Publishes *Missionary Travels* | |
| 1858 | HM Consul Quelimane; *Ma Roberts* reaches Tete; Cabrabassa; 1st Shire expdn.; breaks Tengani blockade | |
| 1859 | 2nd Shire expdn.; Murchison cataracts; Lake Nyasa | |
| 1860 | Takes Makololo to Linyanti | |
| 1861 | Bishop Mackenzie dies | |
| 1862 | Wife dies | |
| 1863 | DL and UMCA mission recalled; sets off for India | |
| 1864 | From India to England | |
| 1865 | Leaves England | |
| 1866 | Arrives at Mikindani | |
| 1867 | Crosses Chambezi | |
| 1868 | Refuge with Arabs; discovers Lake Bangweulu | |
| 1869 | Sets out to plot Lualaba | |
| 1871 | Receives men from Ujiji; reaches Lualaba; Stanley | |
| 1872 | Travels with Stanley; sets out on own for Lake Bangweulu | |
| 1873 | Dies | Pallbearer at DL's funeral |
| 1880 | | |
| 1893 | | Dies |

| | LASZLO MAGYAR | CANDIDO CARDOSO |
|---|---|---|
| 1805 | | Born in Tete |
| 1813 | | |
| 1818 | Born | |
| 1826 | | Marries Francisca Pereira |
| 1831 | | *Prazo* of Soche; begins to trade |
| 1837 | | Travels and trades |
| 1840 | | |
| 1841 | | |
| 1842 | Enrols Naval Academy, Fiume | |
| 1843 | Sails for Brazil | |
| 1844 | Resigns from Navy | |
| 1845 | Sails to S. America and W. Africa | |
| 1846 | Commands King Trudodat's flotilla | Visits Lake Nyasa |
| 1847 | | |
| 1848 | Explores Zaire; arrives Angola | |
| 1849 | Bihe; Msisi; marries Princess Ozoro | |
| 1850 | Katanga; discovers Cassequer tribe | |
| 1851 | | Made *Capitan Mor* |
| 1852 | To Linyanti to meet DL | Becomes important in local affairs |
| 1853 | To Libebe to meet DL; fails | |
| 1854 | Expdn. to Lobal countries | |
| 1855 | | |
| 1856 | Plans return to Hungary | Meets DL; wife dies |
| 1857 | Kajangula murdered; flees | President of Mines Commission; marries again, Helena Nunes Heget |
| 1858 | Expdn. to Munda-Evambo, Lungo, and Kapota countries | Appointed Juiz Privativo |
| 1859 | 1st volume of *Travels in Southern Africa* published | Visited by Kirk to discuss route to Lake Nyasa; visited by R. Thornton |
| 1860 | | Lends DL a donkey |
| 1861 | | |
| 1862 | | |
| 1863 | | Made Knight of Order of Christ by the King of Portugal |
| 1864 | Dies | |
| 1865 | | |
| 1866 | | |
| 1867 | | |
| 1868 | Hungarian Govt. notified of death | Mediates between Pereiras and da Cruz families |
| 1869 | | |
| 1871 | | |
| 1872 | | Attempts alliance with Shire chiefs for Govt. of Mocambique |
| 1873 | Hungarian Academy of Science memorial | |
| 1880 | | Dies |
| 1893 | | |

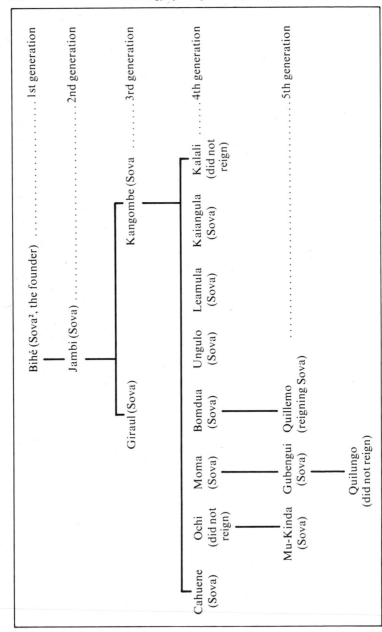

# Appendix

From *William Cotton Oswell*, by W. Edward Oswell, pp. 173–76

ARTICLES, STORES, ETC., REQUIRED FOR A TRIP OF TEN OR TWELVE
MONTHS WITH TWO WAGONS AND SEVEN OR EIGHT SERVANTS.

Coffee, 300 lbs.
Salt, 100 lbs.
Pepper, 10 lbs.
Rice, one bag.
Sago, two lbs.
Spices, etc., qu. suff.
Soap, a box.
Tar, two flasks.
Sugar, 400 lbs.
Mustard, three bottles.
Meal, six muids.
Arrowroot, two lbs.
Cheese.
French brandy, two cases.
Wax candles, 30 lbs.
Snuff, two dozen boxes.
Tobacco, five rolls.

One large baking pot.
One smaller baking pot.
Three saucepans.
Six tin plates.
Six knives and forks.
One fryingpan.
One meat knife.

Four tin canisters for tea, etc.
40 lbs. of beads.
One bale of canvas.
12 riems.
Three saddles and bridles.
Six linchpins.
One spokeshave.
Three axes.
Three picks.
One chisel.
One punch.
Two spare skenes.
Two gimlets.
One saw.
Three spades.
Three sickles.
One cold chisel.
Two kettles.
Two pots.
Four tin dishes.
Six spoons.
One gridiron.
One meat axe.
Three large tin dishes.
One ladle.

Two coffee pots.
One teapot.
Two lanterns.
One flour sieve.
One coffee mill.
Three water casks.
Six needles.
Half pound wicks.
Six tinder boxes.
10 lbs. brass wire.
One candle mould.
Six beakers.
One pair of bellows.
One pestle and mortar.
Two buckets.
Two lbs. of twine.

One dozen knives.
Two dozen boxes lucifers.
One hammer.
Two augers.
Screws, nails, etc.
Thermometer.
Small telescope.
Sextant, etc.
Iron spoon for running bullets.
Coarse powder, 60 lbs.
Fine powder, 20 lbs.
Caps, 3,000.
Lead, 150 lbs.
Tin, 30 lbs.
Flints, 60.
Muskets, 6.

### FOR BOYS.

Six beakers.
Six spoons.
12 common shirts.
Two greatcoats for drivers.
A small tent.

Six scotels.
One piece of moleskin.
Six jackets.
12 blankets.

### PAID BY CHEQUE ON MESSRS. RUTHERFORD.

|  | £ | s. | d. |
|---|---|---|---|
| Mr. James for wagon | 37 | 10 | 0 |
| Mr. James for oxen | 96 | 0 | 0 |
| Krommehout for wagon and span | 130 | 0 | 0 |
| Cockroft for wagon, etc. | 57 | 10 | 0 |
| Wedderburn's bill for stores, etc. | 40 | 5 | 0 |
| Ogilvie's bill for stores, etc. | 30 | 14 | 0 |
| Coffee (3 bags) | 9 | 0 | 0 |
| Canvas | 2 | 8 | 0 |
| Holder, for repairs wagon, etc. | 12 | 10 | 0 |
| Godfrey, for repairs wagon, etc. | 6 | 9 | 0 |
| Wagon box | 0 | 12 | 0 |
| Wagon box | 2 | 0 | 0 |
| Twelve riems | 0 | 10 | 0 |
| Mats | 0 | 9 | 0 |
| Cartels | 2 | 10 | 0 |
|  | 428 | 7 | 0 |

## HORSES

|  | £ | s. | d. |
|---|---|---|---|
| For 3 from Mr. James, £20, £10, £9 | 39 | 0 | 0 |
| For dun pony, Trollop | 15 | 0 | 0 |
| For brown pony, Boer | 15 | 0 | 0 |
| For dun pony | 10 | 0 | 0 |
| Brown | 20 | 0 | 0 |
| Brown chestnut | 15 | 10 | 0 |
| Bay pony | 15 | 0 | 0 |
| Chestnut | 15 | 0 | 0 |
| 'Wildebeest' | 9 | 0 | 0 |
| Mare | 6 | 0 | 0 |
| 'Harry' | 10 | 0 | 0 |
| Chestnut | 9 | 0 | 0 |
|  | 178 | 10 | 0 |
|  |  |  |  |
| Principal expenses as above for stores, repairs, etc. | 428 | 7 | 0 |
| For horses | 178 | 10 | 0 |
|  | 606 | 17 | 0 |

## SERVANTS.

|  | £ | s. | d. |
|---|---|---|---|
| George Fleming, engaged 1st January, 1849, advanced | 15 | 0 | 0 |
| Peat Frer, engaged 1st January, 1849, advanced | 4 | 10 | 0 |
| Claas David, engaged 1st January, 1849, advanced | 1 | 0 | 0 |
| John Thomas, engaged 1st February, 1849, advanced (15s. a month to be drawn by his family) | 8 | 0 | 0 |
| John Scheimen, engaged 26th February, 1849, advanced | 3 | 0 | 0 |
| Ruyter, engaged 26th February, 1849, advanced | 0 | 10 | 0 |
| Hendrick, engaged 26th February, 1849, advanced | 0 | 10 | 0 |
| Claas Henry, engaged 9th March, 1849, advanced | 1 | 0 | 0 |
| Christian, engaged 7th April, 1849, advanced | 1 | 0 | 0 |
| Willem Kurt, engaged 7th April, 1849, advanced | 0 | 17 | 6 |

There is then an entry:

### 'FOR MRS. MOFFAT.

'Cauliflower, peas, broccoli, cabbage, spinach, carrots, turnips, Jerusalem artichokes.'

# Notes

## PART ONE

### Chapter One

1 David Livingstone wrote his name without an 'e' until 1857 when, at his father's request, he restored the original spelling.
2 George Seaver, *David Livingstone: His Life and Letters*, p. 19.
3 Letter to Robert Moffat, September 12, 1855.
4 There had been seven Livingstone children, but two boys died in infancy.
5 Essay by David Livingstone on the Holy Spirit, LMS Archives.
6 The spelling mistakes and erratic use of capitals are copied from the original.
7 The author's italics.
8 George Seaver, op. cit., p. 24; W. G. Blaikie, *The Life of David Livingstone*, p. 20.
9 The LMS, founded in 1795, was entirely non-sectarian.
10 This was Dr Dick's *Philosophy of a Future State*.
11 In a letter to the Rev Joseph Moore, written in "Elisabethtown", South Africa, Livingstone wrote: "I am a very poor preacher, having a bad delivery, and some of them said if they knew I had to preach again they would not enter the chapel."
12 W. G. Blaikie, op. cit., pp. 31–32.
13 W. G. Blaikie, op. cit., p. 27.
14 The Rt Rev George Seaver, author of *David Livingstone: His Life and Letters*, in a letter to the author dated December 15, 1972, said: "I am sure Livingstone would have been quite happy to go out as a lay missionary. But divinity students at Ongar were trained specially for ordination. . . . I think he regarded ordination as a useful adjunct, such as giving its possessor the right to perform marriage ceremonies."

### Chapter Two

1 In *Missionary Travels and Researches in South Africa*, Livingstone wrote: "Returning towards Kuruman, I selected the beautiful valley of Mabotsa (lat. 25°14′ south, long. 26°30′?) as the site of a missionary station; and thither I removed in 1843", p. 11. (Hereafter to be referred to as *Missionary Travels*.) Regarding Mzilikazi see pp. 51 and 71.
2 Ibid., p. 12.
3 W. G. Blaikie, op. cit., pp. 25 and 26.
4 László Magyar, of whom more in later chapters, was another, as was Joseph Thomson, the East African explorer who discovered Lake Rukwa.
5 On December 21, 1844, announcing his engagement in a letter to Dr Tidman, Livingstone wrote: "Various considerations connected with this new sphere of labour and which to you need not be specified in detail, having led me to the conclusion that it was my duty to enter into the marriage relationship, I have made the necessary arrangements for union with Mary, the oldest daughter of Mr Moffat, in the beginning of January, 1845." *Missionary Correspondence*, p. 59.
6 £750 in 1973.

## Chapter Three

1 £10,500 in 1973.
2 From the biography *William Cotton Oswell*, by his son, W. Edward Oswell, published in 1900, p. 38. In future to be referred to as *Oswell*.
3 Ibid., pp. 47–48.
4 Ibid., pp. 55–56.
5 William Cotton was a Director of the Bank of England from 1822 to 1866. In 1841–42 he was Deputy Governor, and from 1842 to 1845 he was Governor of the Bank.
6 In March 1973, the author discussed Oswell with Sir Robert Tredgold, the former Chief Justice of Rhodesia (he resigned over Rhodesia's unilateral declaration of independence) whose mother was a Moffat (and thus related to Mrs David Livingstone). He said that he had been brought up on the legend of Cotton Oswell: "My father admired him exceedingly and always held him up to us as the highest example of a perfect character. By the time he came to South Africa he was perhaps the best shot in the world, yet his modesty was his outstanding trait – he was completely devoid of ambition."

## Chapter Four

1 *Oswell*, pp. 100–101.
2 Mungo Murray of Lintrose, Cupar Angus, Forfarshire.
3 *Oswell*, p. 104.
4 These were the Masarwa Bushmen, who are a foot taller than the short yellow Bushmen of the southern and western Kalahari, and very black. See also, *The Way to Ilala*, by Professor Frank Debenham, p. 55.
5 *Oswell*, p. 107.
6 *Oswell*, pp. 134–35.
7 The great lake they were referring to was Lake Ngami, also known as Noka a Batlatli, or Noka a Mampooré, or Inghabé.
8 From *Madras Journal of Science and Literature* as published in *Oswell*, pp. 150–51.

## Chapter Five

1 For a complete list see the appendix.
2 £4,500 in 1973.
3 Christie's Burn is a rivulet that runs into the Clyde; it has now been covered over and is a culvert under the Stonefield Public Park in Blantyre, Scotland.
4 The Kalahari Desert.
5 Batawana, an off-shoot of the Bamangwato; they had migrated from Shoshong and settled at Lake Ngami c. 1800. I. Schapera, *Livingstone's Missionary Letters*, p. 131.
6 See below; Oswell said that one of them had already visited Lake Ngami and knew the way; Livingstone did not mention this.
7 J. H. Wilson was a trader who came to acquire ivory.
8 The Bushman woman took Oswell to the now famous well of Chokotsa, which has been the saving grace of many caravans since that day.
9 Dated March 23, 1850. *Oswell*, p. 195.
10 *Livingstone's Missionary Correspondence*, edited by I. Schapera, p. 135.
11 *Oswell*, pp. 215–16.
12 August 24, 1850. D. Chamberlin, *Some Letters from David Livingstone*, p. 136. Three days later – August 27, 1850 – Livingstone wrote to the Rev W. Thompson: "Met Mr. Oswell on our return and do not know where he is now." Ibid.
13 Tim Jeal, *Livingstone*, pp. 90–91.

14 Francis Galton had not read the letters Livingstone had written to Dr Moffat and Mr Freeman, or his denigrating references to Cotton Oswell.

15 *Oswell*, Introduction.

## Chapter Six

1 George Seaver, *David Livingstone: His Life and Letters*, p. 129, 1850. His parents-in-law did not agree that it was "as likely to have happened if we had remained at home."

2 *Livingstone's Private Journals*, pp. 70–71, April 1851.

3 *Oswell*, p. 232.

4 Ibid., 231.

5 John Leyland became an explorer and author of *Adventures in the Far Interior of South Africa*.

6 *Missionary Travels*, p. 79.

7 *David Livingstone: Family Letters*, Vol. II, pp. 83–85, edited by I. Schapera, August 24, 1851.

8 June 21, 1851.

9 They settled near present-day Bulawayo.

10 Robert was Livingstone's one year-old son.

11 Years later, in a letter to W. G. Blaikie, Oswell wrote; "He had a way of repeating his intentions boldly and without any explanation. After we had been lying some time on the Chobe River he suddenly announced his intention of going down to the West Coast. We were about 1,800 miles off it. To my re-iterated objection that it would be impossible – 'I'm going down. I mean to go down', was the only answer. . . . Not till long afterwards did I realise that he was speaking of a future intention just then born." W. G. Blaikie, *Autobiography*, p. 289.

12 Silva Porto had been there two years earlier. In his *A Cartografia Antigada Africa Centrale a Travessia entre Angolae Moçambique, 1500–1860*, Alexander Teixeira da Mota says: "Several white Portuguese settlers had been on the Upper Zambezi in the Lobale region already at the end of the 18th century" (p. 215). In future to be referred to *A Cartografia*.

13 *Oswell*, vol. 1, p. 254; October 1, 1851.

14 £170 would be worth about £1,275 in 1973.

15 March 17, 1852. D. Chamberlin, *Some Letters from David Livingstone*, p. 170.

## Chapter Seven

1 *Oswell.*, vol. II, p. 10.

2 About £45,000 in 1973.

3 Ibid., vol. II, pp. 66–67.

4 Tanganyika, January 6, 1872.

5 See Chapter 20 for details of Livingstone's embalming.

## PART TWO

## Chapter Eight

1 His second-in-command was Paul Kruger, who in the battle preceding the burning was hit by two bullets from the five rifles the Bakwain tribe possessed.

2 This was at the time he had taken a short-cut to reach Sebituane, and he and his family had gone for five days without water.

3 *Missionary Travels*, Chapter VIII, p. 177.

4 The meaning of Sesheke is "the place of sand".

5 *Missionary Travels*, p. 215.

6 Based on the now missing 32 page outline for the second volume of Laśzló Magyar's book *Travels in Southern Africa*. A contributory factor to Livingstone's unwillingness to meet Magyar may have been the knowledge that he had a "native wife". Livingstone would have heard this from Sekeletu. Victorian explorers were often racialist in this regard. See also Livingstone's contemptuous references to half-castes.

## Chapter Nine

1 From *A Short Resumé of My Life*, dated April 20, 1851. In future this will be referred to as *A Short Resumé*.

## Chapter Ten

1 The *contre-bande* ship was a slaver, for Britain had outlawed the slave trade in 1807, and Portugal in 1815 (except with her own colonies). The British Navy patrolled the Atlantic Ocean to stop and board vessels suspected of carrying slaves.

2 At the Havana Marine Academy.

3 He died while they were approaching Madras.

4 Sixty years before László Magyar got there an eccentric Hungarian adventurer, Count Móric Benyovszky, died a hero's death on the earthen ramparts of Antongili Bay, fighting with Africans against the French colonisers, who eventually conquered Madagascar.

5 This was a confederation of four South American states, centred around the Argentine, but its members soon fell out with each other, and a war broke out between the Argentine and Uruguay.

6 On August 23, 1845.

7 Don Manuel Rosas lost the war, had to flee from Buenos Aires, and ended his days in Southampton. In November 1972, the followers of ex-President Peron demanded that Don Manuel's body should be returned to the Argentine.

8 Vámosi offered Magyar hospitality for as long as he cared to stay, but he grew restive and for one year he roamed around Brazil, studying its flora and wildlife. See *A Short Resumé*.

9 At that time this was the equivalent of about £600. In 1973 it would be about £4,500.

10 Except for the last paragraph, which is taken from László Magyar's book, *Travels in Southern Africa*, published in Hungarian (Hungarian Academy of Sciences, 1859) and in German (*Petermann Geografische Mitteilungen*, 1860. *Reisen in Süd Afrika in den Jahren 1849 bis 1857*), the rest of this chapter is from his own account, written for his father in April, 1851. He put the date April 20th, 1851, under his signature, and headed the account, *A Short Resumé of My Life*, explaining that, as most of his letters had not arrived, it was best to start at the beginning, keeping it brief, and without chronological order, "as the original is not with me at present". The Hungarian Academy of Sciences published *A Short Resumé* in 1857, which is fortunate as the original documents (Magyar's hand-written diaries and letters) have disappeared from the Academy's archives. By courtesy of Professor László Krizsán, Professor of African History at Moscow University, the author is in possession of a photostat copy of this rare book, which vanished from the Hungarian Academy of Sciences in 1971. All translations from the Hungarian are by the author.

11 This is as far as Boma. As the channel has since been dredged, ships now sail 30 miles further up to Matadi.

12 The Zaire is referred to in semi-fabulous and little known descriptions of the ancient Kingdom of the Congo – *le Bas-Congo*. The Portuguese poet, Luis Vaz de

Camoëns, was the first European to mention the Zaire in his epic, *Os Lusias*, published in 1572. Camoëns had lived for some time in Moçambique, and had considerable knowledge of Africa. He knew that the Zaire delta had been discovered by Diego Cao (or Cam) in 1482. To mark the discovery, the Portuguese erected a pillar on what is now called Shark's Point, from which the river became known as *Rio de Padrao* – Pillar River. To the Africans it was Zaire, a corruption of the Bantu word meaning "river".

13 Eleven years later, in his address to the Hungarian Academy of Sciences, read for him on October 10, 1859, Magyar had this to say about Ambriz:

> In the same year, 1855, a Portuguese armed force, transported to Ambriz from Loanda, did, after several battles, defeat the natives who are now subjected to the Portuguese Government. As a result of this, the slave trade has been abolished, and the place is visibly developing into a town, defended by a newly constructed military fort. Its trading wares are: ivory, wax, and copper (Malequit ford).

> As I have been informed, about the middle of 1856, some 200 miners arrived from Lisbon for the exploitation of the rich copper veins to be found in the centre of the province. They were sent by a company formed by merchants; but so far I do not know how successful their operations have been. I fear that this worthwhile enterprise will end in failure, because it is the general experience that, in spite of the most careful way of life, every year at least half of the newly arrived Europeans fall victims to the deadly climate, which engenders typhus.

14 On July 6, 1816, Captain J. K. Tuckey, R.N., at the head of a well-equipped expedition, began pushing up-river and got as far as Isangila, beyond the lowest series of rapids. But sickness broke out among his men, and Captain Tuckey and sixteen Europeans died. They are buried on Prince's Island, just above Boma.

15 His name was Jerome Mera, and on his return Magyar conveyed him on his barge as far as Ambriz.

16 They are still suspicious. Being a virtually landlocked country they had negligible contact with, or understanding of, seafaring merchant adventurers.

17 Silver currency then prevalent in South America, which had originated in Spain. It was worth about £1 million in the 1840s and about £7,500,000 in 1973.

18 £4 then; £30 now.

19 *Ndele* still means white man.

20 These are the cataracts that tear through the Inga Gorge, one of the great spectacles of the world. It is between Isangila and Matadi; the river drops 163 metres in 9 kilometres. Captain J. K. Tuckey got as far as Isangile (see footnote 14 above); he must have by-passed the Inga rapids by porterage to get to Isangila.

21 Magyar knew of its existence and had seen some of its Journals.

22 The pamphlet about Magyar's Congo exploration, published by the Hungarian Academy of Sciences, was also translated and published in German by *Petermann Geografische Mitteilungen*. Richard Burton, who had been to the Congo delta in 1863, and read both Magyar's account and Stanley's, said that the Hungarian explorer's was the more accurate of the two.

## Chapter Eleven

1 At this time King Gezo ruled Dahomey; possibly Dalaber Almanzor was his viceroy in Calabar; both may have been descended from Trudo Adato?

2 £450 then; about £3,375 now.

3 *A Short Resumé*.

4 In his book, *Travels In Southern Africa*, published in 1859 by the Hungarian Academy of Sciences in Hungarian. From now on all references to this book will be *Travels*.

5 Ibid.
6 This is the little Kuitu. Msisilies on its shores. The big Kuitu flows into the Cubango, which eventually disappears in what is today Botswana.
7 *Travels*, pp. 232–33.
8 This must be a mistake. See genealogy on p. 264. Magyar probably meant that his father-in-law was born on Gualange territory.
9 Ibid., p. 189.
10 Magyar is using the words "African", "Negro", "Kaffer" and "Moor" interchangeably.
11 He was killed at the siege of Komárom, in the anti-Habsburg war of liberation of 1848–49.
12 In his comments on László Magyar's paper, read at the Royal Geographical Society on February 4, 1853, W. D. Cooley said that in 1795 Alexander de Silva Teixeira had been to Yak Quilem, and that Magyar's reports entirely tallied with his.

## Chapter Twelve

1 In his comments on Magyar's letters, read out at the Royal Geographical Society on February 14, 1853, W. D. Cooley said: "It is remarkable that among scattered particulars learned from the Bechuana, and set down as memorandums in the margin of Livingstone's map, the river Kokema occurs in the neighbourhood of the Kuanja or Quanza." *RGS Journal*, 1854, p. 274.
2 Pinto mentions "Ladislau Magiar" as one of Silva Porto's neighbours, but he does not mention that he was an explorer, married to the daughter of Kaiaia Kajangula, p. 164.
3 W. D. Cooley, on p. 8 of his *Livingstone and the Royal Geographical Society*, says: "African rivers in general change their names with the population on their banks."
4 Pombero Pedro Baptista, to our knowledge the first man to cross Africa from west to east, related that the Kazembe, the Great Ruler, appointed *Quilembes* (*quilembe* was an official rank) and *Quilolos* (ditto) to conduct him to Tete. Yam or Yak Quilem, where Magyar settled, could not be found on any map because it meant *the village of the Quilembe*. It may be presumed that it was the same place which according to the Pombero narrative, belonged to the Lord of the Port, or the Lord of the Ferry. Magyar's Yak Quilem was in the Kalunda Province of Morupoland. See *Travels in Southern Africa*.
5 Kunene means "great" in the local African language. *RGS Journal*, 1854, p. 2.
6 This is the big Kuito, not to be mistaken for the little Kuito, where Magyar had his *libata* at Msisi.
7 Silva Porto's African name was Mporotla.
8 Magyar lived five miles south of Belmonte, Silva Porto's house, now restored and open to the public near Silva Porto, a town named after him in Angola. On the first page of the leaflet handed to visitors to Belmonte, "Ladislau Magyar" is named as one of Silva Porto's closest friends.
9 Bashulukompo was the local name of the Kafue river.
10 pp. 180–181. Ch. ix.
11 *A Cartografia* . . . . A. Teixeira de Mota, p. 218.
12 *Livingstone's Private Journals, 1851–53*, ed. I. Schapera: 1853, July 12: "Senhor Porto arrived yesterday evening."
13 Sekeletu allotted 27 men to accompany Livingstone; only two of them were true Makololo.
14 Therefore Livingstone must have realised that Portuguese travellers had been to these areas long before him – in the 17th century – but he never gave them any recognition.

15  p. 181.
16  Ibid., pp. 218–19.
17  This is untrue. Silva Porto went eastward to seek the *pombeiros* and the Moors, and
    returned to Barotseland on finding that they were also going there. (A. Teixeira da
    Mota, *A Cartografia* . . . p. 229–30).
18  Livingstone met Ben Habib at Naliele, the main Barotse town, on December 12,
    1853. He was the leader of a trading party from Zanzibar. *African Journal*, p. 13.
19  Ibid., p. 217.
20  Ibid., p. 231.
21  After 1867, Father Rónay gained a pardon from the Austrian Government and
    was appointed tutor of Crown Prince Rudolf; he had considerable influence on his
    imperial pupil's thinking.
22  Vol. 24, pp. 271–73.
23  MS of Father J. J. Rónay's *Napló Töredékek* (Diary fragments) in the British
    Museum, No C 59 e 2. (BMGC vol. 237 col. 428.)
24  Ibid.

## Chapter Thirteen

1  See the genealogy of Kaiaia Kajangula (from Serpa Pinto's book *How I Crossed
   Africa*, p. 160) on p. 264.
2  *Sova* means Paramount Chief.
3  £30 in 1854; £225 in 1973.
4  About £75; £570 now.
5  Imre Magyar wanted to have his son's MS translated into English or Portuguese,
   for publication in England or Portugal. But László's half-brother, Imre Jr., who on
   this issue thoroughly disagreed with his father, broke open his writing desk, into
   which the MS had been locked. With the help of József Antunovics, he sent it to
   Professor János Hunfalvy, a member of the Academy, who was subsequently commissioned by the Academy to edit it for publication. It saw print in 1859.
6  £150 then; £1,125 now.
7  In the 1850's this was the equivalent of about £50; today its approximate value
   would be £375.
8  See footnote No. 5 above.
9  Kabebe was the capital of Morupoland, not of Bihé. Kombala-an-Bihé was the
   capital of Bihé.

## PART THREE

## Chapter Fourteen

1  *African Journal*, edited by I. Schapera, vol. I, p. 151.
2  On August 9, 1855, he had written in his *Journal*: "I am sorry to hear of that frightful waterfall which exists in the Kabompo . . . and that the Bashukulompo river
   [Kafue] too is spoiled by cataracts. . . . The waterfalls of Mosioatunya [Victoria
   Falls], Kabompo and others explain why commercial enterprise never entered the
   interior of the continent except by foot travellers. I am sorry for it. My dreams of
   establishing a commerce by means of the rivers vanish as I become better acquainted with them."
3  Livingstone's *African Journal*, pp. 326–27. He described the Victoria Falls in his
   diary on November 27, 1855; an edited version appeared in *Missionary Travels*.
4  Ibid., Vol. II, p. 460.
5  Ibid., pp. 469–70. Chissaka's real name was Pedro Caetano Pereira; he was the
   grandson of Gonçalo Caetano Pereira, known as Dombo Dombo (meaning "The
   Terror"), who had come to eastern Africa from Goa about 1770 and was of Indian

origin. Dombo Dombo laid the foundations of the Pereira fortune by trading and gold prospecting, and came to dominate the whole north bank of the Zambezi from the Shire to Zumbo. His daughter, Francisca Pereira, married a man who was to play a decisive role in Livingstone's life.

6 *The Zambesi and its Tributaries*, p. 230, by D. & C. Livingstone.

7 *African Journal*, vol. II, p. 373.

8 Ibid., p. 373.

9 Ibid., p. 374.

10 September, 1853. *Family Letters*, vol. II, p. 228.

11 *Missionary Travels*, p. 604.

12 Ibid.

13 Letter dated March 2, 1856; also *Missionary Correspondence*, edited by I. Schapera, pp. 302–03.

14 Professor I. Schapera says in an editorial note on Livingstone's diary that Pedro da Trindade, who died in 1751, was a Dominican friar who lived at Zumbo for more than 25 years; he was much esteemed by the natives for his good works and for his remedy against poisonous wounds or bites; he was also 'chief captain' (*capitan mor*) of the region, monopolising some of its gold diggings, and controlled about 1,600 slaves. Andrade, *Moçambique Setecentista*, pp. 200–03, 264, 281. Also *Grande Enciclopedia*, article on Zumbo.

15 One of the ways in which the Portuguese had established themselves in Moçambique was by granting long term tenure of land, usually for three generations, known as the *prazo* system. This system gave the lessees a long standing control over their part of Africa, and a thorough acquaintance with local conditions which was bound to make them people of influence. Most *prazos* were granted to women, who were obliged by contract to leave them to their eldest daughter (not son), because – as the author was bluntly told in Tete – with women it was certain who their children were, and because they were willing to stay at home and look after their estates. Determined *donas* could and did leave their *prazos* to male *prazo* owners. Until the 20th century the Portuguese authorities could do little about this, as in Zambezia possession was nine-tenths if not ten-tenths – of the law.

16 At the Congress of Vienna, in 1815, Portugal was induced to agree to outlaw the slave trade by a remission of £450,000 of debt owed to Britain, and by a gift of £300,000, disguised as an "indemnity" for captured slave ships, confining her trade to the transport of slaves from Africa south of the Equator to her "possessions" across the Atlantic. (The pound sterling is now worth approximately $7\frac{1}{2}$ times what it was worth then.) But Portugal passed no punitive legislation against slave traders.

When Brazil became independent in 1825, the Portuguese trade was brought to an end *de jure*, but not *de facto*. In 1817 she had acquiesced to the right of the Royal Navy to search her ships, but in 1835 she stubbornly refused to sign a treaty providing for the seizure of ships found to be equipped with decks, shackles, and other tackle for carrying slaves. This was imperative, for slavers frequently threw their slaves overboard when chased by a British ship. In 1839 the House of Commons passed an Act that Portuguese vessels, if found equipped for the slave trade, might be seized by British cruisers and brought for adjudication by a British court as if they were British vessels. By 1842 slave trading under the Portuguese flag was virtually wiped out, and Portugal signed the treaty declaring the trade piracy. In 1854 France forced Portugal to allow the trade within certain limits in Moçambique; some Portuguese officials, not to mention traders, connived at it and grew rich as a result. Even conscientious governors did not have the force to stop it; but in the 1880's, after the Scramble for Africa, the occupation of Africa by major European

Powers did put an end to it. In 1891 Portugal was compelled to accept a delimita-
tion treaty and British protection over Nyasaland. From that moment on the suppression of the slave trade was only a matter of time.

## Chapter Fifteen

1  p. 640.
2  The photograph was taken by the great-grandson of Cardoso.
3  From M. D. D. Newitt, *Portuguese Settlement on the Zambesi*, p. 134. Francisco
   José de Lacerda e Almeida, *Diario da Viagem de Moçambique para os Rios de Sena*,
   Lisbon, 1889.
4  The four dialects Cardoso spoke.
5  *African Journal*, pp. 449–50.
6  *Missionary Travels*, pp. 641–42.
7  Ibid., p. 641. Livingstone said, "Candido holds the office of judge in all the disputes of the natives and knows the languages of the natives perfectly." A. P. P.
   Gamitto, in his *O Muata Cazembe* says the same on p. 7. (Published in Lisbon in
   1854.)
   Cardoso was also active in the Tete local government. Three documents of 1827
   indicate his activities. On October 4, 1827, in view of trouble with slaves at Mittore,
   one of the Pereira estates, João Costa da Cardoso (Candido's elder brother) as Juiz
   Privativo (judge of the court dealing with customary law), Candido as attorney,
   and Manuel Pereira (Candido's brother-in-law) as *Capitan Mor* of Tete, ordered
   military protection for several *loane* (private houses), including that of Soche. On
   November 22, 1827, elections were held for the Municipal Chamber of Tete, of
   which the Governor was informed, and the document signed by seven distinguished Tete citizens, among them João and Candido da Costa Cardoso, in
   their above capacities. On November 28, 1827, a report was sent to the Governor
   advocating the following: the abolition of the slave trade; the widening of the Zambezi river-bed to promote trade; making Quilimane an international port; creating
   public works to improve the prosperity of the natives; setting up a hospital for the
   natives in Tete, with proper staff; the building of a new elementary school, a new
   Municipal Chamber and a new prison; and making arrangements for artisan training and the setting up of workshops. The report concluded by saying that these
   suggestions were being made after consultation with the responsible citizens of
   Tete, and is signed by eight distinguished citizens, among them João and Candido
   Cardoso. In 1858 Candido succeeded his brother as Juiz Privativo.
8  M. D. D. Newitt, op. cit., p. 235, Judicial Inquiry, May 14, 1822.
9  In 1793 Bisa traders came to see Dombo Dombo at his Java Goldmines, north of
   Tete, and he realised the possibilities of tapping new resources of ivory in the interior. He sent his son Manuel, Cardoso's brother-in-law, to accompany the Bisa on
   their return journey. Six months later Manuel returned with the first detailed
   account that Europeans had had of the coming of the Kazembe's Lunda from the
   Zaire. Manuel told his story to the assembled residents of Tete, and introduced to
   them the ambassadors from the Kazembe's court. The new Governor, F. M. de
   Lacerda e Almeida, had been instructed by the Portuguese Foreign Minister to
   undertake a transcontinental journey to establish a link between Angola and
   Moçambique. Because the British had landed in the Cape in 1795, Lisbon feared
   that they might penetrate the interior and cut any possible contact between the
   Portuguese possessions in east and west Africa. Lacerda set out on his voyage to
   the Kazembe in June 1798; he was already a sick man and died in Kazembe's capital on October 18 of the same year.
10 Marques Sà da Bandeira, *Notas relativas a alguns dos Lagos de Africa Oriental e aos
   Rios Zambeze e Chire*, 1861, in the Arquivo Historico Ultramarino, Maco 1, Sà da
   Bandeira, Sala 12, Lisbon.

11 Oliver Ransford, in *Livingstone's Lake*, p. 57, suggests that Cardoso probably went to Chief Mwase's kraal in Kasungu, from where it was a short march down the escarpment to the lake.

12 Ibid., p. 57; and Engineer Antonio Martins Pires de Carvalho to the author in Tete, March 1973.

13 October 30, 1857. There was trouble with the Africans at Sena; the Zambezi wars, which ended in 1888, had begun in 1840. According to Livingstone the Portuguese authorities had difficulties in putting down the Sena uprising and Tete had to provide such aid as it could. Cardoso played a leading part in this.

14 On July 21, 1858, Register No. 103, Andrade informed the Governor of Quelimane that he had received the instructions of June 20 regarding Livingstone and his party.

15 In May 1858, in a private letter Livingstone wrote: "Got the loan of two donkeys, there being but three in the country. The Portuguese cultivate skin diseases and drunkenness more than horseflesh and are asses themselves."

16 *African Journal*, May 25, 1860.

17 *The Zambezi Papers* of Richard Thornton, p. 45.

18 Ibid., p. 110.

19 From Engineer A. M. P. de Carvalho and from Cardoso's great-grandson, Alvaro Nunes Marques dos Santos.

20 This may be a mis-spelling. Livingstone probably meant Cardoso.

21 In March 1973, de Carvalho told the author that "Senhor Cardoso's ideas were in keeping with the law, as in 1836 the Prime Minister, Marques Sà de Bandeira, had banished slavery from all Portuguese colonies. (The trade in slaves had been banned in 1815.) Therefore such trade had become illegal in Moçambique. The so-called slaves of the time were either captives from native wars, or old slaves, or sons of slaves."

22 He was nicknamed Coimbra because he had swallowed a bill of exchange. David Livingstone's *Journal*, May 11, 1860.

23 The author was told this by Eng. A. M. P. de Carvalho in Tete.

## Chapter Sixteen

1 Livingstone wrote to his brother Charles (who wrote on May 5, 1857, to his wife) that he had decided to accept Lord Clarendon's offer and had accordingly written to him "and the matter will be decided soon."

2 *Kirk of the Zambesi*, pp. 90–91.

3 In March 1858, Livingstone wrote to Rev Adam Sedgwick of Cambridge University: "All this machinery [members and supplies for his expedition] has for its ostensible object the development of African trade but what I tell to no one but such as you in whom I have confidence is this. I hope it may result in an English colony in the healthy high lands of Central Africa – (I have told it only to the Duke of Argyll)."

4 J. P. R. Wallis (ed.), *The Zambezi Expedition of David Livingstone, 1858–1863*, p. 61.

5 José Pedra, *Capitan-Mor* of Zumbo, sent down the canoes by way of experiment.

6 On November 30, 1858.

7 Ibid. The same person who had told Livingstone that there was nothing interesting further on.

8 According to Dr Kirk's diary.

9 J. P. R. Wallis (ed.), *The Zambezi Expedition*, vol. I, p. 71.

10 D. and C. Livingstone, *Narrative of an Expedition to the Zambesi and its Tributaries*, described Tengani: "He was an elderly, well made man, grey haired and over six feet high." p. 75.

11 Dr Kirk wrote in his diary, "We have been the means of opening a slave hunting country." Frank Debenham, *The Way to Ilala*, p. 217. See also George Martelli, *Livingstone's River*, p. 157: "Worse still was the fact that the routes Livingstone had opened up, both to the interior and up the Shire, were now being used by Portuguese Traders, usually half-castes, to increase the traffic in slaves. The method employed was to send out bands of armed slaves, who would incite one tribe to wage war on another and make prisoners of all the able-bodied."

12 J. M. Schoffeleers, *Livingstone and the Mang'anja Chiefs*, pp. 120–21, in *Livingstone, Man of Africa*, edited by Bridglal Pachai. Father Schoffeleers gives his sources for this tragic story: Reginald Coupland, *Kirk of the Zambezi*, pp. 193–43; J. P. R. Wallis,(ed.), *The Zambezi Expedition of David Livingstone*, p. 78; D. and C. Livingstone, *Narrative of an Expedition to the Zambesi and its Tributaries*, p. 76, pp. 355–56, and adds: "Wallis' account is to be compared with the one in Livingstone's *Narrative*, p. 76, which gives an entirely different impression and describes the meeting (with Tengani) as a highly satisfactory one. The *Narrative* appears to be a highly structured account in which the first and later years of the expedition are placed in deliberate contrast to each other."

13 On p. 81 of the *Narrative*.

## Chapter Seventeen

1 See Chapter Fifteen, p. 164.

2 This alleged attack was linked with the Zambezi Wars going on in Moçambique.

3 *Livingstone, Man of Africa*, edited by B. Pachai, p. 122.

4 Reginald Foskett (ed.), *The Zambezi Journal and Letters of Dr John Kirk, 1858–1863*, vol. I, April 18, 1859, p. 194.

5 Ibid.

6 *Narrative*, p. 125.

7 In *David Livingstone: His Life and Letters*, p. 262, George Seaver says that in Tete Livingstone "also exchanged valuable medical and geographical notes with a kindred spirit, Senhor Candido, whose map of the river from Tete to Sena he inserted in his own." (March 2, 1856.) Livingstone genuinely did not know that three Europeans, the Portuguese S. X. Botelho, the Frenchman J. Bourgignon D'Anville, and the Englishman "Mr Alexander", had visited Lake Nyasa earlier in the 19th century, not to mention other Portuguese between the 16th and 19th centuries. See note 1 in the Postscript.

8 On May 5, 1973, at the David Livingstone Seminar organised by Edinburgh University, D. D. Yonge read a paper, *Some Notes on Livingstone's diary from 11th October to 11th November, 1872*, in which he had plotted Livingstone's last journey south of Lake Tanganyika. He said: "It was surprisingly difficult to fit the description in the diary to the ground as I knew it. To a great extent, this was because in Livingstone's day the lake was several feet deeper than it was in 1957, a flooded inlet lay where I saw beach and cultivated valley." And this, unlike the Shire country, is not a volcanic area.

9 Oliver Ransford, *Livingstone's Lake*, p. 56.

10 Antonio Gaspar Bocarro was a wealthy Portuguese trader, who in 1616 visited the lake and wrote in his diary: "There is the great Maganja river or lake which looks like a sea. The river Nanha rises from it, and joins the Zambezi below Sena, where they call the river Chiry." Bocarro's diary was preserved, edited and published under the title, *The Thirteenth Decade*, "in case anyone should have occasion to attempt this journey again."

11 Ransford, op. cit. pp. 55–57.

12 See Chapter Fourteen, p. 155.

## Chapter Eighteen

1 Chapter Fifteen, p.170–71.
2 A South African expression meaning a river-crossing or ford.
3 Out of the original 114 Makololo only sixty could be persuaded to go back to Lin-yanti, and of these thirty bolted back to Tete before Livingstone had reached Cabora Bassa. Eventually he led twenty back to Sekeletu; the rest refused to leave Moçambique, where they had settled, married, and made comfortable lives for themselves.
4 Charles Livingstone to F. F. Fitch, August 8, 1862.
5 D. Livingstone to LMS on November 10, 1860.
6 Ibid.
7 D. Livingstone to John Moffat, November 24, 1861.
8 Tim Jeal, *Livingstone*, p. 184.
9 There is a certain parallel between this and the situation in Rwanda and Burundi. In Rwanda the Hutu managed to overthrow their Tutsi overlords; in Burundi the Tutsi massacred some 140,000 Hutu to maintain their position. The difference is that the Phiri-Marawi rulers never treated the Chewa as their slaves; they only reserved all high positions for themselves.
10 Unpublished *Private Journal* of David Livingstone, National Library of Scotland.
11 Henry Burrup was a member of the UMCA Mission.
12 The ladies' daily ablutions had to be performed on shore, Miss Mackenzie having to be carried there and back. According to Lieutenant Devereaux, the breezy naval paymaster, "she was a pleasant, humorous, good-natured elderly Scotch lady."
13 De Edward Bouverie Pusey, the famous High Churchman, whom Livingstone cordially disliked.
14 The Rev James Stewart came out on the same boat as Mrs Livingstone to join the Mission. Later he became famous as the missionary of Lovedale in South Africa. Before leaving the Zambezi he wrote in his diary:
> In the afternoon I went down the river bank a short way and threw with all my strength into the turbid muddy reed-covered Zambezi my copy of *Missionary Travels in South Africa*. The volume was fragrant with odours of and memories of the earnestness with which I studied the book in days gone by. How different it appeared now! It was nothing short of an eyesore, the very sight of its brown covers. I disliked the book and sent it to sink or swim in the vaunted Zambezi. (*The Zambesi Journal*, p. 190, February 1, 1863.)
15 David Livingstone to William Monk, March 3, 1859.
16 David Livingstone to John Moffat, December 12, 1863.
17 p. 579.
18 Chuma and Wikitani, of whom we will hear again, were members of his small crew.
19 Tengani and Chibisa were killed in March, 1863.
20 J. M. Schoffeleers, *Livingstone and the Mang'anja Chiefs*, p. 127, of *Livingstone, Man of Africa*, (ed. Dr B. Pachai).

## PART FOUR

### Chapter Nineteen

1 January 20, 1863.
2 *David Livingstone's Last Journals*, from Tim Jeal, *Livingstone*, p. 289.
3 Burton reciprocated his feelings; he must also have known of Livingstone's shabby treatment of László Magyar; this may be the reason why he sent the Hungarian explorer money which, unfortunately, only arrived after the latter's death. The best proof that Burton was greatly interested in Magyar is that in 1893, when Isabel

Burton compiled a list of her husband's unpublished works, the second "quite complete" one was *Ladislas Magyar's African Travels* (p. 454, vol. 2, of *Sir Richard Francis Burton* by Isabel Burton). It may have been a translation of the German version of *Magyar's Travels in Southern Africa*, but in view of Burton's intellectual curiosity and thoroughness, there must have been comments, footnotes, and probably a challenging introduction. Burton's diaries must also have contained information about Magyar's last seven years, of which we know very little as the two chests containing his own papers were said to have been burnt "with all their contents" when the man in whose safekeeping they were placed, lost his house in a fire. For reasons best known to herself, Isabel Burton felt differently about her husband's unpublished works than about his diaries. Instead of burning them, this is what she planned: "The Uniform Library will bring out a cheap edition for the people first of all of his hitherto published works, to which will be gradually added his unpublished works as fast as they can be produced that the British public may be made familiar with all that he has written." (Ibid., p. 455.) I had hoped to give this book greater interest by including in it the comments of Sir Richard Burton on László Magyar. All Richard Burton's biographers, and M. N. Penzer, the author of a bibliography of his works as well as works about him, say that Burton's books on László Magyar had been lost. However as Isabel Burton stated in her biography of her husband that she wished it to be published, I felt it was worth looking into.

Leslie Blanche, in her essay on Isabel Burton – in her book *The Wilder Shores Of Love* – said that her papers had been deposited at the Kensington High street and the Campden Hill Public Libraries. I learnt from the first that their Burton papers had been transferred to the Richmond Public Library, and those from the second to the Royal Anthropological Institute. Thanks to the Assistant Librarian of the Richmond Public Library, I found out that Quentin Keynes had bought some Burton MS's, and that an American collector, whose name he did not remember, had also acquired some.

Mr Keynes told me that the MS I was interested in indeed existed, and had been auctioned at Sotheby's in 1963: Bertram Rota had bid for it on behalf of an American client, Mr Edwards H. Metcalf. It was easy to ascertain from the Sotheby catalogue that on April 9, 1963, the manuscript was sold under the title: *Ladislaus Magyar: his residence in South Africa. From the German of Prof. Johann Hunfalvy, by Richard F. Burton. With remarks by Clements R. Markham.* It had formed lot 548, fetched £240, and consisted of 1336 leaves.

I wrote to Mr Metcalf, pointing out that his MS was not an original work of Richard Burton, but a translation from a German translation of Ladislas Magyar's own book, which I repeatedly quote in this book. Moreover the title page is inaccurate textually as well as mis-stating that the author is Professor Hunfalvy, who merely edited Magyar's original Hungarian work. There may be an introduction by Burton, and certainly comments and footnotes, which I am sure are very interesting. It is regretable that I could not go to California to see the work.

Only one more question remained unanswered: where had this MS been from 1896 (when Lady Burton died) until April 9, 1963, when it was auctioned at Sotheby's? Through a mutual friend I obtained the address of John Arundell, the present owner of Wardour Castle, which in Isabel Burton's day belonged to her cousin, the then Lord Arundell of Wardour. Lady Burton had left all her papers to Lord Arundell. Mr John Arundell, who inherited Wardour, brought them with all the other family papers to his new home when Wardour became a school. As for the Ladislaus Magyar manuscript, "I decided," he told me, "to sell it as it was not strictly a family paper."

4 From Bombay Livingstone sailed in the recently refitted *Thule*, which was being presented as a goodwill gift to Sultan Majid bin Said.

5 *Last Journals*, vol. I, pp. 173–76.

6 At this time in Britain the rumour spread that Livingstone had died. On December 5, 1867, *The Times* published a letter from Dr John Kirk which read, "The nine Johanna men of the party which accompanied Livingstone came to Zanzibar reporting that on the west of Nyassa, sometimes between the end of July and September, they were suddenly attacked by a band of Mazite and that Dr Livingstone, with half his party, was murdered. Those who returned escaped, as they say, through being behind and unseen, and they all depose to having helped to bury the dead body of their leader the same evening." All the Johanna men agreed that Livingstone had one wound: that of an axe at the back of the neck.

The Johanna men deserted from Livingstone; they were afraid of getting in trouble with their authorities if Dr Kirk reported them; hence their lies about Livingstone's death.

7 Lake Albert is now called Lake Mobutu Sese Seko.

8 See note 9 in Chapter Fifteen.

9 His real name was Muhammad Ben Garib.

10 *Last Journals*, July 23, 1870, pp. 47–48.

11 Susi had been a boatman on the Zambezi expedition and was a mature man by 1870. Chuma and Gardner were quite young.

12 *Last Journals*, vol. II, p. 72.

13 Herodotus, *History*, Book II.

14 Between the end of 1869 and November, 1870, Kirk had sent three caravans of stores to Ujiji, but the ten men who had joined Livingstone had left the bulk of them in Ujiji.

15 Sherif Basheikh bin Ahmed, called Sherif Bosher by Livingstone.

16 These were the wars the Arabs waged against Mirambo, a minor chief who in the 1860s built up an empire of his own west and north-west of Unyanyembe, now known as Tabora. The all-important Arab caravan route to Ujiji, and to Manyuema beyond Lake Tanganyika, ran west of Unyanyembe, and Mirambo exacted "protection money". The Arabs, incensed at such incursions into their profits, between 1871 and 1875, fought regular wars against Mirambo which almost brought the slave trade to a standstill. Mirambo had some 7,000 well armed and trained men; eventually the Arabs had to sue for peace and pay hongo.

17 November 10, 1871.

18 A tall hat with a piece of material hanging down the back to protect the neck against the sun. The word originates from the Indian *tope*, meaning a tumulus like structure. In Victorian days, in the tropics all Europeans wore topis.

## Chapter Twenty

1 In his *Autobiography*, Henry M. Stanley wrote that on March 3, 1872,

Livingstone reverted again to his charges against the missionaries on the Zambezi and some of his naval officers on the expedition. I have had some intrusive suspicious thoughts that he was not of such an angelic temper as I believed him to be during my first month with him; but for the last month I have been driving them steadily from my mind . . . Livingstone with all his frankness, does not unfold himself at once; and what he leaves untold may be just as vital to the righteous understanding of these disputes as what he has said . . . When however he reiterated his complaints against this man and the other, I felt the faintest fear that his strong nature was opposed to forgiveness and that he was not so perfect as at the first blush of friendship I thought of him. I grew shy of the recurrent theme, lest I should find my fears confirmed (pp. 274–75).

2 David Livingstone to Lord Granville, British Museum, Additional MS 50183.
3 April 27, 1872.
4 *Last Journals*, vol. II, p. 296, April 13, 1873.
5 Litter.
6 The embalming method applied by Susi and Chuma was the same as that used by
  ordinary people in ancient Egypt. They made an incision in the abdomen and
  removed the intestines and internal organs. That is when they noticed a clot of
  blood several inches in diameter obstructing Livingstone's lower intestines. This
  must have caused him great pain. They placed the intestines and internal organs in
  a tin box and buried them at Ilala. Then they filled the open trunk with salt, and allowed the corpse to dry in the sun for a fortnight, moving it a fraction every day.
  They bathed the face in brandy as an extra preservative.

## Chapter Twenty-one

1 £30,000 in 1973.
2 The author has received the following letter from Trevor Griffith-Jones:
  When a cadet in Tanganyika about 1948 (having always been interested in history) I was stationed at Mpwapwa, one of the main stages on the caravan route
  to the Lakes. I was very intrigued that Stanley had never ascertained the whereabouts of Farquar, who had been buried at Mpwapwa when Stanley went on to
  find Livingstone. I therefore set about, over several months, questioning a great
  number of old people; and to cut a long story short, discovered bones, which
  were found to be human. The spot was declared a Preserved Monument. Likewise, about 1959, when I was no longer a District Commissioner, but seconded
  to the Tanganyika Broadcasting Corporation, I visited Tabora and Ujiji, and
  recorded in Swahili a tape of a really quite exceptionally old man, who had been
  in Stanley's party – I photographed him on a colour slide.
  The tape is now in Dar es Salaam, in the Tanzania Broadcasting Corporation's
  library. Details of Farquar's grave are in the District Book of the Mpwapwa
  District Office, and an account of it was published in the *Tanganyika Notes and
  Records*.
3 *Livingstone: Man of Africa* (ed.) Bridglal Pachai.
4 By "Zsenzse" Magyar meant Makololo.
5 Magyar used the words "natives", "Moors", "Kaffers" and "Africans" interchangeably.
6 *Journal* of the RGS, 1859, p. 25.
7 Ibid., 1854, pp. 274–75. Cooley's strictures on Livingstone were much fiercer than
  on Magyar, see his *Dr Livingstone and the Royal Geographical Society*, 1874.
8 Magyar interrupted his explorations of the Kasai to go and meet Livingstone at
  Linyanti.
9 Portuguese claims to have travelled in these areas in previous centuries passed
  unheeded.
10 *Last Journals*, July 14, 1866, p. 72.
11 Muhamed bin Gharib, called Bogharib by Livingstone.
12 Livingstone gave Tippoo Tip a letter of thanks, which was intended to introduce
  him to the British powers in Zanzibar.
13 One of his descendants, the present Nyamwezi Paramount Chief, Muhamed
  Fundi-Kira, is the Chairman of East African Airways, and lives in Nairobi. President Julius Nyerere had de-stooled all the Tanganyikan chiefs.

## Postscript

1 Senhor Abreu was not quite accurate. In 1624 Frei João dos Santos wrote in the
  second volume of his book, *Ethiopia Oriental* (Chapter VIII), about the Shire

River and about Lake Maravi, also called the "Big Nyanja River". In 1663 Father Manuel Godinho in his book, *New Route By Land And By Sea From India To Portugal* (Chapter XXIV) also described Lake Maravi and the route to it. On March 22, 1798, Dr Francisco de Lacerda e Almeida, a Brazilian scientist and explorer, appointed Governor of Moçambique, described some African tribes whose villages he placed quite accurately on the shores of Lake Nyanja, which meant that at this time the lake was already an important landmark. Dr Lacerda quoted a Father Luis Mariano who, in a letter written in 1724, mentioned Lake Hermozura, the source of the Rio Cherim, which was interrupted by rapids. This is the Jesuit to whom Senhor Abreu had referred. In 1835 Sebastiano Xavier Botelho, on p. 22 of his book, *Memorias Estatisticas*, noted the dimensions of the lake, and these tallied completely with those of Father Mariano. In the second volume of *Memorias Estatisticas*, on pp. 64 and 65, Botelho disagreed with the French geographer, J. Bourgignon d'Anville, who had visited the lake on the basis of Father Mariano's instructions. Probably in the same year of 1835, a British officer, referred to by the Portuguese as Mr Alexander, also visited Lake Maravi. Botelho said in his book, "We – d'Anville, Alexander and myself – compared our reciprocal notes which differed slightly." Finally, A. P. Gamitto, in his book *O Muata-Cazembe*, on pp. 48 and 49, described how he crossed Lake Maravi or the Big Nyanja River in 1832. He spent two nights on islands in the lake, and reached the opposite shore on the third day.

Engineer de Carvalho wrote to the author on July 26, 1973: "It is obvious that prior to Livingstone the Shire river and Lake Maravi were frequently visited by the Portuguese. Candido da Costa Cardoso was one of these travellers, who became famous because of Livingstone's ingratitude. Had the Doctor been honest about the information he had received from Cardoso, he would have been a great explorer."

# Bibliography

Bandeira, Marques Sà da, *Notas relativas a alguns dos Lagos de Africa Oriental e dos Rios Zambeze e Chire*, Lisbon, 1861.

Bánfi, János: *Magyar László utazásai és kalandjai*, Budapest, 1892.

Blaikie, William G.: *The Personal Life of David Livingstone*, John Murray, London, 1880.

*Autobiography*, Hodder & Stoughton, London, 1901.

Botelho, Sebastiao Xavier: *Memorias Estatisticas*, Lisbon, 1835.

Burton, Isabel: *The Life of Captain Sir Richard Burton*, 2 vols. Chapman and Hall Ltd. London, 1893.

Camoens, Luis Vas de, *Os Lusias*, Lisbon, 1572.

Chadwick, Owen: *Mackenzie's Grave*, Hodder & Stoughton, London, 1959.

Chamberlin, David: (ed.) *Some Letters from David Livingstone 1840–1872*, Oxford University Press, 1940.

Cooley, W. D.: *Dr Livingstone and the Royal Geographical Society*, published by the author, London, 1874.

Coupland, Sir Reginald: *Kirk of the Zambesi. A Chapter of African History*, Clarendon Press, Oxford, 1928.

*Livingstone's Last Journey*, Collins, London, 1945.

*The British Anti-Slavery Movement*, Thornton and Butterworth, London, 1933.

Cziráky, Gyula: *Szabadak-Dunafőldvár, Magyar László Életéből*, Budapest, 1895.

Dick, Dr T.: *The Philosophy of a Future State*.

Debenham, Frank: *The Way To Ilala: David Livingstone's Pilgrimage*, Longmans, Green & Co. Ltd., London, 1955.

Farwell, Byron: *Burton*, Longmans, Green & Co. Ltd., London, 1963.

Foskett, Reginald: (ed.) *The Zambesi Journal and Letters of Dr John Kirk, 1858–1863*, 2 vols. Oliver & Boyd, Edinburgh, 1965.

Gamitto, A. P.: *O Muata-Casembe*, Lisbon, 1854.

Gelfand, M.: *Livingstone, the Doctor, His Life and Travels*, Blackwell, Oxford, 1957.

Godinho, Father Manuel, *New Route By Land And By Sea From India To Portugal*, Lisbon, 1663.

Grosschmid, G.: *Magyar László életleirása*, Budapest, 1894.

Herodotus: *History*, Leigh & Sotheby, London, 1791.

Hőman, Bálint, és Szekfű, Gyula: *Magyar Történet*, 5 vols. Királyi Magyar Egyetemi Nyomda, Budapest, 1936.

Ingham, Kenneth: *A History of East Africa*, Longmans, Green & Co. Ltd., London, 1962.

Jeal, Tim: *Livingstone*, Heinemann, London, 1973.

Lacerda e Almeida, Dr Francisco José: *Diario da Viagem de Moçambique para os Rios de Sena*, Lisbon, 1889.

Lacerda. José de: *Exame dos Viagem do Dr Livingstone*, Lisbon, 1867.

Lewis, Roy: *The British Empire*, BBC-TV, Time-Life Books Ltd., London, 1972.
Livingstone, David: *Missionary Travels and Researches in South Africa*, John Murray, London, 1857.
*Family Letters 1841–1856*, 2 vols. Chatto & Windus, London, 1959.
*Essay on the Holy Spirit*, MS 1839 in London Missionary Society Archives.
Livingstone, D. & C.: *Narrative of an Expedition to the Zambesi and its Tributaries and of the Discovery of the Lakes Shirwa and Nyassa, 1858–1864*, John Murray, London, 1865.
*Livingstone's Private Journals, 1851–1853*, ed. by Isaac Schapera, Chatto & Windus, London, 1960.
*Livingstone's Missionary Correspondence*, ed. by Isaac Schapera, Chatto & Windus, London, 1960.
*Livingstone's African Journal 1853–1856*, ed. by Isaac Schapera, 2 vols. Chatto & Windus, London, 1963.
Livingstone, David: *Essay on the Holy Spirit*, MS 1839 in London Missionary Society Archives.
Magyar, László: *A Short Resumé of my Life*, April, 1851.
*Explorations of the Zaire Delta*, Hungarian Academy of Sciences, printed by Gusztáv Emich, Pest, 1857.
*Utazások Dél Afrikában*, Hungarian Academy of Sciences, printed by Gusztáv Emich, Pest, 1859.
Martelli, George: *Livingstone's River. A History of the Zambesi Expedition 1858–1864*, Chatto & Windus, London, 1970.
Moffat, The Rev Robert: *Missionary Labours and Scenes in Southern Africa*, John Snow, London, 1846.
Moorhouse, Geoffrey: *The Missionaries*, Eyre Methuen, London, 1973.
Németh, Imre: *Őserdők mélyén, Magyar László regényes életrajza*, Budapest, 1954.
Newitt, M.D.D.: *Portuguese Settlements on the Zambesi*, Longman, London, 1973.
Northcote, the Rev W. C.: *David Livingstone: His Triumph and Fall*, Lutterworth, London, 1973.
Oliver, Roland: *The Missionary Factor in East Africa*, Longmans, Green & Co. Ltd., London, 1952.
Oswell, W. Edward: *William Cotton Oswell*, 2 vols. Heinemann, 1900.
Penzer, Norman M.: *An annotated Bibliography of Sir Richard Francis Burton*, A. M. Philpot Ltd., London, 1923.
Pinto, Alexander de Serpa: *How I Crossed Africa*, Royal Geographical Society, London, 1879.
Ransford, Oliver: *Livingstone's Lake*, John Murray, London, 1966.
Rónay, Father Jacint J.: *Napló Töredékek*, 1857, in the British Museum.
Santos, Frei Joao dos: *Ethiopia Oriental*, Lisbon, 1597.
Schapera, I., see under Livingstone.
Schoffeleers, The Rev J. M.: *Livingstone and the Mang'anja Chiefs*, (essay in *Livingstone, Man of Africa*, ed. Dr B. Pachai) Longman, London, 1973.
Seaver, George: *David Livingstone: His Life and Letters*, Lutterworth Press, London, 1957.
Sedgwick, Rev Adam: *Dr Livingstone's Cambridge Lecture*, Deighton, 1858.
Shepperson, George: *David Livingstone and the Rovuma*, Uniersity Press, Edinburgh, 1965.
Simmons, Jack: *Livingstone and Africa*, English University Press, London, 1955.
Stanley, Henry Morton: *How I Found Livingstone*, Samson Low, London, 1872.
*Autobiography*, Samson Low, London, 1909.
Teixeira, Alexander de Mota: *A Cartografia Antiga da Africa Centrale e a Travessia Entre Angola e Moçambique, 1500–1860*, Tipografia Progresso, Lourenço Marques, 1964.

Thirring, Professor Gusztáv: *Magyar László élete es tudományos működese*, Budapest, 1937.

Thornton, Richard: *The Zambesi Papers of Richard Thornton*, Chatto & Windus, 1963.

Walker, Eric A.: *A History of Southern Africa*, Longmans, Green & Co. Ltd., London, 1957.

Waller, Horace, (ed.) *The Last Journals of David Livingstone in Central Africa*, 2 vols. John Murray, London, 1872.

Wallis, J.P.R. (ed.): *The Zambezi Expedition of David Livingstone 1858–1863*, 2 vols. Central African Archives, Oppenheimer Series No 9, Chatto & Windus, London, 1956.

 *The Zambezi Journal of James Stewart*, 1862–63, Oppenheimer Series No 6, Chatto & Windus, London, 1952.

# Index

R01138 66415